W9-BYP-789

THE CITIZEN-SOLDIER;

OR,

MEMOIRS OF A VOLUNTEER.

BY

JOHN BEATTY.

———•———

CINCINNATI:

WILSTACH, BALDWIN & CO., PUBLISHERS,

Nos. 141 AND 143 RACE STREET.

1879.

TO MY BROTHER,

MAJOR WILLIAM GURLEY BEATTY,

WHOSE GENEROUS SACRIFICE OF HIS OWN INCLINATION AT THE

COMMENCEMENT OF THE WAR, AND FAITHFUL DEVOTION

TO MY FAMILY AND BUSINESS,

ENABLED ME TO ENTER THE ARMY AND REMAIN THREE YEARS,

THIS VOLUME

IS RESPECTFULLY AND AFFECTIONATELY INSCRIBED.

INTRODUCTORY.

In the lifetime of all who arrive at mature age, there comes a period when a strong desire is felt to know more of the past, especially to know more of those from whom we claim descent. Many find even their chief pleasure in searching among parish records and local histories for some knowledge of ancestors, who for a hundred or five hundred years have been sleeping in the grave. Long pilgrimages are made to the Old World for this purpose, and when the traveler discovers in the crowded church-yard a moss-covered, crumbling stone, which bears the name he seeks, he takes infinite pains to decipher the half-obliterated epitaph, and finds in this often what he regards as ample remuneration for all his trouble. How vastly greater would be his satisfaction if he could obtain even the simplest and briefest history of those in whom he takes so deep an interest. Who were they? How were their days spent, and amongst what surroundings? What were their thoughts, fears, hopes, acts? Who were their associates, and on which side of the great questions of the day did they stand? A full or even partial answer to these queries would possess for him an incalculable value.

So, sitting here to-night, in my little library, with wife and children near, and by God's great kindness all in life and health, I look forward one, two, five hundred years, and see in each succeeding century, and possibly in each generation, so long as the name shall last, a wonder-eyed boy, curious youth, or inquisitive old man, exploring closets and libraries for things of the old time, stumbling finally on this volume, which has, by the charity of the State Librarian, still been preserved; he discovers, with quickening pulse, that it bears his own name, and that it was written for him by one whose body has for centuries been dust. Dull and uninteresting as it may be to others, for him it will possess an inexpressible charm. It is his own blood speaking to him from the shadowy and almost forgotten past. The message may be poorly written, the matter in the main may be worthless, and the greater events recorded may be dwarfed by more recent and important ones, but the volume is nevertheless of absorbing interest to him, for by it he is enabled to look into the face and heart of one of his own kin, who lived when the Nation was young. In leaving this unpretentious record, therefore, I seek to do simply what I would have had my fathers do for me.

Kinsmen of the coming centuries, I bid you hail and godspeed!

COLUMBUS, *December* 16, 1878.

The Third Ohio Volunteer Infantry served under two separate terms of enlistment—the one for three months, and the other for three years.

The regiment was organized April 21, 1861, and on

April 27th it was mustered into the United States service, with the following field officers: Isaac H. Marrow, Colonel; John Beatty, Lieutenant Colonel, and J. Warren Keifer, Major.

The writer's record begins with the day on which his regiment entered Virginia, June 22, 1861, and ends on January 1, 1864. He does not undertake to present a history of the organizations with which he was connected, nor does he attempt to describe the operations of armies. His record consists merely of matters which came under his own observation, and of camp gossip, rumors, trifling incidents, idle speculations, and the numberless items, small and great, which, in one way and another, enter into and affect the life of a soldier. In short, he has sought simply to gather up the scraps which fell in his way, leaving to other and more competent hands the weightier matters of the great civil war.

Many errors of opinion and of fact he might now correct, and many items which appear unworthy of a paragraph he might now strike out, but he prefers to leave the record as it was written, when cyclopedias could not be consulted, nor time taken for thorough investigation.

Who can really know what an army is unless he mingles with the individuals who compose it, and learns how they live, think, talk, and act?

THE CITIZEN SOLDIER;

OR,

MEMOIRS OF A VOLUNTEER.

JUNE, 1861.

22. Arrived at Bellaire at 3 P. M. There is trouble in the neighborhood of Grafton. Have been ordered to that place.

The Third is now on the Virginia side, and will in a few minutes take the cars.

23. Reached Grafton at 1 P. M. All avowed secessionists have run away; but there are, doubtless, many persons here still who sympathize with the enemy, and who secretly inform him of all our movements.

24. Colonel Marrow and I dined with Colonel Smith, member of the Virginia Legislature. He professes to be a Union man, but his sympathies are evidently with the South. He feels that the South is wrong, but does not relish the idea of Ohio troops

coming upon Virginia soil to fight Virginians. The Union sentiment here is said to be strengthening daily.

26. Arrived at Clarksburg about midnight, and remained on the cars until morning. We are now encamped on a hillside, and for the first time my bed is made in my own tent.

Clarksburg has apparently stood still for fifty years. Most of the houses are old style, built by the fathers and grandfathers of the present occupants. Here, for the first time, we find slaves, each of the wealthier, or, rather, each of the well-to-do, families owning a few.

There are probably thirty-five hundred troops in this vicinity—the Third, Fourth, Eighteenth, Nineteenth, and part of the Twenty-second Ohio, one company of cavalry, and one of artillery. Rumors of skirmishes and small fights a few miles off; but as yet the only gunpowder we have smelled is our own.

28. At twelve o'clock to-day our battalion left Clarksburg, followed a stream called Elk creek for eight miles, and then encamped for the night. This is the first march on foot we have made. The country through which we passed is extremely hilly and broken, but apparently fertile. If the people of Western Virginia were united against us, it would be almost impossible for our army to advance. In many places the creek on one side, and the perpendicular banks on the other, leave a strip barely wide enough for a wagon road.

Buckhannon, twenty miles in advance of us, is said to be in the hands of the secession troops. To-morrow, or the day after, if they do not leave, a battle will take place. Our men appear eager for the fray, and I pray they may be as successful in the fight as they are anxious for one.

29. It is half-past eight o'clock, and we are still but eight miles from Clarksburg. We were informed this morning that the secession troops had left Buckhannon, and fallen back to their fortifications at Laurel Hill and Rich mountain. It is said General McClellan will be here to-morrow, and take command of the forces in person.

In enumerating the troops in this vicinity, I omitted to mention Colonel Robert McCook's Dutch regiment, which is in camp two miles from us. The Seventh Ohio Infantry is now at Clarksburg, and will, I think, move in this direction to-morrow.

Provisions outside of camp are very scarce. I took breakfast with a farmer this morning, and can say truly that I have eaten much better meals in my life. We had coffee without sugar, short-cake without butter, and a little salt pork, exceedingly fat. I asked him what the charge was, and he said "Ninepence," which means one shilling. I rejoiced his old soul by giving him two shillings.

The country people here have been grossly deceived by their political leaders. They have been made to believe that Lincoln was elected for the sole purpose of liberating the negro; that our army is marching into Virginia to free their slaves, destroy

their property, and murder their families; that we,
not they, have set the Constitution and laws at defiance, and that in resisting us they are simply de-
fending their homes and fighting for their constitutional rights.

JULY, 1861.

---

2. Reached Buckhannon at 5 P. M., and encamped beside the Fourth Ohio, in a meadow, one mile from town. The country through which we marched is exceedingly hilly; or, perhaps, I might say mountainous. The scenery is delightful. The road for miles is cut around great hills, and is just wide enough for a wagon. A step to the left would send one tumbling a hundred or two hundred feet below, and to the right the hills rise hundreds of feet above. The hills, half way to their summits, are covered with corn, wheat, or grass, while further up the forest is as dense as it could well have been a hundred years ago.

3. For the first time to-day, I saw men bringing tobacco to market in bags. One old man brought a bag of natural leaf into camp to sell to the soldiers, price ten cents per pound. He brought it to a poor market, however, for the men have been bankrupt for weeks, and could not buy tobacco at a dime a bagfull.

4. The Fourth has passed off quietly in the little town of Buckhannon and in camp.

At ten o'clock the Third and Fourth Regiments were reviewed by General McClellan. The day was excessively warm, and the men, buttoned up in their dress-coats, were much wearied when the parade was over.

In the court-house this evening, the soldiers had what they call a "stag dance." Camp life to a young man who has nothing specially to tie him to home has many attractions—abundance of company, continual excitement, and all the fun and frolic that a thousand light-hearted boys can devise.

To-night; in one tent, a dozen or more are singing "Dixie" at the top of their voices. In another "The Star-Spangled Banner" is being executed so horribly that even a secessionist ought to pity the poor tune. Stories, cards, wrestling, boxing, racing, all these and a thousand other things enter into a day in camp. The roving, uncertain life of a soldier has a tendency to harden and demoralize most men. The restraints of home, family, and society are not felt. The fact that a few hours may put them in battle, where their lives will not be worth a fig, is forgotten. They think a hundred times less of the perils by which they may be surrounded than their friends do at home. They encourage and strengthen each other to such an extent that, when exposed to danger, imminent though it be, they do not seem to realize it.

7. On the 5th instant a scouting party, under Captain Lawson, started for Middle Fork bridge, a point eighteen miles from camp. At eight o'clock last night, when I brought the battalion from the drill-ground, I found that a messenger had arrived with intelligence that Lawson had been surrounded by a force of probably four hundred, and that, in the en-

gagement, one of his men had been killed and three wounded. The camp was alive with excitement. Each company of the Third had contributed five men to Captain Lawson's detachment, and each company, therefore, felt a special interest in it. The messenger stated that Captain Lawson was in great need of help, and General McClellan at once ordered four companies of infantry and twenty mounted men to move to his assistance. I had command of the detachment, and left camp about nine o'clock P. M., accompanied by a guide. The night was dark. My command moved on silently and rapidly. After proceeding about three miles, we left the turnpike and turned onto a narrow, broken, bad road, leading through the woods, which we followed about eight miles, when we met Captain Lawson's detachment on its way back. Here we removed the wounded from the farm wagon in which they had been conveyed thus far, to an ambulance brought with us for the purpose, countermarched, and reached our quarters about three o'clock this morning.

I will not undertake to give the details of Captain Lawson's skirmish. I may say, however, that the number of the enemy killed and wounded, lacerated and torn, by Corporal Casey, was beyond all computation. Had the rebels not succeeded in getting a covered bridge between themselves and the invincible Irishman, he would, if we may believe his own statement, have annihilated the whole force, and brought back the head of their commanding officer on the point of his bayonet.

8. This morning, at seven o'clock, our tents were struck, and, with General McClellan and staff in advance, we moved to Middle Fork bridge. It was here that Captain Lawson's skirmish on Saturday had occurred. The man killed had been buried by the Fourth Ohio before our arrival. Almost every house along the road is deserted by the men, the women sometimes remaining. The few Union men of this section have, for weeks past, been hiding away in the hills. Now the secessionists have taken to the woods. The utmost bitterness of feeling exists between the two. A man was found to-day, within a half mile of this camp, with his head cut off and entrails ripped out, probably a Union man who had been hounded down and killed. The Dutch regiment (McCook's), when it took possession of the bridge, had a slight skirmish with the enemy, and, I learn, killed two men. On the day after to-morrow I apprehend the first great battle will be fought in Western Virginia.

I ate breakfast in Buckhannon at six o'clock A. M., and now, at six o'clock P. M. am awaiting my second meal.

The boys, I ascertain, searched one secession house on the road, and found three guns and a small amount of ammunition. The guns were hunting pieces, all loaded. The woman of the house was very indignant, and spoke in disrespectful terms of the Union men of the neighborhood, whom she suspected of instigating the search. She said she "had come from a higher sphere than they, and would not lay down with dogs." She was an Eastern Virginia woman, and, although poor as a church mouse, thought herself superior to West Virginia people. As an indication of this lady's refinement and loyalty, it is only necessary to say that a day or two before she had displayed . secession flag made, as she very frankly told the soldiers, of the tail of an old shirt, with J. D. and S. C. on it, the letters standing for Jefferson Davis and the Southern Confederacy.

Four or five thousand men are encamped here, huddled together in a little circular valley, with high hills surrounding. A company of cavalry is just going by my tent on the road toward Beverly, probably to watch the front.

As we were leaving camp this morning, an officer of an Ohio regiment rode at break-neck speed along the line, inquiring for General McClellan, and yelling, as he passed, that four companies of the regiment to which he belongs had been surrounded at Glendale, by twelve hundred secessionists, under O. Jennings Wise. Our men, misapprehending the statement, thought Buckhannon had been attacked, and were in a great state of excitement.

The officers of General Schleich's staff were with me on to-day's march, and the younger members, Captains Hunter and Dubois, got off whatever poetry they had in them of a military cast. "On Linden when the sun was low," was recited to the hills of Western Virginia in a manner that must have touched even the stoniest of them. I could think of nothing but "There was a sound of revelry by

2

night," and as this was not particularly applicable to the occasion, owing to the exceeding brightness of the sun, and the entire absence of all revelry, I thought best not to astonish my companions by exhibiting my knowledge of the poets.

West Virginia hogs are the longest, lankest, boniest animals in creation. I am reminded of this by that broth of an Irish lad, Conway, who says, in substance, and with a broad Celtic accent, that their noses have to be sharpened every morning to enable them to pick a living among the rocks.

Colonel Marrow informs me that an attack is apprehended to-night. We have sent out strong pickets. The cannon are so placed as to shoot up the road. Our regiment is to form on the left of the turnpike, and the Dutch regiment on the right, in case the secession forces should be bold enough to come down on us.

9. Moved from the Middle Fork of the Buckhannon river at seven o'clock this morning, and arrived at Roaring creek at four p. m. We came over the hills with all the pomp and circumstance of glorious war; infantry, cavalry, artillery, and hundreds of army wagons; the whole stretching along the mountain road for miles. The tops of the Alleghanies can now be seen plainly. We are at the foot of Rich mountain, encamped where our brothers of the secession order pitched their tents last night. Our advance guard gave them a few shots and they fled precipitately to the mountains, burning the bridge behind them. When our regiment arrived a few shots were heard,

and the bayonets and bright barrels of the enemy's guns could be seen on the hills.

It clouded up shortly after, and before we had pitched our tents, the clouds came over Rich mountain, settling down upon and hiding its summit entirely. Heaven gave us a specimen of its artillery firing, and a heavy shower fell, drenching us all completely. As I write, the sound of a cannon comes booming over the mountain. There it goes again! Whether it is at Phillippi or Laurel Hill, I can not tell. Certain it is that the portion of our army advancing up the Valley river is in battle, somewhere, and not many miles away.

We do not know the strength of our opponents, nor the character and extent of their fortifications. These mountain passes must be ugly things to go through when in possession of an enemy; our boys look forward, however, to a day of battle as one of rare sport. I do not. I endeavor to picture to myself all its terrors, so that I may not be surprised and dumbfounded when the shock comes. Our army is probably now making one of the most interesting chapters of American history. God grant it may be a chapter our Northern people will not be ashamed to read!

I am not confident of a speedy termination of the war. These people are in the wrong, but have been made to believe they are in the right—that we are the invaders of their hearthstones, come to conquer and destroy. That they will fight with desperation, I have no doubt. Nature has fortified the country for

them. He is foolishly oversanguine who predicts an
easy victory over such a people, intrenched amidst
mountains and hills. I believe the war will run into
a war of emancipation, and when it ends African
slavery will have ended also. It would not, perhaps,
be politic to say so, but if I had the army in my own
hands, I would take a short cut to what I am sure
will be the end—commence the work of emancipation
at once, and leave every foot of soil behind me free.

10. From the best information obtainable, we are
led to believe the mountains and hills lying between
this place and Beverly are strongly fortified and full
of men. We can see a part of the enemy's fortifications very plainly from a hill west of camp. Our
regiment was ordered to be in readiness to march,
and was under arms two hours. During this time
the Dutch regiment (McCook's), the Fourth Ohio,
four pieces of artillery, one company of cavalry, with
General McClellan, marched to the front, the Dutchmen in advance. They proceeded, say a mile, when
they overhauled the enemy's pickets, and in the little
skirmish which ensued one man of McCook's regiment was shot, and two of the enemy captured.
By these prisoners it is affirmed that eight or
nine thousand men are in the hills before us, well
armed, with heavy artillery planted so as to command the road for miles. How true this is we can
not tell. Enough, however, has been learned to satisfy McClellan that it is not advisable to attack to-
day. What surprises me is that the General should
know so little about the character of the country, the

number of the enemy, and the extent of his fortifications.

During the day, Colonel Marrow, apparently under a high state of excitement, informed me that he had just had an interview with George (he usually speaks of General McClellan in this familiar way), that an attack was to be made, and the Third was to lead the column. He desired me, therefore, to get out my horse at once, take four men with me, and search the woods in our front for a practicable road to the enemy. I asked if General McClellan had given him any information that would aid me in this enterprise, such as the position of the rebels, the location of their outposts, their distance from us, and the character of the country between our camp and theirs. He replied that George had not. It occurred to me that four men were rather too few, if the work contemplated was a reconnoissance, and rather too many if the service required was simply that for which spies are usually employed. I therefore spoke distrustingly of the proposed expedition, and questioned the propriety of sending so small a force, so utterly without information, upon so hazardous an enterprise, and apparently so foolish a one. My language gave offense, and when I finally inquired what four men I should take, the Colonel told me, rather abruptly, to take whom I pleased, and look where I pleased. His manner, rather than his words, indicated a doubt of my courage, and I turned from him, mounted my horse, and started for the front, determined to obey the order to the best of my ability, but

to risk the lives of no others on what was evidently a
fool's errand. After proceeding some distance, I
found that the wagon-master was at my heels, and,
together, we traced every cowpath and mountain road
we could find, and passed half a mile beyond the
enemy's outposts, and over ground visited by his
scouts almost hourly. When I returned to make my
report, I was curtly informed that no report was desired, as the plan had been changed.

A little after midnight the Colonel returned from
head-quarters with important information, which he
desired to communicate to the regiment. The men
were, therefore, ordered to turn out, and came hesi-
tatingly and sleepily from their tents. They looked
like shadows as they gathered in the darkness about
their chieftain. It was the hour when graveyards are
supposed to yawn, and the sheeted dead to walk
abroad. The gallant Colonel, with a voice in perfect
accord with the solemnity of the hour, and the
funereal character of the scene, addressed us, in substance, as follows:

"Soldiers of the Third: The assault on the enemy's works will be made in the early morning. The
Third will lead the column. The secessionists have
ten thousand men and forty rifled cannon. They
are strongly fortified. They have more men and
more cannon than we have. They will cut us to
pieces. Marching to attack such an enemy, so intrenched and so armed, is marching to a butcher-
shop rather than to a battle. There is bloody work

ahead. Many of you, boys, will go out who will never
come back again."

As this speech progressed my hair began to stiffen
at the roots, and a chilly sensation like that which
might ensue from the unexpected and clammy touch
of the dead, ran through me. It was hard to die so
young and so far from home. Theological questions
which before had attracted little or no attention,
now came uppermost in our minds. We thought of
mothers, wives, sweethearts—of opportunities lost,
and of good advice disregarded. Some soldiers
kicked together the expiring fragments of a camp-
fire, and the little blaze which sprang up revealed
scores of pallid faces. In short, we all wanted to go
home.

When a boy I had read Plutarch, and knew something of the great warriors of the old time; but I
could not, for the life of me, recall an instance
wherein they had made such an address to their soldiers on the eve of battle. It was their habit, at
such a time, to speak encouragingly and hopefully.
With all due respect, therefore, for the superior rank
and wisdom of the Colonel, I plucked him by the
sleeve, took him one side, and modestly suggested
that his speech had had rather a. depressing effect on
the regiment, and had taken that spirit out of the
boys so necessary to enable them to do well in battle.
I urged him to correct the mistake, and speak to
them hopefully. He replied that what he had said
was true, and they should know the truth.

The morning dawned; but instead of being called

upon to lead the column, we were left to the inglori-
ous duty of guarding the camp, while other regiments
moved forward toward the enemy's line. In half an
hour, in all probability, the work of destruction will
commence. I began this memoranda on the evening
of the 10th, and now close it on the morning of the
11th.

11. At 10 A. M. we were ordered to the front;
passed quite a number of regiments on our way
thither, and finally took position not far from the enemy's works. We were now at the head of the column. A small brook crossed the road at this point,
and the thick woods concealed us from the enemy.
A few rods further on, a bend in the road gave us a
good view of the entire front of his fortifications.
Major Keifer and a few other gentlemen, in their
anxiety to get more definite information in regard to
the position of the secessionists, and the extent of
their works, went up the road, and were saluted by a
shot from their battery. We expected every moment to receive an order to advance. After a time,
however, we ascertained that Rosecrans, with a
brigade, was seeking the enemy's rear by a mountain
path, and we conjectured that, so soon as he had
reached it, we would be ordered to make the assault
in front. It was a dark, gloomy day, and the hours
passed slowly.

Between two and three o'clock we heard shots in
the rear of the fortifications; then volleys of musketry, and the roar of artillery. Every man sprang
to his feet, assured that the moment for making the

attack had arrived. General McClellan and staff
came galloping up, and a thousand faces turned to
hear the order to advance; but no order was given.
The General halted a few paces from our line, and sat
on his horse listening to the guns, apparently in
doubt as to what to do; and as he sat there with in-
decision stamped on every line of his countenance,
the battle grew fiercer in the enemy's rear. Every
volley could be heard distinctly. There would occasionally be a lull for a moment, and then the uproar
would break out again with increased violence. If
the enemy is too strong for us to attack, what must be
the fate of Rosecrans' four regiments, cut off from us,
and struggling against such odds? Hours passed;
and as the last straggling shots and final silence told
us the battle had ended, gloom settled down on every
soldier's heart, and the belief grew strong that Rosecrans had been defeated, and his brigade cut to pieces
or captured. This belief grew to certain conviction
soon after, when we heard shout after shout go up
from the fortifications in our front.

Major Keifer with two companies had, early in
the afternoon, climbed the hill on our right to look
for a position from which artillery could be used
effectively. The ground over which he moved was
broken and covered with a dense growth of trees and
underbrush; finally an elevation was discovered which
commanded the enemy's camp, but before a road could
be cut, and the artillery brought up, it was too late in
the day to begin the attack.

3

Night came on. It was intensely dark. About nine o'clock we were ordered to withdraw our pickets quietly and return to our old quarters. On our way thither a rough voice cried: "Halt! Who comes there?" And a thousand shadowy forms sprang up before us. The challenge was from Colonel Robert McCook, and the regiment his. The scene reminded me of the one where

> "That whistle garrisoned the glen
> At once with full five hundred men,
> As if the yawning hill to heaven
> A subterranean host had given."

12. We were rejoiced this morning to hear of Rosecrans' success, and, at the same time, not well pleased at the escape of the enemy under cover of night. We were ordered to move, and got under way at eight o'clock. On the road we met General Rosecrans and staff. He was jubilant, as well he might be, and as he rode by received the congratulations of the officers and cheers of the men.

Arriving on yesterday's battlefield, the regiment was allowed a half hour for rest. The dead had been gathered and placed in a long trench, which was still open. The wounded of both armies were in hospital, receiving the attention of the surgeons. There were a few prisoners, most of them too unwell to accompany their friends in retreat.

Soon after reaching the summit of Rich mountain, we caught glimpses of Tygart's valley, and of Cheat mountain beyond, and before nightfall reached Beverly and went into camp.

13. Six or eight hundred Southern troops sent in a flag of truce, and surrendered unconditionally. They are a portion of the force which fought Rosecrans at Rich mountain, and Morris at Laurel Hill.

We started up the Valley river at seven o'clock this morning, our regiment in the lead. Found most of the houses deserted. Both Union men and secessionists had fled. The Southern troops, retreating in this direction, had frightened the people greatly, by telling them that we shot men, ravished women, and destroyed property. When within three-quarters of a mile of Huttonville, we were informed that forty or fifty mounted secessionists were there. The order to double-quick was given, and the regiment entered the village on a run. As we made a turn in the road, we discovered a squad of cavalry retreating rapidly. The bridge over the river had been burned, and was still smoking. Our troops sent up a hurrah and quickened their pace, but they had already traveled eleven miles on a light breakfast, and were not in condition to run down cavalry. That we might not lose at least one shot at the enemy, I got an Enfield rifle from one of the men, galloped forward, and fired at the retreating squad. It was the best shot I could make, and I am forced to say it was a very poor one, for no one fell. On second thought, it occurred to me that it would have been criminal to have killed one of these men, for his death could have had no possible effect on the result of the war.

Huttonville is a very small place at the foot of Cheat mountain. We halted there perhaps one hour, to await the arrival of General McClellan; and when he came up, were ordered forward to secure a mountain pass. It is thought fifteen hundred secessionists are a few miles ahead, near the top of the mountain. Two Indiana regiments and one battery are with us. More troops are probably following.

The man who owns the farm on which we are encamped is, with his family, sleeping in the woods tonight, if, indeed, he sleeps at all.

14. The Ninth and Fourth Ohio, Fifteenth Indiana, and one company of cavalry, started up the mountain between seven and eight o'clock. The Colonel being unwell, I followed with the Third. Awful rumors were afloat of fortifications and rebels at the top; but we found no fortifications, and as for the rebels, they were scampering for Staunton as fast as their legs could carry them.

This mountain scenery is magnificent. As we climbed the Cheat the views were the grandest I ever looked upon. Nests of hills, appearing like eggs of the mountain; ravines so dark that one could not guess their depth; openings, the ends of which seemed lost in a blue mist; broken-backed mountains, long mountains, round mountains, mountains sloping gently to the summit; others so steep a squirrel could hardly climb them; fatherly mountains, with their children clustered about them, clothed in birch, pine, and cedar; mountain streams, sparkling now in the sunlight, then dashing down into apparently fathomless abysses.

It was a beautiful day, and the march was delightful. The road is crooked beyond description, but very solid and smooth.

The farmer on whose premises we are encamped has returned from the woods. He has discovered that we are not so bad as we were reported. Most of the negroes have been left at home. Many were in camp to-day with corn-bread, pies, and cakes to sell. Fox, my servant, went out this afternoon and bought a basket of bread. He brought in two chickens also, which he said were presented to him. I suspect Fox does not always tell the truth.

16. The Fourteenth Indiana and one company of cavalry went to the summit this morning to fortify.

The Colonel has gone to Beverly. The boys repeat his Rich mountain speech with slight variations: "Men, there are ten thousand secessionists in Rich mountain, with forty rifled cannon, well fortified. There's bloody work ahead. You are going to a butcher-shop rather than a battle. Ten thousand men and forty rifled cannon! Hostler, you d—d scoundrel, why do n't you wipe Jerome's nose?" Jerome is the Colonel's horse, known in camp as the White Bull.

Conway, who has been detailed to attend to the Colonel's horses, is almost as good a speech-maker as the Colonel. This, in brief, is Conway's address to the White Bull:

"Stand still there, now, or I'll make yer stand

still. Hold up yer head there, now, or I'll make
yer hold it up. Keep quiet; what the h—ll yer
'bout there, now? D—n you! do you want me to hit
you a lick over the snoot, now—do you? Are you a
inviten' me to pound you over the head with a saw-
log? D—n yer ugly pictures, whoa!"

18. This afternoon, when riding down to Huttonville, I met three or four hundred sorry-looking soldiers. They were without arms. On inquiry, I
found they were a part of the secession army, who,
finding no way of escape, had come into our lines
and surrendered. They were badly dressed, and a
hard, dissolute-looking lot of men. To use the language of one of the soldiers, they were " a milk-
sickly set of fellows," and would have died off probably without any help from us if they had been kept
in the mountains a little longer. They were on their
way to Staunton. General McClellan had very gen-
erously provided them with provisions for three days,
and wagons to carry the sick and wounded; and so,
footsore, weary, and chopfallen, they go over the
hills.

An unpleasant rumor is in camp to-night, to the
effect that General Patterson has been defeated at
Williamsport. This, if true, will counterbalance our
successes in Western Virginia, and make the game
an even one.

The Southern soldiers mentioned above are encamped for the night a little over a mile from here.
About dusk I walked over to their camp. They
were gathered around their fires preparing supper.

Many of them say they were deceived, and entered the service because they were led to believe that the Northern army would confiscate their property, liberate their slaves, and play the devil generally. As they thought this was true, there was nothing left for them to do but to take up arms and defend themselves.

While we were at Buckhannon, an old farmer-looking man visited us daily, bringing tobacco, cornbread, and cucumber pickles. This innocent old genman proves to have been a spy, and obtained his reward in the loss of a leg at Rich mountain.

19. To-day, eleven men belonging to a company of cavalry which accompanied the Fourteenth Indiana to the Summit, were sent out on a scouting expedition. When about ten miles from camp, on the opposite side of the mountain, they halted, and while watering their horses were fired upon. One man was killed and three wounded. The other seven fled. Colonel Kimball sent out a detachment to bring in the wounded; but whether it succeeded or not I have not heard.

A musician belonging to the Fourth Ohio, when six miles out of Beverly, on his way to Phillippi, was fired upon and instantly killed. So goes what little there is of war in Western Virginia.

20. The most interesting of all days in the mountains is one on which the sky is filled with floating clouds, not hiding it entirely, but leaving here and there patches of blue. Then the shadows shift from place to place, as the moving clouds either let in the sunshine or exclude it. Standing at my tent-door at

eleven o'clock in the morning, with a stiff breeze going, and the clouds on the wing, we see a peak, now
in the sunshine, then in the shadow, and the lights
and shadows chasing each other from point to point
over the mountains, presenting altogether a panorama most beautiful to look upon, and such an one as
God only can present.

I can almost believe now that men become, to
some extent, like the country in which they live. In
the plain country the inhabitants learn to traffic,
come to regard money-getting as the great object in
life, and have but a dim perception of those higher
emotions from which spring the noblest acts. In a
mountain country God has made many things
sublime, and some things very beautiful. The
rugged, the smooth, the sunshine, and the shadow
meet one at every turn. Here are peaks getting the
earliest sunlight of the morning, and the latest of
the evening; ravines so deep the light of day can
never penetrate them; bold, rugged, perpendicular
rocks, which have breasted the storms for ages; gentle slopes, swelling away until their summits seem
to dip in the blue sky; streams, cold and clear, leap-
ing from crag to crag, and rushing down nobody
knows whither. Like the country, may we not look
to find the people unpolished, rugged and uneven,
capable of the noblest heroism or the most infernal
villainy—their lives full of lights and shadows, eleva-
tions and depressions?

The mountains, rising one above another, suggest,
forcibly enough, the infinite power of the Creator,

and when the peaks come in contact with the clouds
it requires but little imagination to make one feel
that God, as at Sinai, has set His foot upon the earth,
and that earth and heaven are really very near each
other.

21. This morning, at two o'clock, I was rattled up
by a sentinel, who had come to camp in hot haste to
inform me that he had seen and fired upon a body of
twenty-five or more men, probably the advance guard
of the enemy. He desired me to send two companies
to strengthen the outpost. I preferred, however, to
go myself to the scene of the trouble; and, after investigation, concluded that the guard had been alarmed
by a couple of cows.

Another lot of secession prisoners, some sixty
in number, passed by this afternoon. They were
highly pleased with the manner in which they had
been treated by their captors.

The sound of a musket is just heard on the picket
post, three-quarters of a mile away, and the shot is
being repeated by our line of sentinels. * * *
The whole camp has been in an uproar. Many men,
half asleep, rushed from their tents and fired off their
guns in their company grounds. Others, supposing
the enemy near, became excited and discharged theirs
also. The tents were struck, Loomis' First Michigan
Battery manned, and we awaited the attack, but none
was made. It was a false alarm. Some sentinel
probably halted a stump and fired, thus rousing a
thousand men from their warm beds. This is the
first night alarm we have had.

22. We hear that General Cox has been beaten on
the Kanawha; that our forces have been repulsed at
Manassas Gap, and that our troops have been unsuccessful in Missouri. I trust the greater part, if not
all, of this is untrue.

We have been expecting orders to march, but they
have not come. The men are very anxious to be
moving, and when moving, strange to say, always
very anxious to stop.

23. Officers and men are low-spirited to-night.
The news of yesterday has been confirmed. Our
army has been beaten at Manassas with terrible loss.
General McClellan has left Beverly for Washington.
General Rosecrans will assume command in Western
Virginia. We are informed that twenty miles from
us, in the direction of Staunton, some three thousand
secessionists are in camp. We shall probably move
against them.

24. The news from Manassas Junction is a little
more cheering, and all feel better to-day.

We have now a force of about four thousand men
in this vicinity, and two or three thousand at Beverly. We shall be in telegraphic communication
with the North to-morrow.

The moon is at its full to-night, and one of the
most beautiful sights I have witnessed was its rising
above the mountain. First the sky lighted up, then
a halo appeared, then the edge of the moon, not
bigger than a star, then the half-moon, not semi-circu-
lar, but blazing up like a great gaslight, and, finally,
the full, round moon had climbed to the top, and

seemed to stop a moment to rest and look down on the valley.

27. The Colonel left for Ohio to-day, to be gone two weeks.

I came from the quarters of Brigadier-General Schleich a few minutes ago. He is a three-months' brigadier, and a rampant demagogue. Schleich said that slaves who accompanied their masters to the field, when captured, should be sent to Cuba and sold to pay the expenses of the war. I suggested that it would be better to take them to Canada and liberate them, and that so soon as the Government began to sell negroes to pay the expenses of the war I would throw up my commission and go home. Schleich was a State Senator when the war began. He is what might be called a tremendous little man, swears terribly, and imagines that he thereby shows his snap. Snap, in his opinion, is indispensable to a military man. If snap is the only thing a soldier needs, and profanity is snap, Schleich is a second Napoleon. This General Snap will go home, at the expiration of his three-months' term, unregretted by officers and men. Major Hugh Ewing will return with him. Last night the Major became thoroughly elevated, and he is not quite sober yet. He thinks, when in his cups, that our generals are too careful of their men. "What are a th-thousand men," said he, "when (hic) principle is at stake? Men's lives (hic) should n't be thought of at such a time (hic). Amount to nothing (hic). Our generals are too d—d slow" (hic). The Major is a man of excellent natural capacity, the son of Hon. Thomas Ewing, of Lancaster, and brother-in-law of W. T. Sherman, now a colonel or brigadier-general in the army. W. T. Sherman is the brother of John Sherman. The news from Manassas is very bad. The disgraceful flight of our troops will do us more injury, and is more to be regretted, than the loss of fifty thousand men. It will impart new life, courage, and confidence to our enemies. They will say to their troops : " You see how these scoundrels run when you stand up to them."

29. Was slightly unwell this morning ; but about noon accompanied General Reynolds, Colonel Wagner, Colonel Heffron, and a squad of cavalry, up the valley, and returned somewhat tired, but quite well. Lieutenant-Colonel Owen was also of the party. He is fifty or fifty-five years old, a thin, spare man, of very ordinary personal appearance, but of fine scientific and literary attainments. For some years he was a professor in a Southern military school. He has held the position of State Geologist of Indiana, and is the son of the celebrated Robert J. Owen, who founded the Communist Society at New Harmony, Indiana. Every sprig, leaf, and stem on the route suggested to Colonel Owen something to talk about, and he proved to be a very entertaining companion.

General Reynolds is a graduate of West Point, and has the theory of war completely ; but whether he has the broad, practical common sense, more important than book knowledge, time will determine. As yet he is an untried quantity, and, therefore, unknown.

30. About two o'clock P. M., for want of something better to do, I climbed the high mountain in front of our camp. The side is as steep as the roof of a gothic house. By taking hold of bushes and limbs of trees, after a half hour of very hard work, I managed to get to the top, completely exhausted. The outlook was magnificent. Tygart's valley, the river winding through it, and a boundless succession of mountains and ridges, all lay before me. My attention, however, was soon diverted from the landscape to the huckleberries. They were abundant; and now and then I stumbled on patches of delicious raspberries. I remained on the mountain, resting and picking berries, until half-past four. I must be in camp at six to post my pickets, but there was no occasion for haste. So, after a time, I started leisurely down, not the way I had come up, but, as I supposed, down the eastern slope, a way, apparently, not so steep and difficult as the one by which I had ascended. I traveled on, through vines and bushes, over fallen timber, and under great trees, from which I could scarcely obtain a glimpse of the sky, until finally I came to a mountain stream. I expected to find the road, not the stream, and began to be a little uncertain as to my whereabouts. After reflection, I concluded I would be most likely to reach camp by going up the stream, and so started. Trees in many places had fallen across the ravine, and my progress was neither easy nor rapid; but I pushed on as best I could. I never knew so well before what a mountain stream

was. I scrambled over rocks and fallen trees, and
through thickets of laurel, until I was completely
worn out. Lying down on the rocks, which in high
water formed part of the bed of the stream, I took a
drink, looked at my watch, and found it was half-past
five. My pickets were to be posted at six. Having
but a half hour left, I started on. I could see no
opening yet. The stream twisted and turned, keeping no one general direction for twenty rods, and
hardly for twenty feet. It grew smaller, and as the
ravine narrowed the way became more difficult. Six
o'clock had now come. I could not see the sun, and
only occasionally could get glimpses of the sky. I
began to realize that I was lost; but concluded finally
that I would climb the mountain again, and ascertain,
if I could, in what direction the camp lay. I have
had some hard tramps, and have done some hard
work, but never labored half so hard in a whole week
as I did for one hour in getting up that mountain,
pushing through vines, climbing over logs, breaking
through brush. Three or four times I lay down out
of breath, utterly exhausted, and thought I would
proceed no further until morning; but when I
thought of my pickets, and reflected that General
Reynolds would not excuse a trip so foolish and
untimely, I made new efforts and pushed on. Finally
I reached the summit of the mountain, but found it
not the one from which I had descended. Still
higher mountains were around me. The trees and
bushes were so dense I could hardly see a rod before
me. It was now seven o'clock, an hour after the

time when I should have been in camp. I lay down,
determined to remain all night; but my clothing was
so thin that I soon became chilly, and so got up and
started on again. Once I became entangled in a
wilderness of grapevines and briers, and had much
difficulty in getting through them. It was now half-
past seven, and growing dark; but, fortunately, at this
time, I heard a dog bark, a good way off to the right,
and, turning in that direction, I came to a cowpath.
Which end of it should I take? Either end, I concluded, would be better than to remain where I was;
so I worked myself into a dog-trot, wound down
around the side of the mountain, and reached the
road, a mile and a half south of camp, and went to
my quarters fast as my legs could carry me. I found
my detail for picket duty waiting and wondering what
could so detain the officer of the day.

31. The Fifteenth Indiana, Colonel Wagner,
moved up the valley eight miles.

The sickly months are now on us. Considerable
dysentery among the men, and many reported unfit
for duty.

My limbs are stiff and sore from yesterday's exercise, but my adventure proves to have been a lucky
one. The mountain path I stumbled on was unknown to us before, and we find, on inquiry, that it
leads over the ridges. The enemy might, by taking
this path, follow it up during the day, encamp almost
within our picket lines without being discovered, and
then, under cover of night, or in the early morning,

come down upon us while we were in our beds. It will be picketed hereafter.

A private of Company E wrote home that he had killed two secessionists. A Zanesville paper published the letter. When the boys of his company read it they obtained spades, called on the soldier who had drawn so heavily on the credulity of his friends, and told him they had come to bury the dead. The poor fellow protested, apologized, and excused himself as best he could, but all to no purpose. He is never likely to hear the last of it.

I am reminded that when coming from Bellaire to Fetterman, a soldier doing guard duty on the railroad said that a few mornings before he had gone out, killed two secessionists who were just sitting down to breakfast, and then eaten the breakfast himself.

AUGUST, 1861.

1. It is said the pickets of the Fourteenth Indiana and the enemy's cavalry came in collision to-day,
and that three of the latter were killed.

It is now 9 P. M. Sergeants are calling the roll
for the last time to-night. In half an hour taps will
be sounded and the lights extinguished in every private's tent. The first call in the morning, reveille, is
at five; breakfast call, six; surgeon's call, seven;
drill, eight; recall, eleven; dinner, twelve; drill
again at four; recall, five; guard-mounting, half-past
five; first call for dress-parade, six; second call, half-
past six; tattoo at nine, and taps at half-past. So the
day goes round.

Hardee for a month or more was a book of impenetrable mysteries. The words conveyed no idea to my
mind, and the movements described were utterly beyond my comprehension; but now the whole thing
comes almost without study.

2. Jerrolaman went out this afternoon and picked
nearly a peck of blackberries. Berries of various
kinds are very abundant. The fox-grape is also found
in great plenty, and as big as one's thumb.

4

The Indianians are great ramblers. Lieutenant Bell says they can be traced all over the country, for they not only eat all the berries, but nibble the thorns off the bushes.

General Reynolds told me, this evening, he thought it probable we would be attacked soon. Have been distributing ammunition, forty rounds to the man.

My black horse was missing this morning. Conway looked for him the greater part of the day, and finally found him in possession of an Indiana captain. It happened in this way: Captain Rupp, Thirteenth Indiana, told his men he would give forty dollars for a *sesesh* horse, and they took my horse out of the pasture, delivered it to him, and got the money. He rode the horse up the valley to Colonel Wagner's station, and when he returned bragged considerably over his good luck; but about dark Conway interviewed him on the subject, when a change came o'er the spirit of his dream. Colonel Sullivan tells me the officers now talk to Rupp about the fine points of his horse, ask to borrow him, and desire to know when he proposes to ride again.

A little group of soldiers are sitting around a camp-fire, not far away, entertaining each other with stories and otherwise. Just now one of them lifts up his voice, and in a melancholly strain sings:

> Somebody —— " is weeping
> For gallant Andy Gay,
> Who now in death lies sleeping
> On the field of Monterey."

While I write he strikes into another air, and these
are the words as I catch them:

" Come back, come back, my purty fair maid!
   Ten thousand of my *jinture* on you I will bestow
   If you 'll consent to marry me ;
   Oh, do not say me no."

But the maid is indifferent to *jintures*, and replies indignantly:

" Oh, hold your tongue, captain, your words are all in vain ;
   I have a handsome sweetheart now across the main,
   And if I do not find him I 'll mourn continuali."

More of this interesting dialogue between the captain and the pretty fair maid I can not catch.

The sky is clear, but the night very dark. I do
not contemplate my ride to the picket posts with any
great degree of pleasure. A cowardly sentinel is
more likely to shoot at you than a brave one. The
fears of the former do not give him time to consider
whether the person advancing is friend or foe.

3. We hear of the enemy daily. Colonel Kimball, on the mountain, and Colonel Wagner, up the
valley, are both in hourly expectation of an attack.
The enemy, encouraged by his successes at Manassas,
will probably attempt to retrieve his losses in Western
Virginia.

4. At one o'clock P. M. General Reynolds sent for
me. Two of Colonel Wagner's companies had been
surrounded, and an attack on Wagner's position expected to-night. The enemy reported three thousand

strong. He desired me to send half of my regiment and two of Loomis' guns to the support of Wagner. I took six companies and started up the valley. Reached Wagner's quarters at six o'clock. Brought neither tents nor provisions, and to-night will turn in with the Indianians.

It is true that the enemy number three thousand; the main body being ten or fifteen miles away. Their pickets and ours, however, are near each other; but General Reynolds was misinformed as to two of Wagner's companies. They had not been surrounded.

To-morrow Colonel Wagner and I will make a reconnoissance, and ascertain if the rebels are ready to fight. Wagner has six hundred and fifty men fit for duty, and I have four hundred. Besides these, we have three pieces of artillery. Altogether, we expect to be able to hoe them a pretty good row, if they should advance on us. Four of the enemy were captured to-day. A company of cavalry is approaching. "Halt! who comes there?" cries the sentinel. "Lieutenant Denny, without the countersign." "All right," shouts Colonel Wagner, "let him come." I write with at least four fleas hopping about on my legs.

5. To-day we felt our way up the valley eight miles, but did not reach the rebels.

To-night our pickets were sure they heard firing off in the direction of Kanawha. If so, Cox and Wise must be having a pleasant little interchange of lead.

The chaplain of the Thirteenth Indiana is the

counterpart of Scott's Holy Clerk of Copmanhurst,
or the fighting friar of the times of Robin Hood.
In answer to some request he has just said that he will
" go to thunder before doing it." The first time I
saw this fighting parson was at the burnt bridge near
Huttonville. He had two revolvers and a hatchet in
his belt, and appeared more like a firebrand of war
than a minister of peace. I now hear the rough
voice of a braggadocio captain in the adjoining tent,
who, if we may believe his own story, is the most
formidable man alive. His hair-breadth escapes are
innumerable, and his anxiety to get at the enemy is
intense. Is it not ancient Pistol come again to astonish the world by deeds of reckless daring?

We have sent out a scouting party, and hope to
learn something more of the rebels during the night.
Wagner, Major Wood, Captain Abbott, and others
are having a game of whist.

6. Our camp equipage came up to-day, so that we
are now in our own tents.

Four of my companies are on picket, scattered up
the valley for miles, and half of the other two are
doing guard duty in the neighborhood of the camp.
I do not, by any means, approve of throwing out
such heavy pickets and scattering our men so much.
We are in the presence of a force probably twice as
large as our own, and should keep our troops well in
hand.

Our scouts have been busy ; but, although they
have brought in a few prisoners, mostly farmers resid-
ing in the vicinity of the enemy's camp, we have ob-

tained but little information respecting the rebels. I
intend to send out a scouting party in the morning.
Lieutenant Driscoll will command it. He is a brave,
and, I think, prudent officer, and will leave camp at
four o'clock, follow the road six miles, then take to
the mountains, and endeavor to reach a point where
he can overlook the enemy and estimate his strength.

7. The scouting party sent out this morning were
conveyed by wagons six miles up the valley, and were
to take to the mountains, half a mile beyond. I instructed Lieutenant Driscoll to exercise the utmost
caution, and not take his men further than he thought
reasonably safe. Of course perfect safety is not expected. Our object, however, is to get information,
not to give it by losing the squad.

At eleven o'clock a courier came in hot haste from
the front, to inform us that a flag of truce, borne by
a Confederate major, with an escort of six dragoons,
was on the way to camp. Colonel Wagner and I
rode out to meet the party, and were introduced to
Major Lee, the son, as I subsequently ascertained, of
General Robert E. Lee, of Virginia. The Major informed us that his communication could only be im-
parted to our General, and a courier was at once dispatched to Huttonville.

At four o'clock General Reynolds arrived, accompanied by Colonel Sullivan and a company of cavalry.
Wagner and I joined the General's party, and all galloped to the outpost, to interview the Confederate major. His letter contained a proposition to exchange
prisoners captured by the rebels at Manassas for those

taken at Rich mountain. The General appointed a day on which a definite answer should be returned, and Major Lee, accompanied by Lieutenant-Colonel Owen and myself, rode to the outlying picket station, where his escort had been halted and detained.

Major Lee is near my own age, a heavy set, but well-proportioned man, somewhat inclined to boast, not overly profound, and thoroughly impregnated with the idea that he is a Virginian and a Lee withal. As I shook hands at parting with this scion of an illustrious house, he complimented me by saying that he hoped soon to have the honor of meeting me on the battlefield. I assured him that it would afford me pleasure, and I should make all reasonable efforts to gratify him in this regard. I did not desire to fight, of course, but I was bound not to be excelled in the matter of knightly courtesy.

8. Major Wood, Fifteenth Indiana, thought he heard chopping last night, and imagined that the enemy was engaged in cutting a road to our rear.

Lieutenant Driscoll and party returned to-day. They slept on the mountains last night; were inside the enemy's picket lines; heard reveille sounded this morning, but could not obtain a view of the camp.

Have just returned from a sixteen-mile ride, visiting picket posts. The latter half of the ride was after nightfall. Found officers and men vigilant and ready to meet an attack.

Obtained some fine huckleberries and blackberries on the mountain to-day. Had a blackberry pie and pudding for dinner. Rather too much happiness for one day; but then the crust of the pudding was tolerably tough. The grass is a foot high in parts of my tent, where it has not been trodden down, and the gentle grasshopper makes music all the day, and likewise all the night.

Our fortifications are progressing slowly. If the enemy intends to attack at all, he will probably do so before they are complete; and if he does not, the fortifications will be of no use to us. But this is the philosophy of a lazy man, and very similar to that of the Irishman who did not put roof on his cabin: when it rained he could not, and in fair weather he did not need it.

9. Pickets report firing, artillery and musketry, over the mountain, in the direction of Kimball.

The enemy's scouts were within three miles of our camp this afternoon, evidently looking for a path that would enable them to get to our rear. Fifty men have just been sent in pursuit; but owing to a little misunderstanding of instructions, I fear the expedition will be fruitless. Colonel Wagner neither thinks clearly nor talks with any degree of exactness. He has a loose, slip-shod, indefinite way with him, that tends to confusion and leads to misunderstandings and trouble.

I have been over the mountain on our left, hunting up the paths and familiarizing myself with the ground, so as to be ready to defeat any effort that may be made to turn our flank. Colonel Owen has been investigating the mountain on our right. The Colonel is a good thinker, an excellent conversationalist, and a very learned man. Geology is his darling, and he keeps one eye on the enemy, and the other on the rocks.

10. My tent is on the bank of the Valley river. The water, clear as crystal, as it hurries on over the rocks, keeps up a continuous murmur.

There will be a storm to-night. The sky is very dark, the wind rising, and every few minutes a vivid flash of lightning illuminates the valley, and the thunder rolls off among the mountains with a rumbling, echoing noise, like that which the gods might make in putting a hundred trains of celestial artillery in position.

11. Lieutenant Bowen, of topographical engineers, and myself, with ten men, carrying axes and guns, started up the mountain at seven o'clock this morning, followed a path to the crest, or dividing ridge, and felled trees to obstruct the way as much as possible. Returned to camp for dinner.

During the afternoon Lieutenant W. O. Merrill, Lieutenant Bowen, and I, ascended the mountain again by a new route. After reaching the crest, we endeavored to find the path which Lieutenant Bowen and I had traveled over in the morning, but were unable to do so. We continued our search until it became quite dark, when the two engineers, as well as myself, became utterly bewildered. Finally, Lieutenant Merrill took out his pocket compass, and said the camp was in that direction, pointing with his hand. I insisted he was wrong; that he would not reach camp by going

5

that way. He insisted that he would, and must be governed by some general principles, and so started off on his own hook, leaving us to pursue our own course. Finally Bowen lost confidence in me, said I was not going in the right direction at all, and insisted that we should turn squarely around, and go the opposite way. At last I yielded with many misgivings, and allowed him to lead. After going down a thousand feet or more, we found ourselves in a ravine, through which a small stream of water flowed. Following this, we finally reached the valley. We knew now exactly where we were, and by wading the river reached the road, and so got to camp at nine o'clock at night.

Merrill, who was governed by general principles, failed to strike the camp directly, strayed three or four miles to the right of it, came down in Stewart's run valley, and did not reach camp until about midnight.

On our trip to-day, we found a bear trap, made of heavy logs, the lid arranged to fall when the bear entered and touched the bait.

12. This is the fourth day that Captain Cunard's company has been lying in the woods, three miles from camp, guarding an important road, although a very rough and rugged one. Companies upon duty like this, remain at their posts day and night, good weather and bad, without any shelter, except that afforded by the trees, or by little booths constructed of logs and branches. From the main station, where the captain remains, sub-pickets are sent out in

charge of sergeants and corporals, and these often make little houses of logs, which they cover with cedar boughs or branches of laurel, and denominate forts. In the wilderness, to-day, I stumbled upon Fort Stiner, the head-quarters of a sub-picket commanded by Corporal William Stiner, of the Third. The Corporal and such of his men as were off duty, were sitting about a fire, heating coffee and roasting slices of fat pork, preparing thus the noonday meal.

13. At noon Colonel Marrow, Major Keifer, and I, took dinner with Esquire Stalnaker, an old-style man, born fifty years ago in the log house where he now lives. Two spinning-wheels were in the best room, and rattled away with a music which carried me back to the pioneer days of Ohio. A little girl of five or six years stole up to the wheel when the mother's back was turned, and tried her skill on a roll. How proud and delighted she was when she had spun the wool into a long, uneven thread, and secured it safely on the spindle. Surely, the child of the palace, reared in the lap of luxury and with her hands in the mother's jewel-box, could not have been happier or more triumphant in her bearing.

These West Virginians are uncultivated, uneducated and rough, and need the common school to civilize and modernize them. Many have never seen a railroad, and the telegraph is to them an incomprehensible mystery.

Governor Dennison has appointed a Mr. John G. Mitchell, of Columbus, adjutant of the Third.

14. Privates Yincent and Watson, sentinels of a

sub-picket, under command of Corporal Stiner, discovered a man stealing through the woods, and halted him. He professed to be a farm hand; said his employer had a mountain farm not far away, where he pastured cattle. A two-year-old steer had strayed off, and he was looking for him. His clothes were fearfully torn by brush and briars. His hands and face were scratched by thorns. He had taken off his boots to relieve his swollen feet, and was carrying them in his hands. Imitating the language and manners of an uneducated West Virginian, he asked the sentinel if he "had seed anything of a red steer." The sentinel had not. After continuing the conversation for a time, he finally said: "Well, I must be a goin'; it is a gettin' late, and I am durned feared I won't git back to the farm afore night. Good day." "Hold on," said the sentinel; "better go and see the Captain." "O, no; don't want to trouble him; it is not likely he has seed the steer, and it's a gettin' late." "Come right along," replied the sentinel, bringing his gun down; "the Captain will not mind being troubled; in fact, I am instructed to take such men as you to him."

Captain Cunard questioned the prisoner closely, asked whom he worked for, how much he was getting a month for his services, and, finally, pointing to the long-legged military boots which he was still holding in his hands, asked how much they cost. "Fifteen dollars," replied the prisoner." "Fifteen dollars! Is not that rather more than a farm hand who gets but twelve dollars a month can afford to pay for boots?"

inquired the Captain. " Well, the fact is, boots is a gettin' high since the war, as well as every thing else." But Captain Cunard was not satisfied. The prisoner was not well up in the character he had undertaken to play, and was told that he must go to head-quarters. Finding that he was caught, he at once threw off the mask, and confessed that he was Captain J. A. De Lagniel, formerly of the regular army, but now in the Confederate service. Wounded at the battle of Rich mountain, he had been secreted at a farm-house near Beverly until able to travel, and was now trying to get around our pickets and reach the rebel army. He had been in the mountains five days and four nights. The provisions with which he started, and which consisted of a little bag of biscuit, had become moldy. He thought, from the distance traveled, that he must be beyond our lines and out of danger.

De Lagniel is an educated man, and his wife and friends believe him to have been killed at Rich mountain. He speaks in high terms of Captain Cunard, and says, when the latter began to question him, he soon found it was useless to play Major Andre, for Paulding was before him, too sharp to be deceived and too honest to be bribed. When De Lagniel was brought into camp he was wet and shivering, weak, and thoroughly broken down by starvation, cold, exposure, and fatigue. The officers supplied him with the clothing necessary to make him comfortable.

15. I have a hundred axmen in my charge, fell-

ing timber on the mountain, and constructing rough breastworks to protect our left flank.

General Reynolds came up to-day to see De Lagniel. They are old acquaintances, were at West Point together, and know each other like brothers.

The irrepressible Corporal Casey, who, in fact, had nothing whatever to do with the capture of De Lagniel, is now surrounded by a little group of soldiers. He is talking to them about the prisoner, who, since it is known that he is an acquaintance of General Reynolds, has become a person of great importance in the camp. The Corporal speaks in the broadest Irish brogue, and is telling his hearers that he knew the fellow was a *sesesh* at once; that he leveled his musket at him and towld him to halt; that if he had n't marched straight up to him he would have put a minnie ball through his heart; that he had his gun cocked and his finger on the trigger, and was a mind to shoot him anyway. Then he tells how he propounded this and that question, which confused the prisoner, and finally concludes by saying that De Lagniel might be d—d thankful indade that he escaped with his life.

The Corporal is the best-known man in the regiment. He prides himself greatly on the Middle Fork "skrimage." A day or two after that affair, and at a time when whisky was so scarce that it was worth its weight in gold, some officers called the Corporal up and asked him to give them an account of the "skrimage." Before he entered upon the subject, it was suggested that Captain Dubois, who had the little

whisky there was in the party, should give him a
taste to loosen his tongue. The Corporal, nothing
loth, took the flask, and, raising it to his mouth,
emptied it, to the utter dismay of the Captain and
his friends. The dhrap had the effect desired. The
Corporal described, with great particularity, his manner of going into action, dwelt with much emphasis
on the hand-to-hand encounters, the thrusts, the par-
ries, the final clubbing of the musket, and the utter
discomfiture and mortal wounding of his antagonist.
In fact by this time there were two of them; and
finally, as the fight progressed, a dozen or more
bounced down on him. It was lively! There was
no time for the loading of guns. Whack, thump,
crack! The head of one was broken, another lay dying of a bayonet thrust, and still another had per-
ished under the sledge-hammer blow of his fist. The
ground was covered now with the slain. He stood
knee-deep in secesh blood; but a bugle sounded away
off on the hills, and the d—d scoundrels who were
able to get away ran off as fast as their legs could
carry them. Had they stood up like men he
would have destroyed the whole regiment; for, you
see, he was just getting his hand in. "But, Corporal," inquired Captain Hunter, "what were the
other soldiers of your company doing all this time?"
"Bless your sowl, Captain, and do you think I had
nothing to do but to watch the boys? Be jabers, it
was a day when every man had to look after himself."

16. The opinion seems to be growing that the reb-

els do not intend to attack us. They have put it off
too long.

A scouting party will start out in the morning, under the guidance of " old Leather Breeches," a primi-
tive West Virginian, who has spent his life in the
mountains. His right name is Bennett. He wears
an antiquated pair of buckskin pantaloons, and has a
cabin-home on the mountain, twelve miles away.

A tambourine is being played near by, and Fox,
with a heart much lighter than his complexion, is in-
dulging in a double shuffle.

There are many snakes in the mountains: rattle-
snakes, copperheads, blacksnakes, and almost every
other variety of the snake kind; in short, the boys
have snake on the brain. To-day one of the chop-
pers made a sudden grab for his trouser leg; a snake
was crawling up. He held the loathsome reptile
tightly by the head and body, and was fearfully agitated. A comrade slit down the leg of the pantaloon
with a knife, when lo! an innocent little roll of red
flannel was discovered.

The boys are very liberal in the bestowal of titles.
Colonel Hogseye is indebted to them for his commission. The Colonel commands an ax just now. Ordinarily he carries a musket, sleeps and dines with his
subordinates, and is not above traveling on foot.

Fox's real name, I ascertained lately, is William
Washington. His brother, now in the service of-the
surgeon, is called Handsome, and Colonel Marrow's
servant is known by the boys as the Bay Nigger.

17. Was awakened this morning at one o'clock,

by a soldier in search of a surgeon. One of our pickets had been wounded. The post was on the river bank. The sentinel saw a man approaching on the opposite side of the river, challenged, and saw him level his gun. Both fired. The sentinel was wounded in the leg by a small squirrel bullet. The other man was evidently wounded, for after it became light enough he was traced half a mile by blood on the ground, weeds, and leaves. The surgeon is of the opinion that the ball struck his left arm. From information obtained this morning, it is believed this man is secreted not many miles away. A party of ten has been sent to look for him.

This is by far the pleasantest camp we have ever had. The river runs its whole length. The hospital and surgeons' tents are located on a very pretty little island, a quiet, retired spot, festooned with vines, in the shadow of great trees, and carpeted with moss soft and velvety as the best of Brussels.

18. The name of our camp is properly Elk Water, not Elk Fork. The little stream which comes down to the river, from which the camp derives its name, is called Elk Water, because tradition affirms that in early days the elk frequented the little valley through which it runs.

The fog has been going up from the mountains, and the rain coming down in the valley. The river roars a little louder than usual, and its water is a little less clear.

The party sent in pursuit of the bushwhacker has returned. Found no one.

Two men were seen this evening, armed with rifles, prowling among the bushes near the place where the affair of last night occurred. They were fired upon, but escaped.

An accident, which particularly interests my old company, occurred a few minutes ago. John Heskett, Jeff Long, and four or five other men, were detailed from Company I for picket duty. Heskett and Long are intimate friends, and were playing together, the one with a knife and the other with a pocket pistol. The pistol was discharged accidentally, and the ball struck Heskett in the neck, inflicting a serious wound, but whether fatal or not the surgeon can not yet tell. The affair has cast a shadow over the company. Young Heskett bears himself bravely. Long is inconsolable, and begs the boys to shoot him.

20. These mountain streams are unreliable. We had come to regard the one on which we are encamped as a quiet, orderly little river, that would be good enough to notify us when it proposed to swell out and overflow the adjacent country. In fact we had bragged about it, made all sorts of complimentary mention of it, put our tents on its margin, and allowed it to encircle our sick and wounded; but we have now lost all confidence in it. Yesterday, about noon, it began to rise. It had been raining, and we thought it natural enough that the waters should increase a little. At four o'clock it had swelled very considerably, but still kept within its bed of rock and gravel, and we admired it all the more for the energy displayed in hurrying along branches, logs, and some-

times whole trees. At six o'clock we found it was
rising at the rate of one foot per hour, and that the
water had now crept to within a few feet of the hospital tent, in which lay two wounded and a dozen or
more of sick. Dr. McMeens became alarmed and
called for help. Thirty or more boys stripped, swam
to the island, and removed the hospital to higher
ground—to the highest ground, in fact, which the
island afforded. The boys returned, and we felt safe.
At seven o'clock, however, we found the river still
rising rapidly. It covered nearly the whole island.
Logs, brush, green trees, and all manner of drift went
sweeping by at tremendous speed, and the water
rushed over land which had been dry half an hour
before, with apparently as strong a current as that in
the channel. We knew then that the sick and
wounded were in danger. How to rescue them was
now the question. A raft was suggested; but a raft
could not be controlled in such a current, and if it
went to pieces or was hurried away, the sick and
wounded must drown. Fortunately a better way was
suggested; getting into a wagon, I ordered the
driver to go above some distance, so that we could
move with the current, and then ford the stream.
After many difficulties, occasioned mainly by floating
logs and driftwood, and swimming the horses part of
the way, we succeeded in getting over. I saw it was
impossible to carry the sick back, and that there was
but one way to render them secure. I had the horses
unhitched, and told the driver to swim them back and
bring over two or three more wagons. Two more

finally reached me, and one team, in attempting to cross, was carried down stream and drowned. I had the three wagons placed on the highest point I could find, then chained together and staked securely to the ground. Over the boxes of two of these we rolled the hospital tent, and on this placed the sick and wounded, just as the water was creeping upon us. On the third wagon we put the hospital stores. It was now quite dark. Not more than four feet square of dry land remained of all our beautiful island; and the river was still rising. We watched the water with much anxiety. At ten o'clock it reached the wagon hubs, and covered every foot of the ground; but soon after we were pleased to see that it began to go down a little. Those of us who could not get into the wagons had climbed the trees. At one o'clock it commenced to rain again, when we managed to hoist a tent over the sick. At two o'clock the long-roll, the signal for battle, was beaten in camp, and we could just hear, above the roar of the water, the noise made by the men as they hurriedly turned out and fell into line.

It will not do, however, to conclude that this was altogether a night of terrors. It was, in fact, not so very disagreeable after all. There was a by-play going on much of the time, which served to illuminate the thick darkness, and divert our minds from the gloomier aspects of the scene. Smith, the teamster who brought me across, had returned to the mainland with the horses, and then swam back to the island. By midnight he had become very drunk. One of the

hospital attendants was very far gone in his cups, also.
These two gentlemen did not seem to get along ami-
cably; in fact, they kept up a fusillade of words all
night, and so kept us awake. The teamster insisted
that the hospital attendant should address him as Mr.
Smith. The Smith family, he argued, was of the
highest respectability, and being an honored member
of that family, he would permit no man under the
rank of a Major-General to call him Jake. George
McClellan sometimes addressed him by his christian
name; but then George and he were Cincinnatians,
old neighbors, and intimate personal friends, and, of
course, took liberties with each other. This could
not justify one who carried out pukes and slop-buck-
ets from a field hospital in calling him Jake, or
even Jacob.

Mr. Smith's allusions to the hospital attendant were
not received by that gentleman in the most amiable
spirit. He grew profane, and insisted that he was not
only as good a man as Smith, but a much better one,
and he dared the bloviating mule scrubber to get
down off his perch and stand up before him like a
man. But Jake's temper remained unruffled, and
along toward morning, in a voice more remarkable for strength than melody, he favored us with a
song:

> "Ho! gif ghlass uf goodt lauger du me;
>   Du mine fadter, mine modter, mine vife:
> Der day's vork vos done, undt we'll see
>   Vot bleasures der vos un dis life,

Undt ve sit us aroundt mit der table,
    Undt ve speak uf der oldt, oldt time,
Ven we lif un dot house mit der gable,
    Un der vine-cladt banks uf der Rhine;

Undt mine fadter, his voice vos a quiver,
    Undt mine modter, her eyes vos un tears,
Ash da dthot uf dot home un der river,
    Undt kindt friendst uf earlier years;

Undt I saidt du mine fadter be cheerie,
    Du mine modter not longer lookt sadt,
Here's a blace undt a rest for der weary,
    Und ledt us eat, drink, undt be gladt.

So idt ever vos cheerful mitin;
    Vot dtho' idt be stormy mitoudt,
Vot care I vor der vorld undt idts din,
    Ven dose I luf best vos about;

So libft up your ghlass, mine modter,
    Undt libft up yours, Gretchen, my dear,
Undt libft up your lauger, mine fadter,
    Undt drink du long life und good cheer."

21. Francis Union was shot and killed by one of
our own sentinels last night, the ball entering just
under the nose. This resulted from the cowardice of
the soldier who fired. He was afraid to give the nec-
cesary challenge: four simple words: "Halt! who
comes there?" would have saved a life. This illustrates
the danger there is in visiting pickets at night. If the
sentinel halts the man, the man may fire at the sentinel. The latter, if timid, therefore makes sure of

the first shot, and does not challenge. We buried the
dead soldier with all the honors due one of his rank, on
a beautiful hill in the rear of our fortifications. He
was with me on the mountain chopping, a few days
ago, strong, healthy, vigorous, and young. No more
hard work for him!

23. With Wagner, Merrill, and Bowen, I rode
up the mountain on our left this afternoon. We had
one field-glass and two spy-glasses, and obtained a
magnificent view of the surrounding country. Here
and there we could see a cultivated spot or grazing
farm on the top of the mountain; but more frequently
these were on the slopes. We descried one house
with our glasses on the very tiptop of Rich, and so
far away that it seemed no larger than a tent. How
the man of the house gets up to his airy height and
gets down again puzzles us. He has the first gush
of the sunshine in the morning, and the latest gleam
in the evening. Very often, indeed, he must look
down upon the clouds, and, if he has a tender heart,
pity the poor devils in the valley who are being
rained on continually. Is it a pleasant home? Has
he wife and children in that mountain nest? Is
he a man of dogs and guns, who spends his years in
the mountains and glens hunting for bear and deer?
May it not be the baronial castle of "old Leather
Breeches" himself?

Away off to the east a cloud, black and heavy, is
resting on a peak of the Cheat. Around it the
mountain is glowing in the summer sun, and appears
soft and green. A gauze of shimmering blue man-

tles the crest, darkens in the coves, and becomes quite black in the gorges. The rugged rocks and scraggy trees, if there be any, are at this distance invisible, and nothing is seen but what delights the eye and quickens the imagination.

We see by the papers that Ohio is preparing to organize a grand Union party, with a platform on which both Republicans and Democrats can stand. I am glad of this. There should be but one party in the North, and that party willing to make all sacrifices for the Union.

24. Last night a sentinel on one of the picket posts halted a stump and demanded the countersign. No response being made, he fired. The entire Fifteenth Indiana sprang to arms; the cannoniers gathered about their guns, and a thousand eyes peered into the darkness to get a glimpse of the approaching enemy. But the stump, evidently intimidated by the first shot, did not advance, and so the Hoosiers returned again to their couches, to dream, doubtless, of the subject of a song very common now in camp, to wit:

> "Old Governor Wise,
> With his goggle eyes."

25. The Twenty-third Ohio, Colonel Scammon, will be here to-morrow. Stanley Matthews is the lieutenant-colonel of this regiment, and my old friend, Rutherford B. Hayes, the major. The latter is an accomplished gentleman, graduate of Harvard Law School, and will, it is said, in all probability, succeed

Gurley in Congress. Matthews has a fine reputation as a speaker and lawyer, and, I have been told, is the most promising young man in Ohio. Scammon is a West Pointer.

26. Five companies of the Twenty-third Ohio and five companies of the Ninth Ohio arrived to-day, and are encamped in a maple grove about a mile below us. A detachment of cavalry came up also, and is quartered near. Other regiments are coming. It is said the larger portion of the troops in West Virginia are tending in this direction; but on what particular point it ·is proposed to concentrate them rumor saith not.

General McClellan did not go far enough at first. After the defeat of Pegram, at Rich mountain, and Garnett, at Laurel Hill, the Southern army of this section was utterly demoralized. It scattered, and the men composing it, who were not captured, fled, terror stricken, to their homes. We could have marched to Staunton without opposition, and taken possession of the very strongholds the enemy is now fortifying against us. If in our advanced position supplies could not have been obtained from the North, the army might have subsisted off the country. Thus, by pushing vigorously forward, we could have divided the enemy's forces, and thus saved our army in the East from humiliating defeat. This is the way it looks to me; but, after all, there may have been a thousand good reasons for remaining here, of which I know nothing. One thing, however, is, I think, very evi-

6

dent: a successful army, elated with victory, and eager
to advance, is not likely to be defeated by a dispirited
opponent. One-fourth, at least, of the strength of
this army disappeared when it heard of the rebel triumphs on the Potomac.

Latter part of August the writer was sent to Ohio
for recruits for the regiment, and did not return to
camp until the middle of September.

SEPTEMBER 1861.

19. Reached camp yesterday at noon. My recruits arrived to-day.

The enemy was here in my absence in strength and
majesty, and repeated, with a slight variation, the
grand exploit of the King of France, by

> " Marching up the hill with twenty thousand men,
>   And straightway marching down again."

There was lively skirmishing for a few days, and
hot work expected; but, for reasons unknown to us,
the enemy retired precipitately.

On Sunday morning last fifty men of the Sixth
Ohio, when on picket, were surprised and captured.
My friend, Lieutenant Merrill, fell into the hands of
the enemy, and is now probably on his way to Castle
Pinckney. Further than this our rebellious friends
did us no damage. Our men, at this point, killed
Colonel Washington, wounded a few others, and further than this inflicted but little injury upon the enemy. The country people near whom the rebels encamped say they got to fighting among themselves.
The North Carolinians were determined to go home,

and regiments from other States claimed that their term of service had expired, and wanted to leave. I am glad they did, and trust they may go home, hang up their guns, and go to work like sensible people, for then I could do the same.

23. This afternoon I rode by a mountain path to a log cabin in which a half dozen wounded Tennessee-ans are lying. One poor fellow had his leg ampu-tated yesterday, and was very feeble. One had been struck by a ball on the head and a buckshot in the lungs. Two boys were but slightly wounded, and were in good spirits. To one of these—a jovial, pleasant boy—Dr. Seyes said, good humoredly : " You need have no fears of dying from a gunshot; you are too big a devil, and were born to be hung." Colonel Marrow sought to question this same fel-low in regard to the strength of the enemy, when the boy said : " Are you a commissioned officer ?" " Yes," replied Marrow. " Then," returned he, " you ought to know that a private soldier don't know any-thing."

In returning to camp, we followed a path which led to a place where a regiment of the rebels had encamped one night. They had evidently become panic-stricken and left in hot haste. The woods were strewn with knapsacks, blankets, and canteens.

The ride was a pleasant one. The path, first wild and rugged, finally led to a charming little valley, through which Beckey's creek hurries down to the river. Leaving this, we traveled up the side of a ra-

vine, through which a little stream fretted and
fumed, and dashed into spray against slimy rocks,
and then gathered itself up for another charge, and so
pushed gallantly on toward the valley and the sunshine.

What a glorious scene! The sky filled with stars;
the rising moon; two mountain walls so high, apparently, that one might step from them into heaven;
the rapid river, the thousand white tents dotting the
valley, the camp fires, the shadowy forms of soldiers;
in short, just enough of heaven and earth visible to
put one's fancy on the gallop. The boys are in groups
about their fires. The voice of the troubadour is
heard. It is a pleasant song that he sings, and I
catch part of it.

> " The minstrel 's returned from the war,
>   With spirits as buoyant as air,
>   And thus on the tuneful guitar
>   He sings in the bower of the fair:
>   The noise of the battle is over;
>   The bugle no more calls to arms;
>   A soldier no more, but a lover,
>   I kneel to the power of thy charms.
>   Sweet lady, dear lady, I 'm thine;
>   I bend to the magic of beauty,
>   Though the banner and helmet are mine,
>   Yet love calls the soldier to duty."

24. Our Indiana friends are providing for the
winter by laying in a stock of household furniture at
very much less than its original cost, and without

even consulting the owners. It is probable that our
Ohio boys steal occasionally, but they certainly do
not prosecute the business openly and courageously.

26. The Thirteenth Indiana, Sixth Ohio, and two
pieces of artillery went up the valley at noon, to feel
the enemy. It rained during the afternoon, and since
nightfall has poured down in torrents. The poor fellows who are now trudging along in the darkness and
storm, will think, doubtless, of home and warm beds.
It requires a pure article of patriotism, and a large
quantity of it, to make one oblivious for months at a
time of all the comforts of civil life.

This is the day designated by the President for
fasting and prayer. Parson Strong held service in
the regiment, and the Rev. Mr. Reed, of Zanesville,
Ohio, delivered a very eloquent exhortation. I trust
the supplications of the Church and the people may
have effect, and bring that Higher Power to our assistance which hitherto has apparently not been with
our arms especially.

27. To-night almost the entire valley is inundated.
Many tents are waist high in water, and where others
stood this morning the water is ten feet deep. Two
men of the Sixth Ohio are reported drowned. The
water got around them before they became aware of it,
and in endeavoring to escape they were swept down
the stream and lost. The river seems to stretch from
the base of one mountain to the other, and the whole
valley is one wild scene of excitement. Wherever a
spot of dry ground can be found, huge log fires are
burning, and men by the dozen are grouped around

them, anxiously watching the water and discussing the situation. Tents have been hastily pitched on the hills, and camp fires, each with its group of men, are blazing in many places along the side of the mountain. The rain has fallen steadily all day.

28. The Thirteenth Indiana and Sixth Ohio returned. The reconnoissance was unsuccessful, the weather being unfavorable.

OCTOBER, 1861.

2. Our camp is almost deserted. The tents of eight regiments dot the valley; but those of two regiments and a half only are occupied. The Hoosiers have all gone to Cheat mountain summit. They propose to steal upon the enemy during the night, take him by surprise, and thrash him thoroughly. I pray they may be successful, for since Rich mountain our army has done nothing worthy of a paragraph. Rosecrans' affair at Carnifex was a barren thing; certainly no battle and no victory, and the operations in this vicinity have at no time risen to the dignity of a skirmish.

Captain McDougal, with nearly one hundred men and three days' provisions, started up the valley this morning, with instructions to go in sight of the enemy, the object being to lead the latter to suppose the advance guard of our army is before him. By this device it is expected to keep the enemy in our front from going to the assistance of the rebels now threatening Kimball.

3. To-night, half an hour ago, received a dispatch from the top of Cheat, which reads as follows:

" All back. Made a very interesting reconnoissance.

Killed a large number of the enemy. Very small
loss on our side.   J. J. REYNOLDS,
                              Brigadier-General."

Why, when the battle was progressing so advan-
tageously for our side, did they not go on? This,
then, is the result of the grand demonstration on the
other side of the mountain.

McDougal's company returned, and report the enemy fallen back.

The frost has touched the foliage, and the mountain peaks look like mammoth bouquets; green, red,
yellow, and every modification of these colors appear
mingled in every possible fanciful and tasteful way.

Another dispatch has just come from the top of
Cheat, written, I doubt not, after the Indianians had
returned to camp and drawn their whisky ration.   It
sounds bigger than the first.   I copy it:

"Found the rebels drawn up in line of battle one
mile outside of their fortifications, drove them back
to their intrenchments, and continued the fight four
hours. Ten of our men wounded and ten killed.
Two or three hundred of the enemy killed."

If it be true that so many of the rebels were killed,
it is probable that two thousand at least were
wounded; and when three hundred are killed and
two thousand wounded, out of an army of twelve or
fifteen hundred men, the business is done up very
thoroughly. The dispatch which went to Richmond
to-night, I have no doubt, stated that "the Federals
attacked in great force, outnumbering us two or three

7

to one, and after a terrific engagement, lasting five hours, they were repulsed at all points with great slaughter. Our loss one killed and five wounded. Federal loss, five hundred killed and twenty-five hundred wounded." Thus are victories won and histories made. Verily the pen is mightier than the sword.

4. The Indianians have been returning from the summit all day, straggling along in squads of from three to a full company.

The men are tired, and the camp is quiet as a house. Six thousand are sleeping away a small portion of their three weary years of military service. This TIME stretches out before them, a broad, unknown, and extra-hazardous sea, with promise of some smooth sailing, but many days and nights of heavy winds and waves, in which some—how many !— will be carried down.

Their thoughts have now forced the sentinel lines, leaped the mountains, jumped the rivers, hastened home, and are lingering about the old fireside, looking in at the cupboard, and hovering over faces and places that have been growing dearer to them every day for the last five months. Old-fashioned places, tame and uninteresting then, but now how loved! And as for the faces, they are those of mothers, wives, and sweethearts, around which are entwined the tenderest of memories. But at daybreak, when reveille is sounded, these wanderers must come trooping back again in time for "hard-tack" and double quick.

5. Some of the Indiana regiments are utterly beyond discipline. The men are good, stout, hearty, intelligent fellows, and will make excellent soldiers; but they have now no regard for their officers, and, as a rule, do as they please. They came straggling back yesterday from the top of Cheat unofficered, and in the most unsoldierly manner. As one of these stray Indianians was coming into camp, he saw a snake in the river and cocked his gun. He was near the quarters of the Sixth Ohio, and many men were on the opposite side of the stream, among them a lieutenant, who called to the Indianian and begged him for God's sake not to fire; but the latter, unmindful of what was said, blazed away. The ball, striking the water, glanced and hit the lieutenant in the breast, killing him almost instantly.

6. The Third and Sixth Ohio, with Loomis' battery, left camp at half-past three in the afternoon, and took the Huntersville turnpike for Big Springs, where Lee's army has been encamped for some months. At nine o'clock we reached Logan's Mill, where the column halted for the night. It had rained heavily for some hours, and was still raining. The boys went into camp thoroughly wet, and very hungry and tired; but they soon had a hundred fires kindled, and, gathering around these, prepared and ate supper.

I never looked upon a wilder or more interesting scene. The valley is blazing with camp-fires; the men flit around them like shadows. Now some in-

domitable spirit, determined that neither rain nor
weather shall get him down, strikes up:

"Oh! say, can you see by the dawn's early light,
  What so proudly we hailed at the twilight's last gleaming,
  Whose broad stripes and bright stars, through the perilous
    fight,
  O'er the ramparts we watched were so gallantly stream-
    ing?"

A hundred voices join in, and the very mountains,
which loom up in the fire-light like great walls, whose
tops are lost in the darkness, resound with a rude
melody befiting so wild a night and so wild a scene.
But the songs are not all patriotic. Love and fun
make contribution also, and a voice, which may be
that of the invincible Irishman, Corporal Casey,
sings:

"'Twas a windy night. about two o'clock in the morning,
  An Irish lad, so tight, all the wind and weather scorning,
  At Judy Callaghan's door, sitting upon the paling,
  His love tale he did pour, and this is part of his wailing:
  Only say you'll be mistress Brallaghan;
  Don't say nay, charming Judy Callaghan."

A score of voices pick up the chorus, and the hills
and mountains seem to join in the Corporal's appeal
to the charming Judy:

    "Only say you'll be mistress Brallaghan;
      Don't say nay, charming Judy Callaghan."

Lieutenant Root is in command of Loomis' bat-

tery. Just before reaching Logan's one of his provision wagons tumbled down a precipice, severely injuring three men and breaking the wagon in pieces.

7. Left Logan's mill before the sun was up. The
rain continues, and the mud is deep. At eleven
o'clock we reached what is known as Marshall's store,
near which, until recently, the enemy had a pretty
large camp. Halted at the place half an hour, and
then moved four miles further on, where we found the
roads impassable for our artillery and transportation.

Learning that the enemy had abandoned Big
Springs and fallen back to Huntersville, the soldiers
were permitted to break ranks, while Colonel Marrow
and Major Keifer, with a company of cavalry, rode
forward to the Springs. Colonel Nick Anderson, Adjutant Mitchell and I followed. We found on the
road evidence of the recent presence of a very large
force. Quite a number of wagons had been left behind. Many tents had been ripped, cut to pieces, or
burned, so as to render them worthless. A large
number of beef hides were strung along the road.
One wagon, loaded with muskets, had been destroyed.
All of which showed, simply, that before the rebels
abandoned the place the roads had become so bad
that they could not carry off their baggage.

The object of the expedition being now accomplished, we started back at three o'clock in the afternoon, and encamped for the night at Marshall's store.

8. Resumed the march early, found the river
waist high, and current swift; but the men all got
over safely, and we reached camp at one o'clock.

The Third has been assigned to a new brigade, to be commanded by Brigadier-General Dumont, of Indiana.

The paymaster has come at last.

Willis, my new servant, is a colored gentleman of much experience and varied accomplishments. He has been a barber on a Mississippi river steamboat, and a daguerreian artist. He knows much of the South, and manipulates a fiddle with wonderful skill. He is enlivening the hours now with his violin.

Oblivious to rain, mud, and the monotony of the camp, my thoughts are carried by the music to other and pleasanter scenes; to the cottage home, to wife and children, to a time still further away when we had no children, when we were making the preliminary arrangements for starting in the world together, when her cheeks were ruddier than now, when wealth and fame and happiness seemed lying just before me, ready to be gathered in, and farther away still, to a gentle, blue-eyed mother—now long gone—teaching her child to lisp his first simple prayer.

9. The day has been clear. The mountains, decorated by the artistic fingers of Jack Frost, loom up in the sunshine like magnificent, highly-colored, and beautiful pictures.

The night is grand. The moon, a crescent, now rests for a moment on the highest peak of the Cheat, and by its light suggests, rather than reveals, the outline of hill, valley, cove and mountain.

The boys are wide awake and merry. The fair weather has put new spirit in them all, and possibly

the presence of the paymaster has contributed somewhat to the good feeling which prevails.

Hark! This from the company quarters:

> " Her golden hair in ringlets fair;
>   Her eyes like diamonds shining;
>   Her slender waist, her carriage chaste,
>   Left me, poor soul, a pining.
>   But let the night be e'er so dark,
>   Or e'er so wet and rainy,
>   I will return safe back again
>   To the girl I left behind me."

From another quarter, in the rich brogue of the
Celt, we have:

> " Did you hear of the widow Malone,
>   Ohone!
>   Who lived in the town of Athlone,
>   Alone?
>   Oh! she melted the hearts
>   Of the swains in those parts;
>   So lovely the widow Malone,
>   Ohone!
>   So lovely the widow Malone.

10. Mr. Strong, the chaplain, has a prayer meeting in the adjoining tent. His prayers and exhorta-
tions fill me with an almost irresistible inclination to
close my eyes and shut out the vanities, cares, and
vexations of the world. Parson Strong is dull, but
he is very industrious, and on secular days devotes
his physical and mental powers to the work of tan-

ning three sheepskins and a calf's hide. On every fair day he has the skins strung on a pole before his tent to get the sun. He combs the wool to get it clean, and takes especial delight in rubbing the hides to make them soft and pliable. I told the parson the other day that I could not have the utmost confidence in a shepherd who took so much pleasure in tanning hides.

While Parson Strong and a devoted few are singing the songs of Zion, the boys are having cotillion parties in other parts of the camp. On the parade ground of one company Willis is officiating as musician, and the gentlemen go through "honors to partners" and "circle all" with apparently as much pleasure as if their partners had pink cheeks, white slippers, and dresses looped up with rosettes.

There comes from the Chaplain's tent a sweet and solemn refrain :

> " Perhaps He will admit my plea,
>   Perhaps will hear my prayer ;
>   But if I perish I will pray,
>   And perish only there.
>   I can but perish if I go.
>   I am resolved to try,
>   For if I stay away I know
>   I must forever die."

While these old hymns are sounding in our ears, we are almost tempted to go, even if we do perish. Surely nothing has such power to make us forget earth and its round of troubles as these sweet old

church songs, familiar from earliest childhood, and
wrought into the most tender memories, until we
come to regard them as a sort of sacred stream, on
which some day our souls will float away happily to
the better country.

12. The parson is in my tent doing his best
to extract something solemn out of Willis' violin.
Now he stumbles on a strain of "Sweet Home," then
a scratch of "Lang Syne;" but the latter soon breaks
its neck over "Old Hundred," and all three tunes
finally mix up and merge into "I would not live
alway, I ask not to stay," which, for the purpose of
steadying his hand, the parson sings aloud. I look
at him and affect surprise that a reverend gentleman
should take any pleasure in so vain and wicked an instrument, and express a hope that the business of
tanning skins has not utterly demoralized him.

Willis pretends to a taste in music far superior to
that of the common "nigger." He plays a very fine
thing, and when I ask what it is, replies : "Norma,
an opera piece." Since the parson's exit he has been
executing "Norma" with great spirit, and, so far as I
am able to judge, with wonderful skill. I doubt not
his thoughts are a thousand miles hence, among brown-
skinned wenches, dressed in crimson robes, and decorated with ponderous ear-drops. In fact, "Norma"
is good, and goes far to carry one out of the wilderness.

13. It is after tattoo. Parson Strong's prayer-
meeting has been dismissed an hour, and the camp is
as quiet as if deserted. The day has been a duplicate

of yesterday, cold and windy. To-night the moon is sailing through a wilderness of clouds, now breaking out and throwing a mellow light over valley and mountain, then plunging into obscurity, and leaving all in thick darkness.

Major Keifer, Adjutant Mitchell, and Private Jerroloaman have been stretching their legs before my fireplace all the evening. The Adjutant being hopelessly in love, naturally enough gave the conversation a sentimental turn, and our thoughts have been wandering among the rosy years when our hearts throbbed under the gleam of one bright particular star (I mean one each), and our souls alternated between hope and fear, happiness and despair. Three of us, however, have some experience in wedded life, and the gallant Adjutant is reasonably confident that he will obtain further knowledge on the subject if this cruel war ever comes to an end and his sweetheart survives.

14. The paymaster has been busy. The boys are very bitter against the sutler, realizing, for the first time, that " sutler's chips " cost money, and that they have wasted on jimcracks too much of their hard earnings. Conway has taken a solemn Irish oath that the sutler shall never get another cent of him. But these are like the half repentant, but resultless, mutterings of the confirmed drunkard. The " new leaf" proposed to be turned over is never turned.

16. Am told that some of the boys lost in gambling every farthing of their money half an hour after receiving it from the paymaster.

An Indiana soldier threw a bombshell into the fire to-day, and three men were seriously wounded by the explosion.

The writer was absent from camp from October 21st to latter part of November, serving on court-martial, first at Huttonville, and afterward at Beverly.

In November the Third was transferred to Kentucky.

NOVEMBER, 1861.

30. The Third is encamped five miles south of Louisville, on the Seventh-street plank road.

As we marched through the city my attention was directed to a sign bearing the inscription, in large black letters,

" NEGROES BOUGHT AND SOLD."

We have known, to be sure, that negroes were bought and sold, like cattle and tobacco, but it, nevertheless, awakened new, and not by any means agreeable, sensations to see the humiliating fact announced on the broad side of a commercial house. These signs must come down.

The climate of Kentucky is variable, freezing nights and thawing in the day. The soil in this locality is rich, and, where trodden, extremely muddy. We shall miss the clear water of the mountain streams. A large number of troops are concentrating here.

DECEMBER, 1861.

1. Sunday has just slipped away. Parson Strong attempted to get an audience; but a corporal's guard, for numbers, were all who desired to be ministered to in spiritual things.

The Colonel spends much of his time in Louisville. He complains bitterly because the company officers do not remain in camp, and yet fails to set them a good example in this regard. We have succeeded poorly in holding our men. Quite a number dodged off while the boat was lying at the landing in Cincinnati, and still more managed to get through the guard lines and have gone to Louisville. The invincible Corporal Casey has not yet put in an appearance.

The boys of the Sixth Ohio are exceedingly jubilant; the entire regiment has been allowed a furlough for six days. This was done to satisfy the men, who had become mutinous because they were not permitted to stop at Cincinnati on their way hither.

4. Rode to Louisville this afternoon; in the evening attended the theatre, and saw the notorious Adah Isaacs Menken Heenan. The house was packed with soldiers, mostly of the Sixth Ohio. It seemed

probable at one time that there would be a general free fight; but the brawlers were finally quieted and the play went on. One of the performers resembled an old West Virginia acquaintance so greatly that the boys at once y'clepped him Stalnaker, and howled fearfully whenever he made his appearance.

7. Moved three miles nearer Louisville and encamped in a grove. Have had much difficulty in keeping the men in camp; and this evening, to prevent a general stampede, ordered the guards to load their guns and shoot the first man who attempted to break over. Have succeeded also in getting the officers to remain; notified them yesterday that charges would be preferred against all who left without permission, and this afternoon I put my very good friend, Lieutenant Dale, under arrest for disregarding the order.

12. In camp near Elizabethtown. The road over which we marched was excellent; but owing to detention at Salt river, where the troops and trains had to be ferried over, we were a day longer coming here than we expected to be. The weather has been delightful, warm as spring time. The nights are beautiful.

The regiment was greatly demoralized by our stay in the vicinity of Louisville, and on the march hither the boys were very disorderly and loth to obey; but, by dint of much scolding, we succeeded in getting them all through.

13. Have been attached to the Seventeenth Brigade, and assigned to the Third Division; the latter commanded by General O. M. Mitchell. The General

remarked to me this morning, that the best drilled and conditioned regiments would lead in the march toward Nashville.

15. Jake Smith, the driver of the head-quarters wagon, on his arrival in Elizabethtown went to the hotel, and in an imperious way ordered dinner, assuring the landlord, with much emphasis, that he was " no damned common officer, and wanted a good dinner."

18. In camp at Bacon creek, eight miles north of Green river. Have been two days on the way from Elizabethtown; the road was bad. There were nine regiments in the column, which extended as far almost as the eye could reach.

At Louisville I was compelled to bear heavily on officers and men. On the march hither I have dealt very thoroughly with some of the most disorderly, and in consequence have become unpopular with the regiment.

20. General Mitchell called this afternoon and requested me to form the regiment in a square. I did so, and he addressed it for twenty minutes on guard duty, throwing in here and there patriotic expressions, which encouraged and delighted the boys very much. When he departed they gave him three rousing cheers.

21. A reconnoissance was made beyond Green river yesterday, and no enemy found.

We are short of supplies; entirely out of sugar, coffee, and candles, and the boys to-night indicated some faint symptoms of insubordination, but I assured them we had made every effort possible to obtain these articles, and so quieted them.

Major Keifer was officer in charge of the camp yesterday, and when making the rounds last night a sentinel challenged, " Halt! who comes there?" The sergeant responded, " Grand rounds," whereupon the weary and disappointed Irishman retorted in angry tones: " Divil take the grand rounds, I thought it the relafe comin'."

22. The pleasant days have ended. The clouds hang heavy and black, and the rain descends in torrents.

After eleven o'clock last night I accompanied General Mitchell to ten regiments, and with him made the grand rounds in most of them. As we rode from camp to camp the General made the time most agreeable and profitable to me, by delivering a very able lecture on military affairs; laying down what he denominated a simple and sure foundation for the beginner to build upon.

The wind is high and our stove smokes prodigiously. I have been out in the rain endeavoring to turn the pipe, but have not mended the matter at all. The Major insists that it is better to freeze than to be smoked to death, so we shall extinguish the fire and freeze.

Adjutant Mitchell has been commissioned captain and assigned to Company C.

25. Gave passes to all the boys who desired to leave camp. The Major, Adjutant and I had a right royal Christmas dinner and a pleasant time. A fine

fat chicken, fried mush, coffee, peaches and milk, were on the table. The Major is engaged now in heating the second tea-pot of water for punch purposes. His countenance has become quite rosy; this is doubtless the effect of the fire. He has been unusually powerful in argument; but whether his intellect has been stimulated by the fire, the tea, or the punch, we are at this time wholly unable to decide; he certainly handles the tea-pot with consummate skill, and attacks the punch with exceeding vigor.

27. No orders to advance. Armies travel slowly indeed. Within fifteen miles of the enemy and idly rotting in the mud.

Acting Brigadier-General Marrow when informed that Dumont would assume command of the brigade, became suddenly and violently ill, asked for and obtained a thirty-day leave.

I would give much to be home with the children during this holiday time; but unfortunately my health is too good, and will continue so in spite of me. The Major, poor man, is troubled in the same way.

28. Lieutenant St. John goes to Louisville with a man who was arrested as a spy; and strange to say the arrest was made at the instance of the prisoner's uncle, who is a captain in the Union army.

Captain Mitchell assumes command of company C to-morrow. The Colonel is incensed at the Major and me, because of the Adjutant's promotion. He intended to make a place in the company for a non-commissioned officer, who begged money from the

8

boys to buy him a sword. We astonished him, however, by showing three commissions—one for the Adjutant, and one each for a first and second lieutenant, all of the company's own choosing.

30.   Called on General Dumont this morning; he is a small man, with a thin piping voice, but an educated and affable gentleman.   Did not make his acquaintance in West Virginia, he being unwell while there and confined to his quarters.

This is a peculiar country; there are innumerable caverns, and every few rods places are found where the crust of the earth appears to have broken and sunk down hundreds of feet.   One mile from camp there is a large and interesting cave, which has been explored probably by every soldier of the regiment.

31.   General Buell is here, and a grand review took place to-day.

Since we left Elkwater there has been a steadily increasing element of insubordination manifested in many ways, but notably in an unwillingness to drill, in stealing from camp and remaining away for days.   This, if tolerated much longer, will demoralize even the best of men and render the regiment worthless.

JANUARY, 1862.

1.   Albert, the cook, was swindled in the purchase of a fowl for our New Year's dinner; he supposed he was getting a young and tender turkey, but we find it to be an ancient Shanghai rooster, with flesh as tough as whitleather.   This discovery has cast a shade of melancholy over the Major.

The boys, out of pure devilment, set fire to the ·leaves, and to-night the forest was illuminated.   The flames advanced so rapidly that, at one time, we feared they might get beyond control, but the fire was finally whipped out, not, however, without making as much noise in the operation as would be likely to occur at the burning of an entire city.

5.   General Mitchell has issued an immense number of orders, and of course holds the commandants of regiments responsible for their execution.   I have, as in duty bound, done my best to enforce them, and the men think me unnecessarily severe.

To-day a soldier about half drunk was arrested for leaving camp without permission and brought to my quarters; he had two canteens of whisky on his person.   I remonstrated with him mildly, but he grew saucy, insubordinate, and finally insolent and insult-

ing; he said he did not care a damn for what I thought
or did, and was ready to go to the guard-house; in fact
wanted to go there.   Finally, becoming exasperated, I
took the canteens from him, poured out the whisky,
and directed Captain Patterson to strap him to a tree
until he cooled off somewhat.   The Captain failing in
his efforts to fasten him securely, I took my saddle
girth, backed him up to the tree, buckled him to it,
and returned to my quarters.   This proved to be the
last straw which broke the unfortunate camel's back.
It was a high-handed outrage upon the person of a
volunteer soldier; the last and worst of the many
arbitrary and severe acts of which I had been guilty.
The regiment seemed to arise *en masse*, and led on by
a few reckless men who had long disliked me, advanced with threats and fearful oaths toward my tent.
The bitter hatred which the men entertained for me
had now culminated.   It being Sunday the whole
regiment was off duty, and while some, and perhaps
many, of the boys had no desire to resort to violent
measures, yet all evidently sympathized with the prisoner, and regarded my action as arbitrary and cruel.
The position of the soldier was a humiliating one,
but it gave him no bodily pain.   Possibly I had no
authority for punishing him in this way; and had I
taken time for reflection it is more than probable I
should have found some other and less objectionable
mode; confinement in the guard-house, however,
would have been no punishment for such a man; on
the contrary it would have afforded him that relief
from disagreeable duty which he desired.   At any

rate the act, whether right or wrong, had been done, and I must either stand by it now or abandon all hope of controlling the regiment hereafter. I watched the mob, unobserved by it, from an opening in my tent door. Saw it gather, consult, advance, and could hear the boisterous and threatening language very plainly. Buckling my pistol belt under my coat where it could not be seen, I stepped out just as the leaders advanced to the tree for the purpose of releasing the man. I asked them very quietly what they proposed to do. Then I explained to them how the soldier had violated orders, which I was bound by my oath to enforce; how, when I undertook to remonstrate kindly against such unsoldierly conduct, he had insulted and defied me. Then I continued as calmly as I ever spoke, " I understand you have come here to untie him; let the man who desires to undertake the work begin—if there be a dozen men here who have it in their minds to do this thing—let them step forward—I dare them to do it." They saw before them a quiet, plain man who was ready to die if need be; they could not doubt his honesty of purpose. He gave them time to act and answer, they stood irresolute and silent; with a wave of the hand he bade them go to their quarters, and they went.

General Mitchell hearing of my trouble sent for me. I explained to him the difficulties under which I was laboring; told him what I had done and why I had done it. He said he understood my position fully, that I must go ahead, do my duty and he would stand by me, and, if necessary, sustain me with his whole division. I replied that I needed no assistance; that the officers, with but few exceptions, were my friends, and that I believed there were enough good, sensible soldiers in the regiment to see me through. He talked very kindly to me; but I feel greatly discouraged. The Colonel has practically abandoned the regiment in this period of bad weather, when rigorous discipline is to be enforced, and the boys seem to feel that I am taking advantage of his absence to display my authority, and require from them the performance of hard and unnecessary tasks. Many non-commissioned officers have been reduced to the ranks by court-martial for being absent without leave, and many privates have been punished in various ways for the same reason. It was my duty to approve or disapprove the finding of the court. Disapproval in the majority of cases would have been subversive of all discipline. Approval has brought down upon me not only the hatred and curses of the soldiers tried and punished, but in some instances the ill-will also of their fathers, who for years were my neighbors and friends.

Very many of these soldiers think they should be allowed to work when they please, play when they please, and, in short, do as they please. Until this idea is expelled from their minds the regiment will be but little if any better than a mob.

7. We hear of the Colonel occasionally. He is still at Louisville, running his train on the broad gauge. His regiment, he says, has been maneuvering in the face of the enemy beyond Green river, threat-

ened with an attack day and night. Constant vigilance and continued exposure in this most inclement season of the year, so undermined his health that he was compelled to retire a little while to recuperate. He affirms that he has the best regiment of soldiers in the service; but, unfortunately, has not a field officer worth a damn.

Robt. E. Lee was the great man of the rebel army in West Virginia. The boys all talked about Lee, and told how they would pink him if opportunity offered. But Simon Bolivar Buckner is the man here on whom they all threaten to fall violently. There are certainly a hundred soldiers in the Third, each one of whom swears every day that he would whip Simon Bolivar Buckner quicker than a wink if he dared present himself. Simon is in danger.

Had the third sergeants in my school to-night. Am getting to be a pretty good teacher.

10. General Mitchell gave the officers a very interesting lecture this evening. He is indefatigable. The whole division has become a school.

Had five lieutenants before me. Lesson : grand guards and other outposts.

11. The General summoned the officers of his division about him and went through the form of sending out advanced guard, posting picket, grand guards, outposts, and sentinels. During these exercises we rode fifteen or twenty miles, and listened to at least twenty speeches. My horse was very gay, and I had the pleasure of running many races. I learned something, and am learning a little each

day. Had the lieutenants in my school again to-night. Lesson: detachments, reconnoissances, partisans, and flankers.

12. The officers dress better, as a rule, than in West Virginia. The only man who has not, in this regard, changed for the better, is the Major. He continues the careless fellow he was. Occasionally he makes an effort to have his boots polished; but finds the day altogether too short for the work, and abandons the job in despair.

14. Every day we have the roar of artillery, the rattle of musketry, the prancing of impatient steeds, the marching and countermarching of battalions, the roll of the drum, the clash and clatter of sabers, and the thunder of a thousand mounted men, as they hurry hither and yon. But nobody is hurt; it is all practice and drill.

16. People who live in houses would hardly believe one can sleep comfortably with his nose separated from the coldest winter wind by simply a thin cotton canvas; but such is the fact.

19. General Dumont called. He is to-day commandant of the camp. The General is an eccentric genius, and has an inexhaustible fund of good stories. He uses the words "damned" and "be-damned" rather too often; but this adds, rather than detracts, from his popularity. He dispenses good whisky at his quarters very freely, and this has a tendency also to elevate him in the estimation of his subordinates.

General Mitchell never drinks and never swears.

Occasionally he uses the words "confound it" in rather savage style; but further than this I have never heard him go. Mitchell is military; Dumont militia. The latter winks at the shortcomings of the soldier; the former does not.

25. We are not studying so much as we were. The General's grasp has relaxed, and he does not hold us with a tight reign and stiff bit any longer.

There is a great deal of sickness among the troops; many cases of colds, rheumatism, and fever, resulting from exposure. Passing through the company quarters of our regiment at midnight, I was alarmed by the constant and heavy coughing of the men. I fear the winter will send many more to the grave than the bullets of the enemy, for a year to come.

26. A body of cavalry got in our rear last night and attempted to destroy the Nolan creek bridge; but it was driven off by the guard, after a sharp engagement, in which report says nine of the enemy were killed and six of our men.

The enemy is doing but little in our front. A night or two ago he ventured to within a few miles of our forces on Green river, burnt a station-house, and retired.

28. The Colonel returned at noon. I was among the first to visit him. He greeted me very cordially, and called God to witness that he had never spoken a disparaging word of me. Busy bodies and liars, he said, had created all the trouble between us. He had

9

heard that charges were to be preferred against him ; he knew they could not be sustained, and believed it an attempt of his enemies to injure him and prevent his promotion. He affirmed that he had enlisted from the purest of motives, and entered into a general defense of his acts as an officer and gentleman. I listened respectfully to his statement, and then said: " Colonel, if your conduct has been such as you describe, you need not fear an investigation. I hold in my hand the charges and specifications of which you have heard. They are signed by my hand. I make them believing them to be true. If false, the court will so find, and I shall be the one to suffer. If true, you are unfit to command this regiment or any other, and it should be known. I present the charges to you, the commanding officer of the Third Regiment, and with them a written request that they be forwarded to the General commanding the division." He took the package, tore open the envelope, and seated himself while he read.

In less than an hour Captains Lawson and Wing called on me to report that the Colonel would resign if I would withdraw the charges. I consented to do so.

31. Had dress parade this evening, at which the Colonel officiated, it being his first appearance since his return.

Ascertaining that he had not sent in his resignation, I wrote him a note calling attention to the promise made on the 29th instant, and suggesting that it would be well to terminate an unpleasant matter without unnecessary delay.

We had a case of disappointed love in the regiment last night. A sergeant of Captain Mitchell's company was engaged to a girl of Athens county. They were to be married upon his return from the war, and until within a month have been corresponding regularly. Suddenly and without explanation she ceased to write, why he could not imagine. He never, however, doubted that she would be faithful to him. His anxiety to hear from home increased, until finally he learned from her brother, a soldier of the *Eighteenth Ohio*, that she was married. Strong, healthy, good-looking fellow that he was, this intelligence prostrated him completely, and made him crazy as a loon. He imagined that he was in hell, thought Dr. Seyes the devil, and so violent did he become that they had to bind him.

This morning he is more calm, but still deranged. He thought the straws in his bunk were thorns, and would pluck at them with his fingers and exclaim: "My God, ain't they sharp?" Captain Mitchell called, and the boys said: "Sergeant, do n't you know him?" "Yes," he replied, "he is one of the devils." The Captain said: "Sergeant, do n't you know where you are?" "Of course I do; I'm in hell." When they were binding him he said: "That's right; heap on the coals; put me in the hottest place." While Dr. Seyes was preparing something to quiet him— laudanum, perhaps—he said: "Bring on your poison; I'll take it."

The boys, while living roughly, exposed to hardships and dangers, think more of their sweethearts than ever before, and are constantly recurring, in their talk, to the comfortable homes and pleasant scenes from which they are for the present separated.

FEBRUARY, 1862.

1. The Colonel sent in his resignation this morning. It will go to Department head-quarters to-morrow.

Saw the new moon over my right shoulder this evening, which I accept as an omen of good luck. Let it come. It will suit me just as well now as at any time. If deceived, I shall never more have faith in the moon; and as for the man in the moon, I shall call him a cheat to his face.

2. The devil is to pay in the regiment. The Colonel is doing his utmost to create a disturbance. His friends are busy among the privates. At noon an effort was made to get up a demonstration on the color line in his behalf. Now a petition is being circulated among the privates requesting Major Keifer and me to resign.

The night is as dark as pitch. A few minutes ago a shout went up for the Colonel, and was swelled from point to point along the line of company tents, until now possibly five hundred voices have joined in the yell. The Colonel's friends tell the boys that if he were to remain he would obtain leave for the regiment to go back to Camp Dennison to recruit; that he was about to obtain rifles and Zouave uniforms for them, and that there is a conspiracy among the officers to crush him.

3.   Petitions from four companies, embracing two hundred and twenty-five names, have been presented, requesting the Major and Lieutenant-Colonel to resign.

4.   We closed up the day with a dress parade, the Colonel in command. The camp is more boisterous than usual. No more petitions have been presented.

The Major received a package from home to-night containing, among other articles, a pair of slippers, which, greatly to my advantage, were too small for him. They were turned over to me, and it happens that no little thing could have been more acceptable.

The bright moonlight of to-night enlivens our spirits somewhat, and fills us with new courage. The days have been dark and gloomy, and the nights still more so, for many days and nights past.

From the band of the Tenth Ohio, half a mile away, come strains mellow and sweet. The air is full of moonlight and music. The boys are in a happier mood, and a round, full voice comes to us from the tents with the words of an old Scotch song :

" March, march, Ettrick and Teviotdale!
    Why, my lads, dinna ye march forward in order?
  March, march, Eskale and Liddlesdale!
    All the blue bonnets are over the border.
  Many a banner spread flutters above your head,
    Many a crest that is famous in story ;
  Mount and make ready, then, sons of the mountain glen !
    Fight for the King and the old Scottish border !

5. The Major and Mr. Furay are engaged in a tremendous dispute. Furay is positive he can not be mistaken, and the Major laughs him to scorn. When these gentlemen lock horns in dead earnest the clatter of words becomes terrible, and the combat ends only when both fall on their cots exhausted.

6. The Colonel's resignation has been accepted. He delivered his valedictory to the regiment this evening. Subsequently he passed through the company quarters, shaking hands with the boys and bidding them farewell. Still later he made a speech, in which he called God to witness that he was a loyal man, and promised to pray for us all. The regiment is disorderly, if not mutinous even. The best thing he can do for it and himself is to get out.

8. The Colonel has bidden us a final adieu. His most devoted adherents escorted him to the depot, and returned miserably drunk.

One of the color guards, an honest, sensible, good-looking boy, has written me a letter of encouragement. I trust that soon all will feel as kindly toward me as he.

10. We left Bacon creek at noon. There were ten thousand men in advance of us, with immense baggage trains. The roads bad, and our march slow, tedious, and disagreeable. Many of the officers imbibed freely, and the senior surgeon, an educated gentleman, and very popular with the boys, became gloriously elevated. He kept his eye pealed for secesh, and before reaching Munfordsville found a citizen twice as big as himself in possession of a double-

barreled shot-gun. Taking it for granted that he was an enemy, the Doctor drew a revolver and bade him surrender unconditionally. The boys said the Doctor was as tight as a little bull. What phase of inebriety this remark indicated I am unable to say; but certain it is that he did not for a moment lose sight of his gigantic prisoner, nor give him the slightest opportunity to escape. He was quite triumphant in his bearing; directed the movements of the captive in a loud and imperious tone, and favored him with much patriotic advice.

A wagon with six unbroken mules attached is an uncertain conveyance. If the mules are desired to stop suddenly, they are certain not to do so, and if commanded to start suddenly, they are just as sure not to obey. If, after an immense amount of whipping and many fervent asseverations on the part of the driver that all mules should be in Tophet, they conclude to start at all, they go as if determined to reach the place indicated without unnecessary delay. If a mudhole, ditch, tree, or any other obstacle lies in the way, and the driver cries whoa, the mules redouble their speed, and rush forward as if they did not in the slightest degree consider themselves responsible either for the driver's neck or the traps with which the wagon is laden.

It was about eight o'clock in the evening when we crossed the bridge over Green river. The moon had around it a halo, in which appeared very distinctly all the colors of the National flag—red, white, and blue—and the boys said it was a good omen; that they were Union people up there, and had hung out the Stars and Stripes.

12.   To-morrow we start for Bowling Green, our division in the lead.   Before night we shall overtake the rebels, and before the next evening will doubtless fight a battle.

13. Long before sunrise the whole division was astir, and at seven o'clock moved forward, our brigade in the center. Far as the eye could reach, both in front and rear, the road was crowded with men.   A score of bands filled the air with martial strains, while the morning sun brightened the muskets, and made the flags look more cheerful and brilliant.   The day was warm and pleasant.   The country before us was, in a military sense, unexplored, and every ear was open to catch the sound of the first gun.   The conviction that a battle was imminent kept the men steady and prevented straggling. We passed many fine houses, and extensive, well improved farms.   But few white people were seen.   The negroes appeared to have entire possession.

Six miles from Green river a young and very pretty girl stood in the doorway of a handsome farm-house and waved the flag of the Union.   Cheer after cheer arose along the line; officers saluted, soldiers waved their hats, and the bands played " Yankee Doodle" and " Dixie."   That loyal girl captured a thousand hearts, and I trust some gallant soldier who shall win honorable scars in battle may return in good time to crown her his Queen of Love and Beauty.

From this on for fifteen miles we found neither

springs nor streams. The country is cavernous, and the only water is that of the ponds. In all of these we discovered dead and decaying horses, mules, and dogs. The rebels in this way had sought to deprive us of water; but while their action in this regard occasioned a vast deal of profanity among the boys, it did not in the least retard the column. We were, however, delayed somewhat by the felled trees with which they had obstructed miles of the road. At sunset we halted and pitched our tents in a large field, near what is known as Bell's Tavern, on the Louisville and Nashville Railroad. We had marched eighteen miles.

The water used in the preparation of the evening meal was that of the ponds. The thought of the rotting dogs, horses, and mules, could not be banished, and when the Major sipped his coffee in a doubtful way and remarked that it tasted soupy, my stomach quivered on the turning point, and, hungry as I was, the supper gave me no further enjoyment.

14. Resumed the march at daylight. Snow fell last night. The day was exceedingly cold, and the wind pierced through us like needles of ice. I think I never experienced so sudden and extreme a change in the weather. It was too cold to ride, and I dismounted and walked twelve miles. We were certain of a fight, and so pushed on with rapid pace. A regiment of cavalry and Loomis' battery were in advance. When within ten miles of Bowling Green the guns opened in our front. Leaving the regiment in charge of the Major, I rode ahead rapidly as I

could, and reached the river bank opposite Bowling Green in time to see a detachment of rebel cavalry fire the buildings which contained their army stores. The town was ablaze in twenty different places. They had destroyed the bridge over Barren river in the morning, and now, having finished the work of destruction, went galloping over the hills. When the regiment arrived, it was quartered in a camp but recently evacuated by the enemy. The night was bitter cold; but the boys soon had a hundred fires blazing, and made themselves very comfortable.

15. This morning we were called out at daylight to cross the river and take possession of the town; a sorrier, hungrier lot of fellows never rolled out of warm blankets into the icy wind. It was impossible for many of them to get their wet and frozen shoes on, but we hurried down to the river, and were there halted until it was ascertained that our presence on the opposite side was not required, when we went back to our old quarters.

16. To-day we crossed the Big Barren, and are now in Bowling Green. Turchin's brigade preceded us, and has gutted many houses. The rebels burned a million dollars worth of stores, but left enough pork, salt beef, and other necessaries to supply our division for a month; in fact the cigar I am smoking, the paper on which I write, the ink and pen, were all captured.

General Beauregard left the day before our arrival. It is said he was for days reported to be lying in General Hardee's quarters, dangerously ill, and that under cover of this report he left town dressed in citizen's clothes and visited our camps on Green River.

18. The weather is turning warm again, the men are quartered in houses. I room at the hotel. This sort of life, however pleasant it may be, has a demoralizing effect upon the soldier.

19. Spent the forenoon at the river assisting somewhat in getting our transportation over. It is a rainy day, and I got wet to the skin and thoroughly chilled. After dinner I went to bed while William, my servant, put a few necessary stitches in my apparel, and dried my underclothing and boots. I am badly off for clothing; my coat is out at the elbows, and my pantaloons are in a revolutionary condition, the seat having seceded.

The Cincinnati Gazette of the 14th instant reports that I have been promoted. Thanks.

20. We learn from a reliable source that Nashville has been evacuated. The enemy is said to be concentrating at Murfreesboro, twenty or thirty miles beyond.

The river has risen fifteen feet, and many of our teams are still on the other side. The water swelled so rapidly that two teams of six mules each, parked on the river bank last night so as to be in readiness to cross on the ferry this morning, were swept away.

Captain Mitchell returned this evening from a trip North. We are glad to have him back again.

21. Hear that Fort Donelson has been taken after a terrible fight, and ten thousand ears are eager

to hear more about the engagement. No teams crossed the river to-day; we are flood bound.

There was an immense number of deaths in the rebel army while it encamped here. It is said three thousand Southern soldiers are buried in the vicinity of the town. They could not stand the rigorous Northern climate. A Mississippi regiment reported but thirteen men for duty.

22. Moved at seven in the morning toward Nashville without wagons, tents or camp equipage. Marched twenty miles in the rain and were drenched completely. The boys found some sort of shelter during the night in tobacco houses, barns, and straw piles.

23. The day pleasant and sunshiny. The feet of the men badly blistered, and the regiment limps along in wretched style; made fifteen miles.

24. Routed out at daylight and ordered to make Nashville, a distance of thirty-two miles. Many of the boys have no shoes, and the feet of many are still very sore The journey seems long, but we are at the head of the column, and that stimulates us somewhat. Have sent my horse to the rear to help along the very lame, and am making the march on foot.

The martial band of the regiment is doing its utmost to keep the boys in good spirits; the base drum sounds like distant thunder, and the wind of Hughes, the fifer, is inexhaustible; he can blow five miles at a stretch. The members of the band are in good pluck, and when not playing, either sing, tell stories, or indulge in reminiscences of a personal char-

acter.   Russia has been badgering William Heney,
a drummer.   He says that while at Elkwater Heney
sparked one of Esquire Stalnaker's daughters, and
that the lady's little sister going into the room quite
suddenly one evening called back to the father,
"Dad, dad, William Heney has got his arm around
Susan Jane!"   Heney affirms that the story is untrue.
Lochey favors us with a song, which is known as the
warble.

"Thou, thou reignest in this bosom,
    There, there hast thou thy throne;
Thou, thou knowest that I love thee;
    Am I not fondly thine own?

Ya— ya—ya—ya.
Am I not fondly thine own?

CHORUS.

Das unda claus ish mein,
Das unda claus ish mein,
Cants do nic mock un do.

On the banks of the Ohio river,
    In a cot lives my Rosa so fair;
She is called Jim Johnson's darky,
    And has nice curly black hair.
        Tre alo, tre alo, tre ola, ti.

O come with me to the dear little spot,
    And I'll show you the place I was born,
In a little log hut by a clear running brook,
    Where blossom the wild plum and thorn.
        Tre ola, tre ola, treo la ti.

> Mein fadter, mein modter, mein sister, mein frau,
>   Undt swi glass of beer for meinself,
> Undt dey call mein wife one blacksmit shop;
>   Such dings I never did see in my life.
>   Tre ola, tre ola, tre ola ti."

25.   General Nelson's command came up the Cumberland by boat and entered Nashville ahead of us. The city, however, had surrendered to our division before Nelson arrived.   We failed simply in being the first troops to occupy it, and this resulted from detention at the river-crossing.

27.   Crossed the Cumberland and moved through Nashville; the regiment behaved handsomely, and was followed by a great crowd of colored people, who appeared to be delighted with the music.   General Mitchell complimented us on our good behavior and appearance.

28.   Captain Wilson, Fourth Ohio Cavalry, was shot dead while on picket.   One of his sergeants had eight balls put through him, but still lives.

MARCH, 1862.

1.   Our brigade, in command of General **Dumont,**
started for Lavergne, a village eleven miles out on the
Murfreesboro road, to look after a regiment of cavalry said to be in occupation of the place.   Arrived
there a little before sunset, but found the enemy had
disappeared.

The troops obtained whisky in the village, and
many of the soldiers became noisy and disorderly.

A little after nightfall the compliments of a **Mrs.**
Harris were presented to me, with request that **I**
would be kind enough to call.   The handsome little
white cottage where she lived was near our bivouac.
It was the best house in the village; and, as I ascertained afterward, very tastefully if not elegantly
furnished.   She was a woman of perhaps forty.   Her
husband and daughter were absent; the former, I
think, in the Confederate service.   She had only a
servant with her, and was considerably frightened
and greatly incensed at the conduct of some soldiers,
of she knew not what regiment, who had persisted in
coming into her house and treating her rudely.   In
short, she desired protection.   She had a lively
tongue in her head, and her request for a guard was,

I thought, not preferred in the gentlest and most amiable way. Her comments on our Northern soldiers were certainly not complimentary to them. She said she had supposed hitherto that soldiers were gentlemen. I confessed that they ought to be at least. She said, rather emphatically, that Southern soldiers *were* gentlemen. I replied that I did not doubt at all the correctness of her statement; but, unfortunately, the branch of the Northern army to which I had the honor to belong had not been able to get near enough to them to obtain any personal knowledge on the subject.

The upshot of the five minutes' interview was a promise to send a soldier to protect Mrs. Harris' property and person during the night.

Returning to the regiment I sent for Sergeant Woolbaugh. He is one of the handsomest men in the regiment; a printer by trade, an excellent conversationalist, a man of extensive reading, and of thorough information respecting current affairs. I said: "Sergeant, I desire you to brighten up your musket, and clothes if need be, go over to the little white cottage on the right and stand guard." " All right, sir."

As he was leaving I called to him: " If the lady of the house shows any inclination to talk with you, encourage and gratify her to the top of her bent. I want her to know what sort of men our Northern soldiers are."

The Sergeant in due time introduced himself to
        10

Mrs. Harris, and was invited into the sitting room. They soon engaged in conversation, and finally fell into a discussion of the issue between the North and South which lasted until after midnight. The lady, although treated with all courtesy, certainly obtained no advantage in the controversy, and must have arisen from it with her ideas respecting Northern soldiers very materially changed.

2. Started on the return to Nashville at three o'clock in the morning. The boys being again disappointed in not finding the enemy, and considerably under the influence of liquor, conducted themselves in a most disorderly and unsoldierly way.

Have not had a change of clothing since we crossed the Great Barren river.

6. Regiment on picket.

When returning from the front I met a soldier of the Thirty-seventh Indiana, trudging along with his gun on his shoulder. I asked him where he was going; he replied that his father lived four miles beyond, and he had just heard that his brother was home from the Southern army on sick leave, and he was going out to take him prisoner.

8. This afternoon the camp was greatly excited over a daring feat of a body of cavalry under John Morgan. It succeeded in getting almost inside the camps, and was five miles inside of our outposts. It came into the main road between where Kennett's cavalry regiment is encamped and Nashville; captured a wagon train, took the drivers, Captain Braden, of Indiana, who was in charge of the train, and

eighty-three horses, and started on a by-road back for Murfreesboro. General Mitchell immediately dispatched Kennett in pursuit. About fifteen miles out the rebels were overtaken and our men and horses recaptured. Two rebels were killed and two taken; Kennett is still in hot pursuit. Captain Braden says, as the rebels were riding away they were exceedingly jubilant over the success of their adventure, and promised to introduce him to General Hardee in the evening. Without asking the Captain's permission they gave him a very poor horse in exchange for a very good one, put him at the head of the column and guarded him vigilantly; but when Kennett appeared and the running fight occurred he dodged off at full speed, lay down on his horse, and although fired at many times escaped unhurt.

Morgan's men know the country so well that all the by-roads and cow-paths are familiar to them; the citizens keep them informed also as to the location of our camps and picket posts, and if need be are ready to serve them either as guides or spies, hence the success which attended the earlier part of their enterprise does not indicate so great a want of vigilance on the part of our troops, as might at first thought be supposed.

9. The enemy made a descent on one of our outposts, killed one man and wounded another.

16. Went to Nashville this morning to buy a few necessaries. While awaiting dinner at the St. Cloud I took a seat outside the door. Quite a number of Union officers were seated or standing in front of the

hotel, when two well, extremely well, dressed women, followed by a negro lady, approached, and while passing us *held their noses.* What disagreeable thing the atmosphere in our immediate vicinity contained that made it necessary for these lovely women to so pinch their nasal protuberances, I could not discover; certainly the officers looked cleanly, many of them were young men of the "double-bullioned" kind, who had spared no expense in decorating their persons with shoulder straps, golden bugles, and other shining trappings which appertain somehow to glorious war.

After dinner I dropped into a drug store to buy a cake of soap. The druggist gave me, in the way of change, several miserably executed shinplasters. I asked:

"Do you call this money?"

"I do."

"I wonder that every printing office in the South does not commence the manufacture of such money."

"O, no," he replied in a sneering way; "in the North they might do that, but in the South no one is disposed to make counterfeit money."

"Yes," I retorted, "the Southern people are very honest no doubt, but I apprehend there is a better reason for not counterfeiting the money than you have assigned. It is probably not worth counterfeiting."

Private Hawes of the Third is remarkably fond of pies, and a notorious straggler withal. He has just returned to camp after being away for some days, and accounts for his absence by saying that he was in the country looking for pies, when Morgan's men appeared suddenly, shot his horse from under him, mounted him behind a soldier and carried him away. The private is now in the guard-house entertaining a select company with a narrative of his adventures.

We have much trouble with escaped negroes. In some way we have obtained the reputation of being abolitionists, and the colored folks get into our regimental lines, and in some mysterious way are so disposed of that their masters never hear of them again. It is possible the two saw-bones, who officiate at the hospital, dissect, or desiccate, or boil them in the interest of science, or in the manufacture of the villainous compounds with which they dose us when ill. At any rate, we know that many of these sable creatures, who joined us at Bowling Green and on the road to Nashville, can not now be found. Their masters, following the regiment, made complaint to General Buell, and, as we learn, spoke disparagingly of the Third. An order issued requiring us to surrender the negroes to the claimants, and to keep colored folks out of our camp hereafter. I obeyed the order promptly; commanded all the colored men in camp to assemble at a certain hour and be turned over to their masters; but the misguided souls, if indeed there were any, failed to put in an appearance, and could not be found. The scamps, I fear, took advantage of my notice and hid away, much to the regret of all who desire to preserve the Union as it was, and greatly to the chagrin of the gentlemen who expected to take them handcuffed back to Kentucky. One of these fugitives, a handsome mulatto boy, borrowed five dollars of me, and the same amount of Doctor Seyes, not half an hour before the time when he was to be delivered up, but I fear now the money will never be repaid.

18   Started for Murfreesboro. The day is beautiful and the regiment marches well. Encamped for the night near Lavergne. I called on my friend Mrs. Harris. She received me cordially and introduced me to her daughter, a handsome young lady of seventeen or eighteen. They were both extremely Southern in their views, but chatted pleasantly over the situation, and Mrs. Harris spoke of Sergeant Woolbaugh, the guard furnished her on our first visit, in very complimentary terms; in fact, she was surprised to find such men in the ranks of the Federal army. I assured her that there were scores like him in every regiment, and that our army was made up of the flower of the Northern people.

19.   The rebels having burned the bridges on the direct road, we were compelled to diverge to the left and take a longer route; toward evening we went into camp on the plantation of a widow lady, and here for the first time in my life I saw a field of cotton; the old stalks still standing with many bulbs which had escaped the pickers.

20.   Turned out at four o'clock in the morning, got breakfast, struck our tents, and were ready to march at six; but the brigade being now ordered to take the rear, we stood uncovered in a drenching rain

three hours for the division and transportation to pass.
All were thoroughly wet and benumbed with cold,
but as if to show contempt for the weather the Third
sang with great unction:

> " There is a land of pure delight,
>   Where saints immortal reign;
> Infinite day excludes the night,
>   And pleasures banish pain.
>
> There everlasting spring abides,
>   And never withering flowers;
> Death, like a narrow sea, divides
>   This heavenly land from ours."

Soon after getting under way the sky cleared, and
the sun made its appearance; the band struck up,
and at every plantation negroes came flocking to the
roadside to see us.   They are the only friends we
find.   They have heard of the abolition army, the
music, the banners, the glittering arms; possibly the
hope that their masters will be humbled and their
own condition improved, gladdens their hearts and
leads them to welcome us with extravagant manifesta-
tions of joy.   They keep time to the music with feet
and hands, and hurrah " fur de ole flag and de Union,"
sometimes following us for miles.   Parson Strong attempts to do a little missionary work.   A dozen or
more negroes stand in a group by the roadside.   Said
the Parson to an old man: " My friend, are you religious ? "

"No, massa, I is not; seben of my folks is, an dey is all prayen fur your side."

Hailing a little knot, I said: "Boys where do you live?"

"Lib wid Massa ——, sah."

"All Union people, I suppose?"

"Dey say dey is, but dey isn't."

One old woman—evidently a great-grandmother in Israel—climbed on the fence, clapped her hands, shouted for joy, and "bressed de Lord dat dar was de ole flag agin."

To a colored boy who stole into our lines last night, with his little bundle under his arm, the Major said: "Doesn't it make you feel bad to run away from your masters?"

"Oh, no, massa; dey is gone, too."

Reached Murfreesboro in the afternoon.

22. Men at work rebuilding the railroad bridge. General Dumont returns to Nashville. Colonel Lytle, of the Tenth Ohio, will assume command of our brigade.

My servant has imposed upon me for about a month. He arises in the morning when he pleases; prepares my meals when it suits his pleasure, and is disposed in every thing to make me adapt my business to his own notions. This morning I became so provoked over his insolence and laziness that, in a moment of passion, I knocked him down. Since then there has been a decided improvement in his bearing. The blow seems to have awakened him to a sense of his duty.

25. So soon as the railroad is repaired, an immense amount of cotton will be sent East from this section. The crops of two seasons are in the hands of the producer. We are encamped in a cotton field. Peach trees are now in bloom, and many early flowers are to be seen.

26. The boys are having a grand cotillion party on the green in front of my tent, and appear to have entirely forgotten the privations, hardships, and dangers of soldiering.

The army for a temperate, cleanly, cheerful man, is, I have no doubt, the healthiest place in the world. The coarse fare provided by the Government is the most wholesome that can be furnished. The boys oftenest on the sick list are those who are constantly running to the sutler's for gingerbread, sweetmeats, raisins, and nuts. They eat enormous quantities of this unwholesome stuff, and lose appetite for more substantial food. Finding that all desire for hard bread and bacon has disappeared, they conclude that they must be ill, and instead of taking exercise, lie in their tents until they finally become really sick. A contented, temperate, cheerful, cleanly man will live forever in the army; but a despondent, intemperate, gluttonous, dirty soldier, let him be never so fat and strong when he enters the service, is sure to get on the sick list, and finally into the hospital.

The dance on the green is progressing with increased vigor. The music is excellent. At this moment the gentlemen are going to the right; now they

11

promenade all; in a minute more the ladies will be in the center, and four hands round. That broth of an Irish boy, Conway, wears a rooster's feather in his cap, and has for a partner a soldier twice as big as himself, whom he calls Susan. As they swing Conway yells at the top of his voice: "Come round, old gal!"

28. General Mitchell returned from Nashville on a hand-car.

30. This is a pleasant Sunday. The sun shines, the birds sing, and the air stirs pleasantly.

The colored people of Murfreesboro pour out in great numbers on Sunday evenings to witness dress parade, some of them in excellent holiday attire. The women sport flounces and the men canes. Many are nearly white, and all slaves.

Murfreesboro is an aristocratic town. Many of the citizens have as fine carriages as are to be seen in Cincinnati or Washington. On pleasant week-day evenings they sometimes come out to witness the parades. The ladies, so far as I can judge by a glimpse through a carriage window, are richly and elegantly dressed.

The poor whites are as poor as rot, and the rich are very rich. There is no substantial well-to-do middle class. The slaves are, in fact, the middle class here. They are not considered so good, of course, as their masters, but a great deal better than the white trash. One enthusiastic colored man said in my hearing this evening: "You look like solgers. No wonder dat you wip de white trash ob de Southern army. Dey ced dey could wip two ob you, but I guess one ob you could wip two ob dem. You is jest as big as dey is, and maybe a little bigger."

A few miles from here, at a cross roads, is a guide-board: "☞ 15 miles to Liberty." If liberty were indeed but fifteen miles away, the stars to-night would see a thousand negroes dancing on the way thither; old men with their wives and bundles; young men with their sweethearts; little barefooted children, all singing in their hearts:

"De day ob jubilee hab come, ho ho!"

On the march hither we passed a little, contemptible, tumble-down, seven-by-nine frame school-house. Over the door, in large letters, were the words:

CENTRAL ACADEMY.

The boys laughed and said: "If this is called an academy, what sort of things must their common school-houses be?" But Tennessee is a beautiful State. All it lacks is free schools and freemen.

31. Colonel Keifer, in command of four hundred men, started with ninety wagons for Nashville. He will repair the railroad in two or three places and return with provisions.

APRIL, 1862.

3. Struck our tents and started south, at two o'clock this afternoon; marched fifteen miles and bivouacked for the night.

4. Resumed the march at seven o'clock in the morning, the Third in advance. At one place on the road a young negro, perhaps eighteen years old, broke from his hiding in the woods, and with hat in hand and a broad grin on his face, came running to me. "Massa," said he, "I wants to go wid you." "I am sorry, my boy, that I can not take you. I am not permitted to do it." The light went out of the poor fellow's eyes in a moment, and, putting on his slouched hat, he went away sorrowful enough. It seems cruel to turn our backs on these, our only friends. If a dog came up wagging his tail at sight of us, we could not help liking him better than the master, who not only looks sullen and cross at our approach, but in his heart desires our destruction.

As we approach the Alabama line we find fewer, but handsomer, houses; larger plantations, and negroes more numerous. We saw droves of women working in the fields. When their ears caught the first notes of the music, they would drop the hoe and come running to the road, their faces all aglow with pleasure. May we not hope that their darkened minds caught glimpses of the sun of a better life, now rising for them?

Last night my bed-room was as grand as that ever occupied by a prince. The floor was carpeted with soft, green, velvety grass. For walls it had the primeval forest, with its drapery of luxuriant foliage. The ceiling, higher even than one's thoughts can measure, was studded with stars innumerable. The crescent moon added to its beauty for awhile, but disappeared long before I dropped off to sleep.

We entered Shelbyville at noon. There are more Union people here than at Murfreesboro, and we saw many glad faces as we marched through the streets. The band made the sky ring with music, and the regiment deported splendidly. One old woman clapped her hands and thanked heaven that we had come at last. Apparently almost wild with joy, she shouted after us, "God be with you!"

We went into camp on Duck river, one mile from the town.

5.   General Mitchell complimented me on the good behavior and good appearance of the Third. He said it was the best regiment in his division. At Bacon creek, Kentucky, he was particularly severe on us, and attributed all our trouble to defective discipline and bad management on the part of the officers. On the evening when the acceptance of Marrow's resignation was read, the General was present. After parade was dismissed, I shook hands with him and

said: "General, give us a little time and we will make the Third the best regiment in your division." The old gentleman was glad to hear me say so, but smiled dubiously. I am glad to have him acknowledge so soon that we have fulfilled the promise.

At Murfreesboro heavy details were made for bridge building, and one day, while superintending the work, the General addressed the detail from the Third in a very uncomplimentary way: "You lazy scoundrels, go to work! Your regiment is the promptest in the division to report for duty, but you will not work." At another time he gave an order to a soldier which was not obeyed with sufficient alacrity, when he yelled: "What regiment do you belong to?" "The Third." "Well, sir, I thought you were one of the obstinate devils of that regiment." At another time he rode into our camp, and the boys failed to rise at his approach, when he reined in his horse suddenly and shouted: "Get up here, you lazy scoundrels, and treat your superiors with respect!" Riding on a little further, a private passed without touching his cap: "Hold on, here," said the General, "don't you know how to salute a superior?" "Yes," stammered the boy, "but I did not see you." "Hold up your head like a soldier, and you will see me."

One night I was making the rounds in the Second Ohio with the General. The guard did not turn out promptly and he became angry; diving into the guard-tent to rout them up, he ran against a big fellow so violently that he was nearly thrown off his legs. This increased his fury, and seizing the soldier by the coat collar he shook him roughly, and said: "You insolent dog, I'll stand insolence from no man. Officer, put this man under arrest immediately."

On the same night the guard of the Thirty-third Ohio turned out slowly, and some of them were found to have stolen off to their quarters. The General was still in a bad humor. "Where is the officer of the day?" he asked. "At his quarters, sir," replied a sergeant. "Present him the compliments of the General commanding, and tell him if he does not come to the guard-tent at once, I will send a file of soldiers after him." The officer appeared very soon. I refer to these incidents to show simply that the men of other regiments received reprimands as well as those of my own.

6. Late in the evening the officers of the regiment, with the string band, started on a serenading expedition. After playing sundry airs and singing divers songs, Ethiopian and otherwise, at the residence of a Mr. Warren, Miss Julia Gurnie, sister of Mrs. Warren, appeared on the veranda and made to us a very pretty Union speech. After a general introduction to the family and a cordial reception, we bade them good-night, and started for another portion of the village. On the way thither we dropped into the store of a Mr. Armstrong, and imbibed rather copiously of apple-jack, to protect us against the night air, which, by the way, is always dangerous when apple-jack is convenient. After thus fortifying ourselves, we proceeded to the residence of a Mr.

Storey. His doors were thrown open, and we entered his parlors. Here we had the honor to be introduced to Miss Storey, a handsome young lady, and Lieutenant O'Brien, nephew of Parson Brownlow.

Lieutenant O'Brien is an officer of the rebel army. He accompanied Parson Brownlow to Nashville under a flag of truce, and has been loitering on his way back until the present time. He wears the Confederate gray, and when we entered the room was seated on the sofa with Miss Storey. After being introduced in due form, I placed myself by the young lady and endeavored to at least divide her attention with my Confederate friend. The apple-jack dilated most engagingly on the remarkable beauty of the evening, the pleasantness of the weather generally, and the delightfulness of Shelbyville. There was a piano in the room, and finally, after having occupied her attention jointly with O'Brien for some time, I took the liberty to ask her to favor us with a song; but she pleaded an awful cold, and asked to be excused. The apple-jack excused her. The Storeys are pleasant people, and I trust that, full as we were, we did nothing to lessen their respect for us.

From Mr. Storey's we went to the house of Mr. Cooper, President of the Shelbyville Bank, but were not invited in, the family having retired.

Our last call was at the residence of Mr. Weasner, whilom member of the Tennessee Legislature. The doors were here thrown open, and a cordial invitation given us to enter. A pitcher of good wine was set out, and soon after Miss Weasner, a very pretty young lady, appeared, and played and sang many patriotic songs. When finally we bade this pleasant family good night, it was bordering on the Sabbath, and we returned to camp.

7. Colonel Kennett, at the head of three hundred cavalry, made a dash into the country toward the Tennessee river, captured and destroyed a train on a branch of the Nashville and Chattanooga Railroad, and returned to camp to-night with fifteen prisoners.

8. Party at Mr. Warren's, to which many of the officers have gone.

9. Moved at six o'clock in the morning. Roads sloppy, and in many places overflowed. Marched sixteen miles.

10. Resumed the march at six o'clock A. M. Reached Fayetteville at noon. Passed through the town and encamped one mile beyond. General Mitchell, with Turchin's and Sill's brigades and two batteries, left for Huntsville on our arrival.

There are various and contradictory rumors afloat respecting the condition of affairs at Shiloh. The rebel sympathizers here are jubilant over what they claim is reliable intelligence, that our army has been surprised and defeated. Another report, coming via Nashville, says that a part of our army was terribly beaten on Sunday; but reinforcements arriving on Monday, the rebels were driven back, and our losses of the first day retrieved.

A courier arrived about dark with dispatches for General Mitchell; but they were forwarded to him unopened.

13. Confused and unsatisfactory accounts still reach us of the great battle at Pittsburg Landing.

It is strange what fortune, good or ill, our division has had. Taking the lead at Green river, we doubted not that a battle awaited us at Bowling Green. In advance again on the march to Nashville, we were sure of fighting when we reached that place. Starting again, the division pushed on alone to Murfreesboro, Shelbyville, Fayetteville, and finally to Huntsville and Decatur, Alabama, at each place expecting a battle, and yet meeting with no opposition. With but one division upon this line, we looked for hard work and great danger, and yet have found neither. As we advanced the honors we expected to win have receded or gone elsewhere, to be snatched up by other divisions. The boys say the Third is fated never to see a battle; that the Third Ohio in Mexico saw no fighting; that there is something magical in the number which preserves it from all danger.

14. The Fifteenth Kentucky remains here. The Third and Tenth Ohio moved at three in the afternoon. Roads bad and progress slow. Bivouacked for the night near a distillery. Many of the men drunk; the Tenth Ohio particularly wild.

15. Resumed the march at six in the morning. Passed the plantation of Leonidas Polk Walker. He is said to be the wealthiest man in North Alabama. His domain extends for fifteen miles along the road. The overseer's house and the negro huts near it make quite a village.

Met a good many young men returning from

Corinth and Pittsburg Landing. Quite a number of them had been in the Sunday's battle, and, being wounded, had been sent back to Huntsville. General Mitchell had captured and released them on parole. Some had their heads bandaged, others their arms, while others, unable to walk, were conveyed in wagons. As they passed, our men made many good-natured remarks, as, " Well, boys, you're tired of soldiering, ar'n't you?"   " Goin' home on furlough, eh?"   "Played out."   "Another bold soger boy!"   "See the soger!"

At one point a hundred or more colored people, consisting of men, women, and children, flocked to the roadside. The band struck up, and they accompanied the regiment for a mile or more, crowding and jostling each other in their endeavors to keep abreast of the music. The boys were wonderfully amused, and addressed to the motley troupe all the commands known to the volunteer service : "Steady on the right ;" "Guide center;" "Forward, double quick."

Reached Huntsville at five in the afternoon.

16.   Just after sunset Colonel Keifer and I strolled into the town, stopped at the hotel for a moment, where we saw a rebel officer in his gray uniform running about on parole. Visited the railroad depot, where some two hundred rebels are confined. The prisoners were variously engaged; some chatting, others playing cards, while a few of a more devotional turn were singing

> " Come thou fount of every blessing,
>   Tune my heart to sing thy praise."

By his timely arrival General Mitchell cut a division of rebel troops in two. Four thousand got by, and were thus enabled to join the rebel army at Corinth, while about the same number were obliged to return to Chattanooga.

20. At Decatur. The Memphis and Charleston Railroad crosses the Tennessee river at this point. The town is a dilapidated old concern, as ugly as Huntsville is handsome.

There is a canebrake near the camp, and every soldier in the regiment has provided himself with a fishing-rod; very long, straight, beautiful rods they are, too.

The white rebel, who has done his utmost to bring about the rebellion, is lionized, called a plucky fellow, a great man, while the negro, who welcomes us, who is ready to peril his life to aid us, is kicked, cuffed, and driven back to his master, there to be scourged for his kindness to us. Billy, my servant, tells me that a colored man was whipped to death by a planter who lives near here, for giving information to our men. I do not doubt it. We worm out of these poor creatures a knowledge of the places where stores are secreted, or compel them to serve as guides, and then turn them out to be scourged or murdered. There must be a change in this regard before we shall be worthy of success.

21. A detachment went to Somerville yesterday. While searching for buried arms forty-two hundred dollars, in gold, silver, and bank-notes, were found.

The money is, undoubtedly, private property, and will, I presume, be returned to the owner.

Fine, large fish are caught in the Tennessee. We have a buffalo for supper—a good sort of fish—weighing six pounds.

General Mitchell has been made a Major-General. He is a deserving officer. No other man with so few troops has ventured so far into the enemy's country, and accomplished so much. Battles if they result favorably are great helps to the cause, but the general who by a bold dash accomplishes equally imporant results, without loss of life, is entitled to as great praise certainly as he who fights and wins a victory.

Colonel Keifer and I have been on horseback most of the afternoon, examining all the roads leading from Decatur. On our way back to camp we called at Mr. Rather's. He was a member of the Alabama Senate, favored the secession movement, but claims now to be heartily sorry for it. He received us cordially; introduced us to to Mrs. Rather, brought in wine of his own manufacture, and urged us to drink heartily.

23. A beautiful day has gone by and a beautiful starlit night has come. The camp is very still. The melody of the frog, if melody it•can be called, and the ripple of the Tennessee, are the only sounds to be heard. Thoughts of home and the quiet evenings; of youth and the gay visions; of the thousand and one pleasant scenes in life; of what we might have been and where we might have been, had the cards of our life been shuffled differently; of the deeds we might do, if peradventure the opportunity

were offered, and the little we have done; all come up to-night, and we chew the cud over and over, without being able to determine whether it is bitter or sweet.

The enemy, three hundred strong, made a dash on our picket last night, wounded one man, and made an unsuccessful effort to retake a bridge.

24. Our forces are on the alert. I lay down in my clothes last night, or rather this morning, for it was between one and two o'clock when I retired. The division is stretched over a hundred miles of railway, but in position to concentrate in a few hours.

Before leaving this place, the rebels built a cotton fort, using in its construction probably five hundred bales.

To-day we filled the bridge over the Tennessee with combustible material, and put it in condition to burn readily, in case we find it necessary to retire to the north side.

A man with his son and two daughters arrived to-night from Chattanooga, having come all the way— one hundred and fifty miles probably—in a small skiff.

25. Price, with ten thousand men, is reported advancing from Memphis. Turchin had a skirmish with his advance guard near Tuscumbia.

26. Turchin's brigade returned from Tuscumbia and crossed the Tennessee.

27. The Tenth and Third crossed to the north side of the river, and Lieutenant-Colonel Burke of the Tenth applied the torch to the bridge; in a few

minutes the fire extended along its whole length, and as we marched away, the flames were hissing among its timbers, and the smoke hung like a cloud above it.

28. Ordered to move to Stevenson. Took a freight train and proceeded to Bellefonte, where we found a bridge had been burned; leaving the cars we marched until twelve o'clock at night, and then bivouacked on the railroad track.

29. Resumed the march at daylight; one mile beyond Stevenson we found the Ninth Brigade, Colonel Sill, in line of battle; formed the Third in support of Loomis' Battery, and remained in this position until two in the afternoon, when General Mitchell arrived and ordered the Ninth Brigade, Loomis' Battery and my regiment to move forward. At Widow's creek we met a detachment of the enemy; a few shots from the battery and a volley from our skirmish line drove it back, and we hastened on toward Bridgeport, exchanging shots occasionally with the enemy on the way.

About five o'clock we formed in line of battle, on high ground in the woods, one-half mile from Bridgeport, the Third having the right of the column, and moved steadily forward until we came in sight of the town and the enemy. The order to double quick was then given, and we dashed into the village on a run. The enemy stood for a moment and then left as fast as legs could carry him; in fact he departed in such haste that but few muskets and one shot from a six pound gun were fired at us; one piece of his artillery was found still loaded.   We captured fifty prisoners, a number of horses, two pieces of artillery and many muskets.   The bridge over the Tennessee had already been filled with combustible material, and when the rear of the rebel column passed over the match was applied ; the fire extended rapidly, and we found it impossible to proceed further.

The fright of the enemy was so great that, after getting beyond the river a mile or more, he threw away over a thousand muskets, and abandoned every thing that could impede his flight.   Unfortunately, however, before a raft could be constructed to convey our troops across the river, the rebels recovered from their panic, backed down a railroad train, and gathered up most of their arms and camp equipage.

A little more coolness on the part of our troops would have enabled us to capture twenty-five or thirty cavalrymen, who came riding into Bridgeport, supposing it to be still in the hands of their friends.   As they approached, a few scattering shots were fired at them by the excited soldiers, when they wheeled and succeeded in making their escape.

30.   The troops are short of provisions ; there is a grist mill near, but the owner claims that it is out of repair, and can not be put in running order for some days, as part of the machinery is missing.   On inquiry, I found that the owner of the mill was a rebel, and that the missing machinery had probably been hidden by himself.   I therefore said to him that if he did not have the mill going by noon, I would burn it down ;

by ten o'clock it was running, and at three in the afternoon we had an abundance of corn meal.

A detachment of the Third under Colonel Keifer crossed the river and reconnoitered the country beyond. It found no enemy, but returned to camp with an abundance of bacon—an article very greatly needed by our troops.

Started at nine o'clock P. M. for Stevenson; marched all night. Whenever we stopped on the way to rest, the boys would fall asleep on the roadside, and we found much difficulty in getting them through.

12

MAY, 1862.

1. Moved to Bellefonte.

2. Took the cars for Huntsville.

At Paint Rock the train was fired upon, and six or eight men wounded. As soon as it could be done, I had the train stopped, and, taking a file of soldiers, returned to the village. The telegraph line had been cut, and the wire was lying in the street. Calling the citizens together, I said to them that this bushwhacking must cease. The Federal troops had tolerated it already too long. Hereafter every time the telegraph wire was cut we would burn a house; every time a train was fired upon we should hang a man; and we would continue to do this until every house was burned and every man hanged between Decatur and Bridgeport. If they wanted to fight they should enter the army, meet us like honorable men, and not, assassin-like, fire at us from the woods and run. We proposed to hold the citizens responsible for these cowardly assaults, and if they did not drive these bushwhackers from amongst them, we should make them more uncomfortable than they would be in hell. I then set fire to the town, took three citizens with me, returned to the train, and proceeded to Huntsville.

Paint Rock has long been a rendezvous for bushwhackers and bridge burners. One of the men taken is a notorious guerrilla, and was of the party that made the dash on our wagon train at Nashville.

The week has been an active one. On last Saturday night I slept a few hours on the bridge at Decatur. The next night I bivouacked in a cotton field; the next I lay from midnight until four in the morning on the railroad track; the next I slept at Bridgeport on the soft side of a board, and on the return to Stevenson I did not sleep at all. My health is excellent.

5. Captain Cunard was sent yesterday to Paint Rock to arrest certain parties suspected of burning bridges, tearing up the railroad track, and bushwhacking soldiers. To-day he returned with twenty-six prisoners.

General Mitchell is well pleased with my action in the Paint Rock matter. The burning of the town has created a sensation, and is spoken of approvingly by the officers and enthusiastically by the men. It is the inauguration of the true policy, and the only one that will preserve us from constant annoyance.

The General rode into our camp this evening, and made us a stirring speech, in which he dilated upon the rapidity of our movements and the invincibility of our division.

8. The road to Shelbyville is unsafe for small parties. Guerrilla bands are very active. Two or

three of our supply trains have been captured and destroyed. Detachments are sent out every day to capture or disperse these citizen cut-throats.

10. Have been appointed President of a Board of Administration for the post of Huntsville. After an ineffectual effort to get the members of the Board together, I concluded to spend a day out of camp, the first for more than six months; so I strolled over to the hotel, took a bath, ate dinner, smoked, read, and slept until supper time, dispatched that meal, and returned to my quarters in the cool of the evening.

We have in our camp a superabundance of negroes. One of these, a Georgian, belonged to a captain of rebel cavalry, and fell into our hands at Bridgeport. Since that affair he has attached himself to me. The other negroes I do not know. In fact they are too numerous to mention. Whence they came or whither they are going it is impossible to say. They lie around contentedly, and are delighted when we give them an opportunity to serve us. All the colored people of Alabama are anxious to go " wid yer and wait on you folks." There are not fifty negroes in the South who would not risk their lives for freedom. The man who affirms that they are contented and happy, and do not desire to escape, is either a falsifier or a fool.

11. Attended divine service with Captain Mc-Dougal at the Presbyterian Church. The edifice is very fine. The audience was small; the sermon tolerable. Troubles, the preacher said, were sent to discipline us. The army was of God; they should,

therefore, submit to it, not as slaves, but as Christians, just as they submitted to other distasteful and calamitous dispensations.

12.   My letters from home have fallen into the hands of John Morgan.   The envelopes were picked up in the road and forwarded to me.   My wife should feel encouraged.   It is not every body's letters that are pounced upon at midnight, taken at the point of the bayonet, and read by the flickering light of the camp-fire.

Moved at two o'clock this afternoon.   Reached Athens after nightfall, and bivouacked on the Fair Ground.

13.   Marched to Elk river.   A great many negroes from the neighboring plantations came to see us, among them an elderly colored man, whose sanctimonious bearing indicated that he was a minister of the Gospel.   The boys insisted that he should preach to them, and, after some hesitation, the old man mounted a stump, lined a hymn from memory, sang it, and then commenced his discourse.   He had not proceeded very far when he uttered this sentence: "De good Lord He hab called me to preach de Gospil.   Many sinners hab been wakened by my poor words to de new life.   De Lord He hab been very kind to me, an' I can nebber pay Him fur all He done fur me."

"Never pay the Lord?" broke in the boys; "never pay the Lord?   Oh! you wicked nigger!   Just hear him!   He says he is never going to pay the Lord!"

The preacher endeavored to explain: the kindness

and mercy of the Lord had been so great that it was impossible for a poor sinner to make any sufficient return; but the boys would accept no explanation. "Here," they shouted, "is a nigger who will not pay the Lord!" and they groaned and cried, "Oh! Oh!" and swore that they never saw so wicked a man before. Fortunately for the poor colored man, a Dutchman began to interrogate him in broken English, and the two soon fell into a discussion of some point in theology, when the boys espoused the negro's side of the question, and insisted that the Dutchman was no match for him in argument. Finally, by groans and hisses, they compelled the Dutchman to abandon the controversy, leaving the colored man well pleased that he had vanquished his opponent and re-established himself in the good opinion of his hearers.

14. Resumed the march at two o'clock in the morning, and proceeded to a point known as the Lower Ferry. Ascertaining here that the enemy had recrossed the Tennessee, and was pushing southward, we abandoned pursuit and turned to retrace our steps to Huntsville. Leaving the regiment in command of Colonel Keifer, I accompanied General Mitchell on the return, and reached camp a little after dark.

16. Appointed Provost Marshal of the city. Have been busy hearing all sorts of complaints, signing passes for all sorts of persons, sending guards to this and that place in the city, and doing the numerous other things necessary to be done in a city under

martial law. Captain Mitchell and Lieutenant Wilson are my assistants, and, in fact, do most of the work. The citizens say I am the youngest Governor they ever had.

17. Captain Mitchell and I were invited to a strawberry supper at Judge Lane's. Found General Mitchell and staff, Colonel Kennett, Lieutenant-Colonel Birdsall, and Captain Loomis, of the army, there. Mr. and Mrs. Judge Lane, Colonel and Major Davis, and a general, whose name I can not recall, were the only citizens present. General Mitchell monopolized the conversation. He was determined to make all understand that he was the greatest of living soldiers. Had his counsel prevailed, the Confederacy would have been knocked to pieces long ago. The evening was a very pleasant one.

A few days ago we had John Morgan utterly annihilated; but he seems to have gathered up the dispersed atoms and rebuilt himself. In the destruction of our supply trains he imagines, doubtless, that he is inflicting a great injury upon our division; but he is mistaken. The bread and meat we fail to get from the loyal States are made good to us from the smoke-houses and granaries of the disloyal. Our boys find Alabama hams better than Uncle Sam's sidemeat, and fresh bread better than hard crackers. So that every time this dashing cavalryman destroys a provision train, their hearts are gladdened, and they shout "Bully for Morgan!"

19. Rumor says that Richmond is in the hands of our troops; and from the same source we learn that

a large force of the enemy is between us and Nashville. Fifteen hundred mounted men were within seventeen miles of Huntsville yesterday. A regiment with four pieces of artillery, under command of Colonel Lytle, was sent toward Fayetteville to look after them.

20. The busiest time in the Provost Marshal's office is between eight o'clock in the morning and noon. Then many persons apply for passes to go outside the lines and for guards to protect property. Others come to make complaints that houses have been broken open, or that horses, dogs, and negroes, have strayed away or been stolen.

23. The men of Huntsville have settled down to a patient endurance of military rule. They say but little, and treat us with all politeness. The women, however, are outspoken in their hostility, and marvelously bitter. A flag of truce came in last night from Chattanooga, and the bearers were overwhelmed with visits and favors from the ladies. When they took supper at the Huntsville Hotel, the large diningroom was crowded with fair faces and bright eyes; but the men prudently held aloof.

A day or two ago one of our Confederate prisoners died. The ladies filled the hearse to overflowing with flowers, and a large number of them accompanied the soldier to his last resting-place.

The foolish, yet absolute, devotion of the women to the Southern cause does much to keep it alive. It encourages, nay forces, the young to enter the army, and compels them to continue what the more sensible

Southerners know to be a hopeless struggle. But we must not judge these Huntsville women too harshly. Here are the families of many of the leading men of Alabama; of generals, colonels, majors, captains, and lieutenants in the Confederate army; of men, even, who hold cabinet positions at Richmond, and of many young men who are clerks in the departments of the rebel Government. Their wives, daughters, sisters, and sweethearts feel, doubtless, that the honor of these gentlemen, and possibly their lives, depend upon the success of the Confederacy.

To-day two young negro men from Jackson county came in with their wives. They were newly married, and taking their wedding journey. The vision of a better and higher life had lured them from the old plantation where they were born. At midnight they had stolen quietly away, plodded many weary miles on foot, confident that the rainbow and the bag of gold were in the camp of the Federal army.

25. This in-door life has made me ill. I am as yellow as an orange. The doctors say I have the jaundice.

13

JUNE, 1862.

3.   Have requested General Mitchell to relieve me
from duty as Provost Marshal; am now wholly unfit
to do business.

We have heard of the evacuation of Corinth.   The
simple withdrawal of the enemy amounts to but little,
if anything; he still lives, is organized and ready to
do battle on some other field.

5.   Go home on sick leave.

*   *   *   *   *

25.   There were three little girls on the Louisville
packet, about the age of my own children.   They
were great romps.   I said to one, "what is your
name?"   She replied " Pudin' an' tame."   So I called
her Pudin', and she became very angry, so angry indeed that she cried.   The other little girls laughed
heartily, and called her Pudin' also, and then asked
my name.   I answered John Smith; they insisted
then that Pudin' was my wife, and called her Pudin'
Smith.   This made Pudin' furious, and she abused her
companions and me terribly; but John Smith invested a little money in cherries, and thus pacified
Pudin', and so got to Louisville without getting his
hair pulled.   I saw no more of Pudin' until she got
off the cars at Elizabethtown.   Going up to her, we

shook hands, and I said, "Good-by, Pudin'." She hung her head for a moment, and tried to look angry, but finally breaking into a laugh she said, " I do n't like you at all any way, good-by."

27. Reached Huntsville. The regiment in good condition, boys well; weather hot. General Buell arrived last night. McCook's Division is here; Nelson, Crittenden, and Wood on the road hither.

JULY, 1862.

2.   We know, or think we know, that a great battle has been fought near Richmond, but the result for some reason is withheld.   We speculate, talk, and compare notes, but this makes us only the more eager for definite information.

I am almost as well as ever, not quite so strong, but a few days will make me right again.

3.   It is exceedingly dull; we are resting as quietly and leisurely as we could at home.   There are no drills, and no expeditions.   The army is holding its breath in anxiety to hear from Richmond.   If McClellan has been whipped, the country must in time know it; if successful, it would be rejoiced to hear it. Why, therefore, should the particulars, and even the result of the fighting, be suppressed.   Rumor gives us a thousand conflicting stories of the battle, but rumor has many tongues and lies with all.

General Mitchell departed for Washington yesterday.

The rebels at Chattanooga claim that McClellan has been terribly whipped, and fired guns along their whole line, within hearing of our troops, in honor of the victory.

A lieutenant of the Nineteenth Illinois, who fell

into the enemy's hands, has just returned on parole, and claims to have seen a dispatch from the Adjutant-General of the Southern Confederacy, stating that McClellan had been defeated and his army cut to pieces. He believes it.

My horse is as fat as a stall-fed ox. He has had a very easy time during my absence.

To-morrow is the Fourth, hitherto glorious, but now, like to-day's meridian sun, clouded, and sending out a somewhat uncertain light. Has the great experiment failed? Shall we hail the Fourth as the birth-day of a great Nation, or weep over it as the beginning of a political enterprise which resulted in dissolution, anarchy and ruin? Let us lift up our eyes and be hopeful. The dawn may be even now breaking.

The boys propose to have a barbecue to-morrow, and roast a corpulent, good-natured Ethiopian, named Cæsar. They are now discussing the matter very voluminously, in Cæsar's presence. He thinks they are probably joking; but still they seem to be greatly in earnest, and he knows little of these Yankees, and thinks maybe his "massa tole him de truff about dem, after all." "The Fourth is a great day," the boys go on to say, "whereon Yankees always dine on roast nigger. It is a part of their religion. It is this which makes colored folks so scarce in the North." Shall Cæsar be stuffed or not? That is really the only question. One party claims that if Cæsar be stuffed with vegetables and nicely roasted, he will be delicious. The other party insists that Cæsar is sufficiently stuffed already; vegetables would not improve him. They have eaten roast nigger both ways and know. So the discussion waxes hot, and the dusky Alabamian has some fear, even, that his last day may be drawing very near.

4. Thirty-four guns were fired at noon.

5. An Atlanta paper of the 1st instant says the Confederates have won a decisive victory at Richmond. No Northern papers have been allowed to come into camp.

6. McCook moved toward Chattanooga. General W. S. Smith has command of our division.

The boys have a great many game chickens. Not long ago Company G, of the Third, and Company G, of the Tenth, had a rooster fight, the stakes being fifteen dollars a side. After numerous attacks, retreats, charges, and counter-charges, the Tenth rooster succumbed like a hero, and the other was carried in triumph from the field. General Mitchell made his appearance near the scene at the conclusion of the conflict; but, supposing the crowd to be an enthusiastic lot of soldiers who were cheering him, passed on, well pleased with them and himself.

The boys have a variety of information from Richmond to-day. One party affirms that McClellan has been cut to pieces; that a dispatch to that effect has been received by General Buell. Another insists that he has obtained a decided advantage, and is heating the shot to burn Richmond; while still another affirms that he has utterly destroyed Richmond, and, Marius-like, is sitting amid the ruins of that ill-fated city, eating sow belly and doe-christers.

7. Am detailed to serve on court-martial.

DETAIL FOR THE COURT.

General James A. Garfield.
Colonel Jacob Ammen.
Colonel Curren Pope.
Colonel Jones.
Colonel Marc Mundy.
Colonel Sedgewick.
Colonel John Beatty.

Convened at Athens at ten o'clock this morning. Organized and adjourned to meet at ten to-morrow.

General Buell proposes, I understand, to give General Mitchell's administration of affairs in North Alabama a thorough overhauling. It is asserted that the latter has been interested in cotton speculations; but investigation, I am well satisfied, will show that General Mitchell has been strictly honest, and has done nothing to compromise his honor, or cast even the slightest shadow upon his good name.

The first case to be tried is that of Colonel J. B. Turchin, Nineteenth Illinois. He is charged with permitting his command, the Eighth Brigade, to steal, rob, and commit all manner of outrages.

10. Our court has been adjourning from day to day, until Colonel Turchin should succeed in procuring counsel; but it is now in full blast.

Nelson's division is quartered here. The town is enveloped in a dense cloud of dust.

14.   There are many wealthy planters in this section.   One of the witnesses before our court has a cotton crop on hand worth sixty thousand dollars. Another swears that Turchin's brigade robbed him of twelve hundred dollars' worth of silver plate.

Turchin's brigade has stolen a hundred thousand dollars' worth of watches, plate, and jewelry, in Northern Alabama.   Turchin has gone to one extreme, for war can not justify the gutting of private houses and the robbery of peaceable citizens, for the benefit of individual officers or soldiers; but there is another extreme, more amiable and pleasant to look upon, but not less fatal to the cause.   Buell is likely to go to that.   He is inaugurating the dancing-master policy: "By your leave, my dear sir, we will have a fight; that is, if you are sufficiently fortified; no hurry; take your own time."   To the bushwhacker: "Am sorry you gentlemen fire at our trains from behind stumps, logs, and ditches.   Had you not better cease this sort of warfare?   Now do, my good fellows, stop, I beg of you."   To the citizen rebel: "You are a chivalrous people; you have been aggravated by the abolitionists into subscribing cotton to the Southern Confederacy; you had, of course, a right to dispose of your own property to suit yourselves, but we prefer that you would, in future, make no more subscriptions of that kind, and in the meantime we propose to protect your property and guard your negroes." Turchin's policy is bad enough; it may indeed be the policy of the devil; but Buell's policy is that of the amiable idiot.   There is a better policy than either.

It will neither steal nor maraud; it will do nothing for the sake of individual gain, and, on the other hand, it will not crouch to rebels; it will not fear to hurt the feelings of traitors; it will not fritter away the army and the revenue of the Government in the insane effort to protect men who have forfeited all right to protection. The policy we need is one that will march boldly, defiantly, through the rebel States, indifferent as to whether this traitor's cotton is safe, or that traitor's negroes run away; calling things by their right names; crushing those who have aided and abetted treason, whether in the army or out. In short, we want an iron policy that will not tolerate treason; that will demand immediate and unconditional obedience as the price of protection.

15.   The post at Murfreesboro, occupied by two regiments of infantry and one battery, under Critten-den, of Indiana, has surrendered to the enemy. A bridge and a portion of the railroad track between this place and Pulaski have been destroyed. A large rebel force is said to be north of the Tennessee. It crossed the river at Chattanooga.

18.   The star of the Confederacy appears to be rising, and I doubt not it will continue to ascend until the rose-water policy now pursued by the Northern army is superseded by one more determined and vigorous. We should look more to the interests of the North, and less to those of the South. We should visit on the aiders, abettors, and supporters of the Southern army somewhat of the severity which hitherto has been aimed at that army only. Who are

most deserving of our leniency, those who take arms and go to the field, or those who remain at home, raising corn, oats, and bacon to subsist them? Plain people, who know little of constitutional hair-splitting, could decide this question only one way; but it seems those who have charge of our armies can not decide it in any sensible way. They say: "You would not disturb peaceable citizens by levying contributions from them?" Why not? If the husbands, brothers, and fathers of these people, their natural leaders and guardians, do not care for them, why should we? If they disregard and trample upon that law which gave all protection, and plunge the country into war, why should we be perpetually hindered and thwarted in our efforts to secure peace by our care fo those whom they have abandoned? If we make th country through which we pass furnish supplies to our army, the inhabitants will have less to furnish our enemies. The surplus products of the country should be gathered into the Federal granaries, so that they could not, by possibility, go to feed the rebels. The loyal and innocent might occasionally and for the present suffer, but peace when once establshed would afford ample opportunity to investigate and repay these sufferers. Shall we continue to protect the property of our enemies, and lose the lives of our friends? It is said that it is hard to deprive men of their horses, cattle, grain, simply because they differ from us in opinion; but is it not harder still to deprive men of their lives for the same reason? The opinions from which we differ in this instance are treasonable. The man who, of his own free will, supplies the wood is no whit better than he who kindles the fire; and the man who supplies the ammunition neither better nor worse than he who does the killing. The severest punishment should be inflicted upon the soldier who appropriates either private or public property to his own use; but the Government should lay its mailed hand upon treasonable communities, and teach them that war is no holiday pastime.

19. Returned to Huntsville this afternoon; General Garfield with me. He will visit our quarters tomorrow and dine with us.

General Rousseau has been assigned to the command of our division. I am glad to hear that he discards the rose-water policy of General Buell under his nose, and is a great deal more thorough and severe in his treatment of rebels than General Mitchell. He sent the Rev. Mr. Ross to jail to-day for preaching a secession sermon last Sunday. He damns the rebel sympathizers, and says if the negro stands in the way of the Union he must get out. Rousseau is a Kentuckian, and it is very encouraging to learn that he talks as he does.

Turchin has been made a brigadier.

21. An order issued late last evening transferring our court from Athens to Huntsville.

Colonel Turchin's case is still before us. No official notice of his promotion has been communicated to the court.

23. Garfield and Ammen are our guests. They

are sitting with Colonel Keifer, in the open air, in front of our tent. We have eaten supper, and Colonel Ammen has the floor; he always has it. He is somewhat superstitious. He never likes to see the moon through brush. He is to some extent a believer in dreams. On one occasion he dreamed that his father, who was drowned, came up from the muddy water, looked angrily at him, and endeavored to stab him with a rusty knife. In his effort to escape he awoke. Falling to sleep again, his father reappeared and made a second attempt to stab him. This so thoroughly aroused and troubled him that he could not sleep. In the morning he told this dream to a friend, and was informed that two members of his family would soon die. Soon after he was summoned home, when he found his mother dead and his sister dying of cholera. At another time he felt a sharp pain in the back of his neck, and was impressed with the idea that he had been shot. Soon afterward he learned that his brother in the South had been shot in the back of the neck and killed. He believes that his own sensation of pain was experienced at the very instant when his brother received the fatal wound; but as he could not remember the precise hour when he was startled by the disagreeable impression, he could not be positive that the occurrences were simultaneous. When going into battle at Greenbrier and at Shiloh, the belief that his time to die had not come rendered him cool and fearless. He never felt more at ease or more secure. So when, at two different times, he was very ill, and informed that he could not live through the night, he felt absolutely sure that he would recover.

Garfield had a very impressionable relative. The night before his fight with Humphrey Marshall, she wrote a very accurate general description of the battle, giving the position of the troops; referring to the reinforcements which came up, and the great shout with which they were welcomed.

These mysterious impressions suggested the existence of an undiscovered, or possibly an undeveloped principle in nature, which time and investigation would ultimately make familiar.

Colonel Ammen says, " If superstition, or a belief in the supernatural, is an indication of weakness, Napoleon and Sir Walter Scott were the weakest of men."

With General Garfield I called on General Rousseau this morning. He is a larger and handsomer man than Mitchell, but I think lacks the latter's energy, culture, system, and industry.

24. We can not boast of what is occurring in this department. The tide seems to have set against us everywhere. The week of battles before Richmond was a week of defeats. I trust the new policy indicated by the confiscation act, just passed by Congress, will have good effect. It will, at least, enable us to weaken the enemy, as we have not thus far done, and strengthen ourselves, as we have hitherto not been able to do. Slavery is the enemy's weak point, the key to his position. If we can tear down this institution, the rebels will lose all interest in the Confed-

eracy, and be too glad to escape with their lives, to be very particular about what they call their rights.

Colonel Ammen has just received notice of his confirmation as brigadier. He is a strange combination of simplicity and wisdom, full of good stories, and tells those against himself with a great deal more pleasure than any others.

Colonels Turchin, Mihalotzy, Gazley, and Captain Edgerton form a group by the window; all are smoking vigorously, and speculating probably on the result of the present and prospective trials. Mihalotzy is what is commonly termed " Dutch ;" but whether he is from the German States, Russia, Prussia, or Poland, I know not.

Ammen left camp early this morning, saying he would go to town and see if he could find an idea, he was pretty nearly run out. He talks incessantly ; his narratives abound in episode, parenthesis, switches, side-cuts, and before he gets through, one will conclude a dozen times that he has forgotten the tale he entered upon, but he never does.

Colonel Stanley, Eighteenth Ohio, has just come in. He has in his time been a grave and reverend senator of Ohio ; he never loses sight of this fact, and never fails to impress it upon those with whom he comes in contact.

An order has just been issued, and is now being circulated among the members of the court, purporting to come from General Ammen, and signed with his name. It recites the fact of his promotion, and forbids any one hereafter to call him Uncle Jacob,

that title being entirely too familiar and undignified
for one of his rank. All who violate the order are
threatened with the direst punishment.

The General says if such orders please the court,
he will not object to their being issued; it certainly
requires but very little ability to get them up.

The General prides himself on what he calls deli-
cate irony. He says, in the town of Ripley, men who
can not manage a dray successfully criticise the conduct of this and that general with great severity;
when they appeal to him, he tells them quietly he
has not the capacity to judge of such matters; it requires a great mind and a thorough understanding of
all the circumstances.

After all I have said about General Ammen, it is
hardly necessary to remark that he does most of the
talking.

To-day Garfield and Keifer, who of course entertain the kindliest feelings, and the greatest respect for
the General, in a spirit of fun, entered into a conspiracy against him. They proposed for one night to do
all the talking themselves, and not allow him to edge
in even a word. After supper Garfield was to commence with the earliest incidents of his childhood, and
without allowing himself to be interrupted, continue
until he had given a complete narrative of his life and
adventures; then Keifer was to strike in and finish up
the night. General Ammen was not to be permitted
to open his mouth except to yawn.

We ate supper and immediately adjourned to the
adjoining tent. Before Garfield was fairly seated on

his camp stool, he began to talk with the easy and deliberate manner of a man who had much to say. He dwelt eloquently on the minutest details of his early life, as if they were matters of the utmost importance. Keifer was not only an attentive listener, but seemed wonderfully interested. Uncle Jacob undertook to thrust in a word here and there, but Garfield was too much absorbed to notice him, and so pushed on steadily, warming up as he proceeded. Unfortunately for his scheme, however, before he had gone far he made a touching reference to his mother, when Uncle Jacob, gesticulating energetically, and with his forefinger leveled at the speaker, cried: "Just a word—just one word right there," and so persisted until Garfield was compelled either to yield or be absolutely discourteous. The General, therefore, got in his word; nay, he held the floor for the remainder of the evening. The conspirators made brave efforts to put him down and cut him off, but they were unsuccessful. At midnight, when Keifer and I left, he was still talking; and after we had got into bed, he, with his suspenders dangling about his legs, thrust his head into our tent-door, and favored us with the few observations we had lost by reason of our hasty departure. Keifer turned his face to the wall and groaned. Poor man! he had been hoisted by his own petard. I think Uncle Jacob suspected that the young men had set up a job on him.

The regiment went on a foraging expedition yesterday, under Colonel Keifer, and was some fifteen miles from Huntsville, in the direction of the Tennessee river.

At one o'clock last night our picket was confronted by about one hundred and fifty of the enemy's cavalry; but no shots were exchanged.

29. The rebel cavalry were riding in the mountains south of us last night. A heavy mounted patrol of our troops was making the rounds at midnight. There was some picket firing along toward morning; but nothing occurred of importance.

Our forces are holding the great scope of country between Memphis and Bridgeport, guarding bridges, railroads, and towns, frittering away the strength of a great army, and wasting our men by permitting them to be picked up in detail. In short, we put down from fifty to one hundred, here and there, at points convenient to the enemy, as bait for them. They take the bait frequently, and always when they run no risk of being caught. The climate, and the insane effort to garrison the whole country, consumes our troops, and we make no progress. May the good Lord be with us, and deliver us from idleness and imbecility; and especially, O! Lord, grant a little every-day sense—that very common sense which plain people use in the management of their business affairs—to the illustrious generals who have our armies in hand!

30. We have just concluded Colonel Turchin's case, and forwarded the proceedings to General Buell.

General Ammen for many years belonged to a club, the members of which were required either to sing a

14

song or tell a story. He could not sing, and, consequently, took to stories, and very few can tell one better. The General is a member of the Episcopal Church, and, although a pious man, emphasizes his language occasionally by an oath. When conducting his brigade from the boat at Pittsburg Landing to position on the field, he was compelled to pass through the immense crowd of skedaddlers who had sought shelter under the bluffs from the storm of bullets. A chaplain of one of the disorganized regiments was haranguing the mob in what may be termed the whangdoodle style: "Rally, men; rally, and we may yet be saved. O! rally! For God and your country's sake rally! R-a-l-l-y! O-h! r-a-l-l-y around the flag of your c-o-w-n-try, my c-o-wn-tryme-n!" "Shut up, you God damned old fool!" said Ammen, "or I'll break your head! Get out of the way!"

General Garfield is lying on the lounge unwell. He has an attack of the jaundice, and will, I think, start home to-morrow.

I find an article on the tables of the South, which, with coffee, I like very much. The wheat dough is rolled very thin, cut in strips the width of a table-knife, and about as long, baked until well done; if browned, all the better. They become crisp and brittle, and better than the best of crackers.

31. General Ammen is so interesting to me that I can not avoid talking about him, especially when items are scarce, as they are now. Our court takes a recess at one, and assembles again at half-past three, giving us two hours and a half for dinner. To-day

the conversation turned on the various grasses North and South. After the General had described the peculiar grasses of many sections, he drifted to the people South who lived on farms, where he had seen a variety of grass unknown in the North, and the following story was told:

In the part of Mississippi where he resided for a number of years, there lived a Northern family named Greenfield. When he was there the farm was known as the Greenfield farm. It was the peculiar grass on this farm which suggested the story. The Greenfields were Quakers, originally from Philadelphia. One of the wealthiest members of the family was a little weazen-faced old maid, of fifty years or more. Her overseer was a large, fine looking young man named Roach. After he had been in her service a year she took a fancy to him, and proposed to give him twenty thousand dollars if he would marry her. He accepted, and they were duly married. A year after she grew tired of wedlock, and proposed to give thirty thousand dollars to be unmarried. He accepted this proposition also. They united in a petition for a divorce and obtained it. Roach took the fifty thousand dollars thus made and invested it in the Yazoo country. The property increased in value rapidly, and he soon became a millionaire. When General Ammen saw him, he had married again more to his liking, and was one of the prominent men in his section.

The farm of the Gillyards lay near that of the Greenfields, and this suggested another story. A

Miss Gillyard was a great heiress; owned plantations in Mississippi, and an interest in a large estate in South Carolina. A doctor of prepossessing appearance came from the latter State, and commenced practice in the neighborhood, and an acquaintance of a few months resulted in a marriage. After living together a year very happily, they started on a visit to South Carolina; she to visit relatives and look after her interest in the estate mentioned, and he to see his friends. On the way it was agreed that he should attend to his wife's business, and so full power to sell or dispose of the property, or her interest therein, was given him. At Charleston she was met by the relatives with whom she was to remain, while the Doctor proceeded to a different part of the State to see his friends, and afterward attend to business. When about to separate, like a jolly soul, he proposed that they should drink to each other's health during the separation. The wine was produced; they touched glasses, and raised them to their lips, when the door opened suddenly and the Doctor was called. Setting his wine on the table, he stepped out of the room, and the wife, more affectionate, possibly, than most women, took the glass which his lips had touched and put her own in its place. The husband reappeared shortly, and they drank off the wine. In an hour he was dead, and she in the deepest affliction. After she had recovered somewhat from the shock, she left Charleston to visit his people. She found them poor, and that he had a wife and three children. The truth then broke in upon her; he had drank the wine prepared for her.

This story suggested one involving some of Miss Gillyard's relations.

Two lady cousins resided in the same town. The father of one had amassed a handsome fortune in the tailoring business. The father of the other had been a saddler, and, carrying on the business extensively, had also become wealthy. The descendant of the saddler would refer to her cousin's father as the tailor, and intimate that his calling was certainly not that of a gentleman. The other hearing of this, and meeting her one evening at a large party, said: "Cousin Julia, I hear that you have said my father was nothing but a tailor. Now, this is true; he was a tailor, and a very good one, too. By his industry and judgment he made a large fortune, which I am enjoying. I respect him; am grateful, and not ashamed of him, if he was a tailor. Your father was a saddler, and a very good one. He, by industry and good management, accumulated great wealth, which you are enjoying. I see no reason, therefore, why we should not both be proud of our fathers, and I certainly can see no reason why a man-tailor should not be just as good as a horse-tailor."

AUGUST, 1862.

1. The Judge-Advocate, Captain Swayne, was unwell this morning. The court, therefore, took a recess until three o'clock. Captain Edgerton's case was disposed of last evening. Colonel Mihalotzy's will come before us to-day. A court-martial proceeds always with due respect to red tape. The questions to witnesses are written out; the answers are written down; the statement of the accused is in writing, and the defense of the accused's counsel is written; so that the court snaps its fingers at time, as if it were of no consequence, and seven men, against whom there are no charges, are likely to spend their natural lives in investigating seven men, more or less, against whom there are charges. It is thus the rebels are being subjugated, the Union re-united, the Constitution and the laws enforced.

3. Among the curiosities in camp are two young coons and a pet opossum. The latter is the property of Augustus Cæsar, the esquire of Adjutant Wilson. Cæsar restrains the opossum with a string, and looks forward with great pleasure to the time when he will be fat enough to eat. The coons are just now playing on the wild cherry tree in front

of my tent, and several colored boys are watching them with great interest. One of these, a native Alabamian, tells me "de coon am a great fiter; he can wip a dog berry often; but de possum can wip de coon, for he jist takes one holt on de coon, goes to sleep, an' nebber lets go; de coon he scratch an' bite, but de possum he nebber min'; he keeps his holt, shuts his eyes, and bimeby de coon he knocks under. De she coon am savager dan de he coon. I climbed a tree onct, an' de she coon come out ob her hole mitey savage, an' I leg go, an' tumbled down to de groun', and like ter busted my head. De she coon am berry savage. De possum can't run berry fast, but de coon can run faster'n a dog. You can tote a possum, but you can't tote a coon, he scratch an' bite so."

The gentlemen of the South have a great fondness for jewelry, canes, cigars, and dogs. Out of forty white men thirty-nine, at least, will have canes, and on Sunday the fortieth will have one also. White men rarely work here. There are, it is true, tailors, merchants, saddlers, and jewelers, but the whites never drive teams, work in the fields, or engage in what may be termed rough work.

Judging from the number of stores and present stocks, Huntsville, in the better times, does a heavier retail jewelry business than Cleveland or Columbus. Every planter, and every wealthy or even well-to-do man, has plate. Diamonds, rings, gold watches, chains, and bracelets are to be found in every family. The negroes buy large amounts of cheap jewelry, and the trade in this branch is enormous. One may walk a whole day in a Northern city without seeing a ruffled shirt. Here they are very common.

The case of Colonel Mihàlotzy was concluded to-day.

5. General Ammen was a teacher for years at West Point, at Natchez, Mississippi, in Kentucky, Indiana, and recently at Ripley, Ohio. He has devoted particular attention to the education of children, and has no confidence in the usual mode of teaching them. He labors to strengthen or cultivate, first: *attention*, and to this end never allows their interest in anything to flag; whenever he discovers that their minds have become weary of a subject, he takes the book from them and turns their thought in a new direction. Nor does he allow their attention to be divided between two or three objects at the same time. By his method they acquire the power to concentrate their whole mind upon a given subject. The next thing to be cultivated is *observation;* teach them to notice whatever may be around, and describe it. What did you see when you came up street? The child may answer a pig. What is a pig, how did it look, describe it. Saw a man, did you? Was he large or small? How was he dressed? A room? What is a room? Thus will they be taught to observe everything, and to talk about what they observe, and learn not only to think but to express their thoughts. He often amuses them by what he terms opposites. To illustrate: He will say "black," the child will answer "white." Long, short; good, bad; heavy,

light; dark, light. "What kind of light," he will ask, "is that kind which is the opposite of heavy?" Here is a puzzle for them. Next in importance to observation, and to be strengthened at the same time, is the *memory*. They are required to learn little pieces; short stories perhaps, or songs that their minds can comprehend; not too long, for neither the memory nor the attention should be overtaxed.

7. As General Ammen and I were returning to camp this evening, we were joined by Colonel Fry, of General Buell's staff, who informed us that General Robert McCook was murdered, near Winchester, yesterday, by a small band of guerrillas. McCook was unwell, riding in an ambulance some distance in advance of the column; while stopping in front of a farm-house to make some enquiry, the guerrillas made a sudden dash, the escort fled, and McCook was killed while lying in the ambulance defenseless. When the Dutchmen of his old regiment learned of the unfortunate occurrence they became uncontrollable, and destroyed the buildings and property on five plantations near the scene of the murder. McCook had recently been promoted for gallantry at Mill Springs. He was a brave, bluff, talented man, and his loss will be sorely felt.

Captain Mitchell started home in charge of a recruiting party this morning. I am anxious to fill the regiment to a thousand strong.

8. General Ammen was at Buell's quarters this evening, and ascertains that hot work is expected soon.

15

The enemy is concentrating a heavy force between Bridgeport and Chattanooga.

The night is exceedingly beautiful; our camp lies at the foot of a low range of mountains called the Montesano; the sky seems supported by them. A cavalry patrol is just coming down the road, on its return to camp, and the men are singing:

" An exile from home, splendor dazzles in vain,
  Oh ! give me my lowly thatched cottage again ;
  The birds singing gayly, that came at my call,
  Give me them, with the peace of mind dearer than all.
    Home, home, sweet home, there is no place like home ;
      There is no place like home.''

9. I have sometimes wondered how unimportant occurences could suggest so much, but the faculty of association brings similar things before the mind, and a thousand collateral subjects as well. The band of the Tenth Ohio is playing. Where, and under what circumstances, have I heard other bands? The question carries my thoughts into half the States of the Union, into a multitude of places, into an innumerable variety of scenes—faces, conversations, theatres, balls, speeches, songs—the chain is endless, and it might be followed for a lifetime.

10. The enemy, a thousand strong, is said to be within five miles of us. One hundred and sixty-five men of the Third, under Major Lawson, and five companies of cavalry, the whole commanded by Colonel Kennett, left at two o'clock to reconnoiter the

front; they will probably go to the river unless the enemy is met on the way.

A negro came in about four o'clock to report that the enemy's pickets were at his master's house, five miles from here, at the foot of the other slope of the mountain. He was such an ignorant fellow that his report was hardly intelligible. We sent him back, telling him to bring us more definite information. He was a field hand, bare-footed, horny-handed, and very black, but he knew all about "de mountings; dey can't kotch him nohow. If de sesesh am at Massa Bob's when I git back, I come to-night an' tell yer all." With these words, this poor proprietor of a dilapidated pair of pants and shirt, started over the mountains. What are his thoughts about the war, and its probable effects on his own fortunes, as he trudges along over the hills? Is it the desire for freedom, or the dislike for his overseer, that prompts him to run five miles of a Sunday to give this information? Possibly both.

Cæsar said to the Adjutant, "Massa Wilson, may I go to church?" "What do you want to go church for, Cæsar?" "To hear de Gospel." One day Cæsar said to me, "Co'nel, you belongs to de meetin do n't you?" "Why so, Cæsar?" "Kase I nebber heard you swar any."

To-day one of the pet coons got after a chicken. A young half-naked negro took after the coon; and a long and crooked chase the chicken, coon, and negro had of it.

12.   At five o'clock the members of the court met

to say good-by, and drink a dozen bottles of Scotch ale at General Ammen's expense. This was quite a spree for the General, and quite his own spree. It was a big thing, equal almost to the battle of "Shealoh." They were pint bottles, and the General would persist in acting upon the theory that one bottle would fill all our glasses. Seeing the glasses empty he would call for another bottle, and say to us, "Gentlemen, I have ordered another bottle." The General evidently drinks, when he imbibes at all, simply to be social, and a thimble-full would answer his purpose as well as a barrel.

The court called on General Buell; he is cold, smooth-toned, silent, the opposite of Nelson, who is ardent, loud-mouthed, and violent.

17. Colonel Keifer has just received a telegram informing him that he has been appointed Colonel of the One Hundred and Tenth Ohio. I regret his departure too much to rejoice over his promotion. He has been a faithful officer, always prompt and cheerful; much better qualified to command the regiment than its Colonel.

Watermelons, peaches, nectarines, are abundant. Peaches thrive better in this climate than apples. I have eaten almost the whole of a watermelon to-day, and am somewhat satiated. The melon had a cross (+) on the rind. I enquired of the negro who brought it in, what the mark meant, and he replied, "de patch war owned principally by a good many niggars, sah, an' dey dewided dem afore day got ripe, an' put de mark on de rine, to show dat de p'tic'lar melon belonged to a p'tic'lar niggar, sah."

Governor Tod is damaging the old regiments by injudicious promotions. He does in some instances, it is true, reward faithful soldiers; but often complaining, unwilling, incompetent fellows are promoted, who get upon the sick list to avoid duty; lay upon their backs when they should be on their feet, and are carousing when they should be asleep. On the march, instead of pushing along resolutely at the head of their command, they fall back and get into an ambulance. The troops have no confidence in them; their presence renders a whole company worthless, and this company contributes greatly to the demoralization of a regiment.

22.   A little vine has crept into my tent and put out a handsome flower.

General Buell and staff, with bag and baggage, left this morning.

25.   Ordered to move.

29.   We are at Decherd, Tennessee. I am weak, discouraged, and worn out with idleness.

The negroes are busily engaged throwing up earth works and building stockades.   To-night, as they were in line, I stopped a moment to hear the sergeant call the roll, "Scipio McDonald."   "Here I is, sah," "Cæsar—Cæsar McDonald."   "Cæsar was 'sleep las' I saw ob him, sah."   These negroes take the family name of their masters.

The whole army is concentrated here, or near here; but nobody knows anything, except that the water is bad, whisky scarce, dust abundant, and the air loaded with the scent and melody of a thousand mules. These long-eared creatures give us every variety of sound of which they are capable, from the deep bass bray to the most attenuated whinny.

The Thirty-third Ohio was shelled out of its fortifications at Battle creek yesterday. Colonel Moore is in the adjoining tent, giving an account of his trials and tribulations to Shanks of the New York Herald.

Fifty of the Third, under Lieutenant Carpenter, went to Stevenson yesterday; on their return they were fired upon by guerrillas. Jack Boston shot a man and captured a horse.

SEPTEMBER, 1862.

4.   Army has fallen back to Murfreesboro.

5.   At Nashville.

6.   To-night we cross the Cumberland.

7.   Bivouacked in Edgefield, at the north end of the railroad bridge.   Troops pouring over the bridge and pushing North rapidly.   One of Loomis' men was shot dead last night while attempting to run by a sentinel.

10.   The moving army with its immense transportation train, raises such a cloud of dust that it is impossible to see fifty yards ahead.

11.   Arrived at Bowling Green.   The two armies are running a race for the Ohio river.   At this time Bragg has the lead.

OCTOBER, 1862.

3. At Taylorsville, Kentucky. Our first day's march out of Louisville was disagreeable beyond precedent. The boys had been full of whisky for three days, and fell out of the ranks by scores. The road for sixteen miles was lined with stragglers. The new men bore the march badly. Rain fell yesterday afternoon and during the night; I awoke at three o'clock this morning to find myself lying in a puddle of water. A soldier of Captain Rossman's company was wrestling with another, and being thrown, died almost instantly from the effect of the fall.

4. At Bloomfield. Shelled the rebels out of the woods in which we are now bivouacking, and picked up a few prisoners. The greater part of the rebel army is, we are told, at Bardstown—twelve miles away.

5. Still at Bloomfield, in readiness to move at a moment's notice.

7. Moved to Maxville, and bivouacked for the night.

PERRYVILLE.

8. Started in the early morning toward Perryville.

The occasional boom of guns at the front notified us that the enemy was not far distant. A little later the rattle of musketry mingled with the roar of artillery, and we knew the vanguard was having lively work. The boys marched well and were in high spirits; the long-looked for battle appeared really near, and that old notion that the Third was fated never to see a fight seemed now likely to be exploded. At ten o'clock we were hastened forward and placed in battle line on the left of the Maxville and Perryville road; the cavalry in our front appeared to be seriously engaged, and every eye peered eagerly through the woods to catch a glimpse of the enemy. But in a little while the firing ceased, and with a feeling of disappointment the boys lounged about on the ground and logs awaiting further orders.

They came very soon. At 11 A. M. the Third was directed to take the head of the column and move forward. We anticipated no danger, for Rousseau and his staff were in advance of us, followed by Lytle and his staff. The regiment was marching by the flank, and had proceeded to the brow of the hill overlooking a branch of the Chaplin river, and was about to descend into the valley, when the enemy's artillery opened in front with great fury. Rousseau and his staff wheeled suddenly out of the road to the left, accompanied by Lytle. After a moment spent by them in consultation, I was ordered to countermarch my regiment to the bottom of the hill we had just ascended, and file off to the right of the road.

Loomis' and Simonson's Batteries were soon put in

position, and began to reply to the enemy. A furious interchange of shell and solid shot occurred, but after a little while our batteries ceased firing, and we had comparative silence.

About 2 o'clock the rebel infantry was seen advancing across the valley, and I ordered the Third to ascend the hill and take position on the crest. The enemy's batteries now reopened with redoubled fury, and the air seemed filled with shot and exploding shells. Finding the rebels were still too far away to make our muskets effective, I ordered the boys to lie down and await their nearer approach. They advanced under cover of a house on the side hill, and having reached a point one hundred and fifty yards distant, deployed behind a stone fence which was hidden from us by standing corn. At this time the left of my regiment rested on the Maxville and Perryville road; the line extending along the crest of the hill, and the right passing somewhat behind a barn filled with hay. In this position, with the enemy's batteries pouring upon us a most destructive fire, the Third arose and delivered its first volley. For a time, I do not know how long thereafter, it seemed as if all hell had broken loose; the air was filled with hissing balls; shells were exploding continuously, and the noise of the guns was deafening; finally the barn on the right took fire, and the flames bursting from roof, windows, doors, and interstices between the logs, threw the right of the regiment into disorder; the confusion, however, was but temporary. The boys closed up to the left, steadied themselves on the colors, and stood bravely to the work. Nearly two hundred of my five hundred men now lay dead and wounded on the little strip of ground over which we fought.

Colonel Curren Pope, of the Fifteenth Kentucky, whose regiment was being held in reserve at the bottom of the hill, had already twice requested me to retire my men and allow him to take the position. Finding now that our ammunition was exhausted, I sent him notice, and as his regiment marched to the crest the Third was withdrawn in as perfect order, I think, as it ever moved from the drill-ground. The Fifteenth made a gallant fight, and lost heavily both in officers and men; in fact, the Lieutenant-Colonel and Major fell mortally wounded while it was moving into position. Colonel Pope was also wounded, but not so seriously as to prevent his continuing in command. The enemy getting now upon its right and rear, the regiment was compelled to retire from the crest.

After consultation with Colonel Pope, it was determined to move our regiments to the left, and form line perpendicular to the one originally taken, and thus give protection to the rear and right of the troops on our left. The enemy observing this movement, and accepting it as an indication of withdrawal, advanced rapidly toward us, when I about faced my regiment, and ordered the men to fix bayonets and move forward to meet him; but before we had proceeded many yards, I was overtaken by Lientenant Grover, of Colonel Lytle's staff, with an order to retire.

Turning into a ravine a few rods distant, we found an ammunition wagon, and, under a dropping fire from the enemy, refilled our empty cartridge boxes. Ascertaining while here that Colonel Lytle was certainly wounded, and probably killed, I reported at once for duty to Colonel Len. Harris, commanding Ninth Brigade of our division; but night soon thereafter put an end to the engagement.

We bivouacked in a corn-field. The regiment had grown suddenly small. It was a sorry night for us indeed. Every company had its long list of killed, wounded, and missing. Over two hundred were gone. Nearly two hundred, we felt quite sure, had fallen dead or disabled on the field. Many eyes were in tears, and many hearts were bleeding for lost comrades and dear friends. General Rousseau rides up in the darkness, and, as we gather around him, says, in a voice tremulous with emotion: " Boys of the Third, you stood in that withering fire like men of iron." They did.

They are thirsty and hungry. Few, however, think either of food or water. Their thoughts are on the crest of that little hill, where Cunard, McDougal, St. John, Starr, and scores of others lie cold in death. They think of the wounded and suffering, and speak to each other of the terrible ordeal through which they have passed, with bated breath and in solemn tones, as if a laugh, or jest, or frivolous word, would be an insult to the slain.

They have long sought for a battle, and often been disappointed and sore because they failed to find one; but now, for the first time, they really realize what a battle is. They see it is to men what an arctic wind is to autumn leaves, and are astonished to find that any have outlived the furious storm of deadly missiles.

The enemy is in the woods before us, and as the sentinels occasionally exchange shots, we can see the flash of their guns and hear the whistle of bullets above our heads. The two armies are too near to sleep comfortably, or even safely, so the boys cling to their muskets and keep ready for action. It is a long night, but it finally comes to an end.

9. The enemy has disappeared, and we go to the hill where our fight occurred. Within the compass of a few rods we find a hundred men of the Third and Fifteenth lying stiff and cold. Beside these there are many wounded, whom we pick up tenderly, carry off and provide for. Men are already digging trenches, and in a little while the dead are gathered together for interment. We have looked upon such scenes before; but then the faces were strange to us. Now they are the familiar faces of intimate personal friends, to whom we are indebted for many kindly acts. We hear convulsive sobs, see eyes swollen and streaming with tears, and as our fallen comrades are deposited in their narrow grave, the lines of Wolfe recur to us:

> " No useless coffin inclosed his breast;
>   Not in sheet or in shroud we wound him,
> But he lay like a warrior taking his rest,
>   With his martial cloak around him.
>   *   *   *   *

Slowly and sadly we laid him down
 From the field of his fame fresh and gory;
We carved not a line, we raised not a stone,
 But left him alone with his glory."

13. We are in a field near Harrodsburg. Moved yesterday from Perryville. We are without tents. Rain is falling, and the men uncomfortable.

Many, perhaps most, of the boys of the regiment disliked me thoroughly. They thought me too strict, too rigid in the enforcement of orders; but now they are, without exception, my fast friends. During the battle of Chaplin Hills, while the enemy's artillery was playing upon us with terrible effect, I ordered them to lie down. The shot, shell, and canister came thick as hail, hissing, exploding, and tearing up the ground around us. There was a universal cry from the boys that I should lie down also; but I continued to walk up and down the line, watching the approaching enemy, and replied to their entreaties, "No; it is my time to stand guard now, and I will not lie down."

Meeting Captain Loomis yesterday, he said: "Do you know you captured a regiment at Chaplin Hills?" "I do not." "Yes, you captured the Third. You have not a man now who would n't die for you."

I have been too much occupied of late to record even the most interesting and important events. I should like to preserve the names of the private soldiers who behaved like heroes in the battle; but I have only time to mention the fact that our colors changed hands seven times during the engagement. Six of our color bearers were either killed or wounded, and as the sixth man was falling, a soldier of Company C, named David C. Walker, a boyish fellow, whose cheeks were ruddy as a girl's, and who had lost his hat in the fight, sprang forward, caught the falling flag, then stepping out in front of the regiment, waved it triumphantly, and carried it to the end of the battle.

On the next morning I made him color bearer, and undertook to thank him for his gallantry, but my eyes filled and voice choked, and I was unable to articulate a word. He understood me, doubtless.

If it had not been for McCook's foolish haste, it is more than probable that Bragg would have been most thoroughly whipped and utterly routed. As it was, two or three divisions had to contend for half a day with one of the largest and best disciplined of the Confederate armies, and that, too, when our troops in force were lying but a few miles in the rear, ready and eager to be led into the engagement. The whole affair is a mystery to me. McCook is, doubtless, to blame for being hasty; but may not Buell be censurable for being slow? And may it not be true that this butchery of men has resulted from the petty jeolousies existing between the commanders of different army corps and divisions?

19. Encamped in a broken, hilly field, five miles south of Crab Orchard. From Perryville to this place, there has been each day occasional cannonading; but this morning I have heard no guns. The

Cumberland mountains are in sight. We are pushing forward as fast probably as· it is possible for a great army to move. Buell is here superintending the movement.

24. In the woods near Lebanon, and still without tents. Bragg has left Kentucky, and is thought to be hastening toward Nashville. We shall follow him. Having now twice traveled the road, the march is likely to prove tedious and uninteresting. The army has been marching almost constantly for two months, and bivouacking at night with an insufficiency of clothing.

The troops are lying in an immense grove of large beech. We have had supper, and a very good one, by the way: pickled salmon, currant jelly, fried ham, butter, coffee, and crackers. It is now long after nightfall, and the forest is aglow with a thousand campfires. The hum of ten thousand voices strikes the ear like the roar of a distant sea. A band away off to the right is mingling its music with the noise, and a mule now and then breaks in with a voice not governed by any rules of melody known to man.

NOVEMBER, 1862.

9. In camp at Sinking Spring, Kentucky. Thomas commands the Fourteenth Army Corps, consisting of Rousseau's, Palmer's, Dumont's, Negley's, and Fry's divisions; say 40,000 men. McCook has Sill's, Jeff C. Davis', and Granger's; say 24,000. Crittenden has three divisions, say 24,000. A large army, which ought to sweep to Mobile without difficulty.

Sinking Spring, as it is called by some, Mill Spring by others, and by still others Lost river, is quite a large stream. It rises from the ground, runs forty rods or more, enters a cave, and is lost. The wreck of an old mill stands on its banks. Bowling Green is three miles southward.

When we get a little further south, we shall find at this season of the year persimmons and opossums in abundance. Jack says: "Possum am better dan chicken. In de fall we hunt de possum ebbery night 'cept Sunday. He am mitey good an' fat, sah; sometimes he too fat."

We move at ten o'clock to-morrow.

11. We have settled down at Mitchellville for a

16

few days. After dinner Furay and I rode six miles beyond this, on the road to Nashville, to the house of a Union farmer whose acquaintance I made last spring. The old gentleman was very glad to see us, and insisted upon our remaining until after supper. In fact, he urged us to stay all night; but we consented to remain for supper only, and would not allow him to put our horses in the stable.

We learned that a little over a week ago the rebels endeavored to enforce the conscription law in this neighborhood, and one of Mr. Baily's sons was notified to appear at Gallatin to enter the Southern army. He was informed that if he did not appear voluntarily at the appointed time, he would be taken, either dead or alive. He did not go, and since has been constantly on the watch, expecting the guerrilla bands, which rendezvous at Tyree Springs, ten miles distant, to come for the purpose of taking him away. When, therefore, he saw Furay and me galloping up to the house, he mounted his horse and rode for the woods as fast as his steed could carry him. After we had been there half an hour, he returned, and, while shaking hands with us, said : " You scared me out of a full year's growth."

Morgan, with a force, the strength of which is variously estimated, passed near this a few days ago. Many of Mr. Baily's neighbors are members of the guerrilla bands, and all of them willing spies and informers.

We had a splendid supper : chicken, pork, ham, milk, pumpkin pie ; in short, there was every thing on the table that a hungry man could desire.

I had introduced Mr. Furay as the correspondent of the Cincinnati Gazette; but the good folks, not understanding this long title exactly, dubbed him Doctor. There were three strapping girls in the family, who did not make their appearance until they had taken time to put on their Sunday clothes. To one of these the Doctor paid special attention, and finally won his way so far into her good favor as to induce her to play him a tune on the dulcimer, an abominable instrument, which she pounded with two little sticks. The Doctor declared that the music was good—excellent—charming. He now attempts to get out of this outrageous falsehood by affirming that he referred simply to the air—the tune—and not to the manner in which it was executed by the young lady. This, however, is a mere quibble.

It was quite dark when we said good-by to this kind-hearted, excellent family, and started on our way back to camp. The woods were on fire for miles along the road. Many fences and farm buildings had caught. One large house tumbled in as we were passing, and the fences, out-buildings, and trees were all enveloped in flames. While riding slowly forward, and looking back upon the dense cloud of smoke, the flames stretching as far almost as the eye could reach, the dry trees standing up like immense pillars of fire, we were startled not a little by the sentinel's challenge, "Halt!" There had been no pickets on the road when we were going out, and we were, therefore, uncertain whether the challenge came from our own men or those of John Morgan. "Who

comes there?" continued the sentinel. "Friends."
"Advance friends, and give the countersign." Going
up to the sentinel, I told him who we were, and that
we had not the countersign. After a little delay, the
officer of the guard came and allowed us to proceed.

12. To-day farmer Baily came to see us. I sent
his good wife a haversack of coffee, to remunerate her
somewhat for the excellent dinner she had given us.
He urged us to come again, and said they would
have a turkey prepared for us this afternoon; but I
declined with thanks.

15. At eight o'clock to-morrow morning we shall
move to Tyree Springs, a little village situated in the
heart of a wild, broken tract of country, which, of
late, has been a favorite rendezvous for guerrillas and
highwaymen. Citizens and soldiers traveling to and
from Nashville, during the last two months, have, at
or near this place, been compelled to empty their
pockets, and when their clothes were better than
those of their captors, have been compelled to spare
them also.

We have no certain information as to the enemy's
whereabouts. One rumor says he is at Lavergne, another locates him at Murfreesboro, and still another
puts him at Chattanooga. General Rosecrans is now
in command, and, urged on by the desires of the North,
may follow him to the latter place this winter. A
man from whom the people are each day expecting
some extraordinary action, some tremendous battle, in
which the enemy shall be annihilated, is unfortunately
situated, and likely very soon to become unpopular.

It takes two to make a fight, as it does to make a bargain. General John Pope is the only warrior of modern times who can find a battle whenever he wants to, and take any number of prisoners his heart desires. Even his brilliant achievements, however, afford the people but temporary satisfaction, for, upon investigation, they are unable to find either the captives or the discomfited hosts.

I predict that in twelve months Rosecrans will be as unpopular as Buell. After the affair at Rich mountain, the former was a great favorite. When placed in command of the forces in Western Virginia, the people expected hourly to hear of Floyd's destruction; but after a whole summer was spent in the vain endeavor to chase down the enemy and bring him to battle, they began to abuse Rosecrans, and he finally left that department, much as Buell has left this. Our generals should, undoubtedly, do more, but our people should certainly expect less.

19. At Tyree Springs. Am the presiding officer of a court-martial.

The supplies for the great army at Nashville and beyond, are wagoned over this road from Mitchellville to Edgefield Junction. Immense trains are passing continually.

20. General Bob Mitchell dined with me to-day. He is on the way to Nashville. Blows his own trumpet, as of old, and expects that a division will be given him.

30. This is a delightful Indian summer day. I have been in the forest, under the persimmon and

butternut trees. It is the first ramble I have had at this season for years, and I thought of the many quiet places in the thick woods of the old homestead, where long ago I hunted for hickory-nuts and walnuts; then of its hazel thickets, through which were scattered the wild plum, black-haw, and thorn-apple—perfect solitudes, in which the squirrels and birds had the happiest of times. How pleasant it is to recur to those days; and how well I remember every path through the dense woods, and every little open grassy plot, made brilliant by the summer sunshine.

DECEMBER, 1862.

2. We move to-morrow, at six o'clock in the morning, to Nashville.

9. Nashville. Every thing indicates an early move-ment. Whether a reconnoissance is intended or a per-manent advance, I do not even undertake to guess. The capture of a brigade, at Hartsville, by John Morgan, has awakened the army into something like life; before it was idly awaiting the rise of the Cum-berland, but this bold dash of the rebels has made it bristle up like an angry boar; and this morning, I am told, it starts out to show its tusks to the enemy. Our division has been ordered to be in readiness.

The kind of weather we desire now, is that which is generally considered the most disagreeable, namely, a long rain; two weeks of rain-fall is necessary to make the Cumberland navigable, and thus ensure to us abundant supplies.

The whole army feels deeply mortified over the loss of the brigade at Hartsville; report says it was cap-tured by an inferior force. One of our regiments did not fire a gun, and certainly the other two could not have made a very obstinate resistance. I am glad

Ohio does not have to bear the whole blame; two-thirds is rather too much.

10.   During all of the latter part of last night troops were pouring through Nashville, and going southward.   Our division, Rousseau's, moved three miles beyond the city, and went into camp on the Franklin road.

14.   Our court has been holding its sessions in the city, but to-day it adjourned to meet at division head-quarters to-morrow at ten o'clock A. M.

The most interesting character of our court-martial is Colonel H. C. Hobart, of the Twenty-first Wisconsin; a gentleman who has held many important public positions in his own State, and whose knowledge of the law, fondness for debate, obstinacy in the maintenance of his opinions, love of fun, and kind-heartedness, are immense.   He makes use of the phrase, "in my country," when he refers to any thing which has taken place in Wisconsin; from this we infer that he is a foreigner, and pretend to regard him as a savage from the great West.   He has, therefore, been dubbed Chief of the Wisconsins.   The court occasionally becomes exceedingly mellow of an evening, and then the favorite theme is the "injin."   Such horrible practices as dog eating and cannibalism are imputed to the Chief. To-night we visited the theater to witness Ingomar. On returning to our room at Bassay's restaurant, the members took solemn Irish oaths that the man with the sheep-skin on his back, purporting to be Ingomar, was no other than Hobart, the Wisconsin savage; and the supposition that such an individual could ever reform, and become fitted for civilized society, was a monstrous fiction, too improbable even for the stage.

It should not be presumed from this, however, that the subject of our raillery holds his tongue all the time. On the contrary, he expresses the liveliest contempt for the opinions of his colleagues of the court-martial, and professes to think if it were not for the aid which the Nation receives from his countrymen, the Wisconsins, the effort to restore the Union would be an utter failure.

Bassay's restaurant is a famous resort for military gentlemen. Major-General Hamilton just now took dinner; Major-General Lew Wallace, Brigadier-Generals Tyler and Schoepf, and Major Donn Piatt occupy rooms on the floor above us, and take their meals here; so that we move in the vicinity of the most illustrious of men. We are hardly prepared now to say that we are on intimate terms with the gentlemen who bear these historic names; but we are at least allowed to look at them from a respectful distance. A few years hence, when they are so far away as to make contradiction improbable, if not impossible, we may claim to have been their boon companions, and to have drank and played whist with them in the most genial and friendly way.

16. This afternoon Negley sent over a request for help, stating that his forage train had been attacked. The alarm, however, proved groundless. A few shots only had been fired at the foragers.

17. The news from Fredericksburg has cast a

17

shadow over the army. We did hope that Burnside would be successful, and thus brighten the prospect for a speedy peace; but we are in deeper gloom now than ever. The repulse at Fredericksburg, while it has disabled thousands, has disheartened, if not demoralized a great army, and given confidence and strength to the rebels every-where. It may be, however, that this defeat was necessary to bring us clearly to the point of extinguishing slavery in all the States. The time is near when the strength of the President's resolution in this regard will be put to the test. I trust he will be firm. The mere reconstruction of the Union on the old basis would not pay humanity for all the blood shed since the war began. The extinction of slavery, perhaps, will.

While the North raises immense numbers of men, and scatters them to the four winds, the enemy concentrates, fortifies, and awaits attack. Will the man ever come to consolidate these innumerable detachments of the National army, and then sweep through the Confederacy like a tornado?

It is said that many regiments in the Eastern army number less than one hundred men, and yet have a full complement of field and company officers. This is ridiculous; nay, it is an outrage upon the tax-payers of the North. Worse still, so long as such a skeleton is called a regiment, it is likely to bring discredit upon the State and Nation; for how can it perform the work of a regiment when it has but one-tenth of a regiment's strength? These regiments should be consolidated, and the superfluous officers either sent home or put into the ranks.

20. This morning, at one o'clock, we were ordered to hold ourselves in readiness to march at a moment's notice, with five days' rations. Court has adjourned to meet at nine o'clock A. M. Monday. It is disposing of cases quite rapidly, and I think next week, if there be no interruptions, it will be able to clear the docket.

A brigade, which went out with a forage train yesterday, captured a Confederate lieutenant at a private house. He was engaged at the moment of his capture in writing a letter to his sweetheart. The letter was headed Nashville, and he was evidently intent upon deceiving his lady-love into the belief that he had penetrated the Yankee lines, and was surrounded by foes. Had the letter reached her fair hands, what earnest prayers would have gone up for the succor of this bold and reckless youth.

There was a meeting of the generals yesterday, but for what purpose they only know.

21. The dispatches from Indianapolis speak of the probable promotion of Colonel Jones, Forty-second Indiana. This seems like a joke to those who know him. He can not manage a regiment, and not even his best friends have any confidence in his military capacity. In Indiana, however, they promote every body to brigadierships. Sol Meredith, who went into the service long after the war began, and who, in drilling his regiment, would say : "Battalion, right or left face, as the case may be, march," was made a

brigadier some time ago. Milroy, Crittenden, and many others were promoted for inconsiderable services in engagements which have long since been forgotten by the public. Their promotions were not made for the benefit of the service, but for the political advancement of the men who caused them to be made.

Last evening, a little after dark, we were startled by heavy cannonading on our left, and thought the enemy was making an attack. The boys in our division were all aglow with excitement, and cheered loudly; but after ten or fifteen minutes the firing ceased, and I have heard no more about it.

The rebels are before us in force. The old game of concentration is probably being played. The repulse of our army at Fredericksburg will embolden them. It will also enable them to spare troops to reinforce Bragg. The Confederates are on the inside of the circle, while we are on the outside, scattered far and wide. They can cut across and concentrate rapidly, while we must move around. They can meet Burnside at Fredericksburg, and then whip across the country and face us, thus making a smaller army than ours outnumber us in every battle.

In the South the army makes public opinion, and moves along unaffected by it. In the North the army has little or nothing to do with the creation of public sentiment, and yet is its servant. The people of the North, who were clamoring for action, are probably responsible for the fatal repulse at Fredericksburg and the defeat at Bull run. The North must be patient, and get to understand that the work before us is not one that can be accomplished in a day or month. It should be pushed deliberately, yet persistently. We should get rid of a vast number of men who are forever in hospital. They are an expense to the country, and an incumbrance to the army. We should consolidate regiments, and send home thousands of unnecessary officers, who draw pay and yet make no adequate return for it.

23. The court met this morning as usual. We are now going on the fifth week of the session. New cases arise just about as fast as old ones are disposed of.

The boys in front of my tent are singing:

> " We are going home, we are going home,
> To die no more."

Were they to devote as much time to praying as they do to singing, they would soon establish a reputation for piety; but, unfortunately for them, after the hymn they generally proceed to swear, instead of prayer, and one is left in doubt as to what home they propose to go to.

25. About noon there were several discharges of artillery in our front, and last night occasional shots served as cheerful reminders that the enemy was near.

At an expense of one dollar and seventy-five cents, I procured a small turkey and had a Christmas dinner; but it lacked the collaterals, and was a failure.

For twenty months now I have been a sojourner in

camps, a dweller in tents, going hither and yon, at all hours of the day and night, in all sorts of weather, sleeping for weeks at a stretch without shelter, and yet I have been strong and healthy. How very thankful I should feel on this Christmas night! There goes the boom of a cannon at the front.

26. This morning we started south on the Franklin road. When some ten miles away from Nashville, we turned toward Murfreesboro, and are now encamped in the woods, near the head-waters of the Little Harpeth. The march was exceedingly unpleasant. Rain began to fall about the time of starting, and continued to pour down heavily for four hours, wetting us all thoroughly.

I have command of the brigade.

27. We moved at eight o'clock this morning, over a very bad dirt road, from Wilson's pike to the Nolansville road, where we are now bivouacking. About ten the artillery commenced thundering in our front, and continued during the greater portion of the day. Marched two miles toward Triune to support McCook, who was having a little bout with the enemy; but the engagement ending, we returned to our present quarters in a drenching rain. Saw General Thomas, our corps commander, going to and returning from the front. We are sixteen miles from Nashville, on a road running midway between Franklin and Murfreesboro. The enemy is supposed to be in force at the latter place.

28. At four o'clock P. M. we were ordered to leave baggage and teams behind, and march to Stewart's

creek, a point twenty miles from Nashville. Night had set in before the brigade got fairly under way. The road runs through a barren, hilly, pine district, and was exceedingly bad. At eleven o'clock at night we reached the place indicated, and lay on the damp ground until morning.

29. At eight o'clock A. M. the artillery opened in our front; but after perhaps two hours of irregular firing, it ceased altogether, and we were led to the conclusion that but few rebels were in this vicinity, the main body being at Murfreesboro, probably. Going to the front about ten o'clock, I met General Hascall. He had had a little fight at Lavergne, the Twenty-sixth Ohio losing twenty men, and his brigade thirty altogether. He also had a skirmish at this place, in which he captured a few prisoners. Saw General Thomas riding to the front. Rosecrans is here, and most of the Army of the Cumberland either here or hereabouts. McCook's corps had an inconsiderable engagement at Triune on Saturday. Loss small on both sides.

Riding by a farm-house this afternoon, I caught a glimpse of Miss Harris, of Lavergne, at the window, and stopped to talk with her a minute. The young lady and her mother have experienced a great deal of trouble recently. They were shelled out of Lavergne three times, two of the shells passing through her mother's house. She claims to have been shot at once by a soldier of the One Hundred and Nineteenth Illinois, the ball splintering the window-sill near her head. Her mother's house has been converted into a hospital, and the clothes of the family taken for bandages. She is, therefore, more rebellious now than ever. She is getting her rights, poor girl!

30. A little after daylight the brigade moved, and proceeded to within three miles of Murfreesboro, where we have been awaiting orders since ten o'clock A. M.

The first boom of artillery was heard at ten o'clock. Since then there has been almost a continuous roar. McCook's corps is in advance of us, perhaps a mile and a half, and, with divisions from other corps, has been gradually approaching the enemy all day, driving his skirmishers from one point to another.

About four o'clock in the afternoon the artillery firing became more vigorous, and, with Colonel Foreman, of the Fifteenth Kentucky, I rode to the front, and then along our advanced line from right to left. Our artillery stationed on the higher points was being fired rapidly. The skirmishers were advancing cautiously, and the contest between the two lines was quite exciting. As I supposed, our army is feeling its way into position. To-morrow, doubtless, the grand battle will be fought, when I trust the good Lord will grant us a glorious victory, and one that will make glad the hearts of all loyal people on New-Year's Day.

I saw Lieutenant-Colonel Given, Eighteenth Ohio. Twelve of his men had been wounded. Met Colonel Wagner, Fifteenth Indiana. Starkweather's brigade

lost its wagon train this forenoon. Jeff C. Davis, I
am told, was wounded this evening. A shell exploded near a group, consisting of General Rosecrans and staff, killing two horses and wounding
two men.

STONE RIVER.

31. At six o'clock in the morning my brigade
marches to the front and forms in line of battle. The
roar of musketry and artillery is incessant. At nine
o'clock we move into the cedar woods on the right to
support McCook, who is reported to be giving way.
General Rousseau points me to the place he desires me
to defend, and enjoins me to "hold it until hell freezes
over," at the same time telling me that he may be
found immediately on the left of my brigade with
Loomis' battery. I take position. An open wood is
in my front; but where the line is formed, and to the
right and left, the cedar thicket is so dense as to render it impossible to see the length of a regiment.
The enemy comes up directly, and the fight begins.
The roar of the guns to the right, left, and front
of my brigade sounds like the continuous pounding
on a thousand anvils. My men are favorably situated, being concealed by the cedars, while the enemy,
advancing through the open woods, is fully exposed.
Early in the action Colonel Foreman, of the Fifteenth Kentucky, is killed, and his regiment retires
in disorder. The Third Ohio, Eighty-eighth, and
Forty-second Indiana, hold the position, and deliver

their fire so effectively that the enemy is finally forced back. I find a Michigan regiment and attach it to my command, and send a staff officer to General Rousseau to report progress; but before he has time to return, the enemy makes another and more furious assault upon my line. After a fierce struggle, lasting from forty to sixty minutes, we succeed in repelling this also. I send again to General Rousseau, and am soon after informed that neither he nor Loomis' battery can be found. Troops are reported to be falling back hastily, and in disorder, on my left. I send a staff officer to the right, and ascertain that Scribner's and Shepperd's brigades are gone. I conclude that the contingency has arisen to which General Rousseau referred—that is to say, that hell has frozen over—and about face my brigade and march to the rear, where the guns appear to be hammering away with redoubled fury. In the edge of the woods, and not far from the Murfreesboro pike, I find the new line of battle, and take position. Five minutes after the enemy strike us. For a time—I can not even guess how long—the line stands bravely to the work; but the regiments on our left get into disorder, and finally become panic-stricken. The fright spreads, and my brigade sweeps by me to the open field in our rear. I hasten to the colors, stop them, and endeavor to rally the men. The field is by this time covered with flying troops, and the enemy's fire is most deadly. My brigade, however, begins to steady itself on the colors, when my horse is shot under me, and I fall heavily to the ground. Before I have time to recover my feet, my troops, with thousands of others, sweep in disorder to the rear, and I am left standing alone. Going back to the railroad, I find my men, General Rousseau, Loomis, and, in fact, the larger part of the army. The artillery has been concentrated at this point, and now opens upon the advancing columns of the enemy with fearful effect, and continues its thunders until nightfall. The artillery saved the army. The battle during the whole day was terrific.

I find that soon after the fight began in the cedars, our division was ordered back to a new line, and that the order had been delivered to Scribner and Shepperd, but not to me. They had, consequently, retired to the second position under fire, and had suffered most terribly in the operation; while my brigade, being forgotten by the division commander, or by the officer whose duty it was to convey the order, had held its ground until it had twice repulsed the enemy, and then changed position in comparative safety. A retrograde movement under fire must necessarily be extremely hazardous. It demoralizes your own men, who can not, at the moment, understand the purpose of the movement, while it encourages the enemy. The one accepts it as an indication of defeat; the other as an assurance of victory.

McCook had been surprised and shattered in the morning. This unexpected success had inspired the rebels and dispirited us. They fought like devils, and the victory—if victory there was to either army—belonged to them.

When the sun went down, and the firing ceased, the Union army, despondent, but not despairing, weary and hungry, but still hopeful, lay on its arms, ready to renew the conflict on the morrow.

JANUARY, 1863.

1. At dawn we are all in line, expecting every moment the re-commencement of the fearful struggle. Occasionally a battery engages a battery opposite, and the skirmishers keep up a continual roar of small arms; but until nearly night there is no heavy fighting. Both armies want rest; both have suffered terribly. Here and there little parties are engaged burying the dead, which lie thick around us. Now the mangled remains of a poor boy of the Third is being deposited in a shallow grave. A whole charge of canister seems to have gone through him. Generals Rosecrans and Thomas are riding over the field, now halting to speak words of encouragement to the troops, then going on to inspect portions of the line. I have been supplied with a new horse, but one far inferior to the dead stallion. A little before sundown all hell seems to break loose again, and for about an hour the thunder of the artillery and volleys of musketry are deafening; but it is simply the evening salutation of the combatants. The darkness deepens; the weather is raw and disagreeable. Fifty thousand hungry men are stretched beside their guns again on the field. Fortunately I have a piece of raw pork

and a few crackers in my pocket. No food ever tasted sweeter. The night is gloomy enough; but our spirits are rising. We all glory in the obstinacy with which Rosecrans has clung to his position. I draw closer to the camp-fire, and, pushing the brands together, take out my little Bible, and as I open it my eyes fall on the xci Psalm:

"I will say of the Lord, He is my refuge and my fortress, my God; in Him will I trust. Surely He shall deliver thee from the snare of the fowler, and from the noisome pestilence. He shall cover thee with His feathers, and under His wings shall be thy trust. His truth shall be thy shield and buckler. Thou shalt not be afraid for the terror by night, nor for the arrow that flieth by day; nor for the pestilence that walketh in darkness, nor for the destruction that wasteth at noonday. A thousand shall fall by thy side, and ten thousand at thy right hand; but it shall not come nigh thee."

Camp-fires innumerable are glimmering in the darkness. Now and then a few mounted men gallop by. Scattering shots are heard along the picket line. The gloom has lifted, and I wrap myself in my blanket and lie down contentedly for the night.

2. At sunrise we have a shower of solid shot and shell. The Chicago Board of Trade battery is silenced. The shot roll up the Murfreesboro pike like balls on a bowling alley. Many horses are killed. A soldier near me, while walking deliberately to the rear, to seek a place of greater safety, is struck between the shoulders by a ricochetting ball, and in-

stantly killed. We are ordered to be in readiness to
repel an attack, and form line of battle amid this
fearful storm of iron. Gaunther and Loomis get
their batteries in position, and, after twenty or thirty
minutes' active work, silence the enemy and compel
him to withdraw. Then we have a lull until one or
two o'clock, when Van Cleve's division on the left is
attacked. As the volume of musketry increases, and
the sound grows nearer, we understand that our
troops are being driven back, and brigade after
brigade double quicks from the right and center, across
the open field, to render aid. Battery after battery
goes in the same direction on the run, the drivers
lashing the horses to their utmost speed. The thunder of the guns becomes more violent; the volleys of
musketry grow into one prolonged and unceasing roll.
Now we hear the yell which betokens encouraged
hearts; but whose yell? Thank God, it is ours! The
conflict is working southward; the enemy has been
checked, repulsed, and is now in retreat. So ends
another day.

The hungry soldiers cut steaks from the slain
horses, and, with the scanty supplies which have come
forward, gather around the fires to prepare supper,
and talk over the incidents of the day. The prospect
seems brighter. We have held the ground, and in
this last encounter have whipped the enemy. There
is more cheerful conversation among the men
They discuss the battle, the officers, and each other,
and give us now and then a snatch of song. Officers
come over from adjoining brigades, hoping to find a

little whisky, but learn, with apparent resignation and well-feigned composure, that the canteens have been long empty; that even the private flasks, which officers carry with the photographs of their sweethearts, in a side pocket next to their hearts, are destitute of even the flavor of this article of prime necessity. My much-esteemed colleague of the court-martial, Colonel Hobart, stumbles up in the thick darkness to pay his respects. The sentinel, mistaking him for a private, tells him, with an oath, that this is neither the time nor place for stragglers, and orders him back to his regiment; and so the night wears on, and fifty thousand men lay upon their guns again.

3. Colonel Shanklin, with a strong detachment from my brigade, was captured last night while on picket. Rifle pits are being dug, and I am ordered to protect the workmen. The rebels hold a strip of woods in our immediate front, and we get up a lively skirmish with them. Our men, however, appear loth to advance far enough to afford the necessary protection to the workers. Vexed at their unwillingness to venture out, I ride forward and start over a line to which I desire the skirmishers to advance, and discover, before I have gone twenty yards, that I have done a foolish thing. A hundred muskets open on me from the woods; but the eyes of my own brigade and of other troops are on me, and I can not back out. I quicken the pace of my horse somewhat, and continue my perilous course. The bullets whistle like bees about my head, but I ride the whole length of the proposed skirmish line, and get back to the

brigade in safety. Colonel Humphrey, of the Eighty-eighth Indiana, comes up to me, and with a tremor in his voice, which indicates much feeling, says: " My God, Colonel, never do that again !" The caution is unnecessary. I had already made up my mind never to do it again. We keep up a vigorous skirmish with the enemy for hours, losing now and then a man ; but later in the day we are relieved from this duty, and retire to a quieter place.

About nightfall General Rousseau desires me to get two regiments in readiness, and, as soon as it becomes quite dark, charge upon and clean out the woods in our front. I select the Third Ohio and Eighty-eighth Indiana for this duty, and at the appointed time we form line in the open field in front of Gaunther's battery, and as we start, the battery commences to shell the woods. As we get nearer the objective point, I put the men on the double quick. The rebels, discovering our approach, open a heavy fire, but in the darkness shoot too high. The blaze of their guns reveals their exact position to us. We reach the rude log breastworks behind which they are standing and grapple with them. Colonel Humphrey receives a severe thrust from a bayonet; others are wounded, and some killed. It is pitch dark under the trees. Some of Gaunther's shells fall short, and alarm the men. Unable to find either staff officer or orderly, I ride back and request him to elevate his guns. Returning, I find my troops blazing away with great energy ; but, so far as I can discover,

18

their fire is not returned. It is difficult, however, in the noise, confusion, and darkness, to direct their movements, and impossible to stop the firing. In the meantime a new danger threatens. Spear's Tennesseeans have been sent to support us, probably without any definite instructions. They are, most of them, raw troops, and, becoming either excited or alarmed at the terrible racket in the woods, deliver scattering shots in our rear. I ride back and urge them either to cease firing or move to the left, go forward and look after our flank. One regiment does move as directed; but the others are immovable, and it is with great difficulty that I succeed in making them understand that in firing they are more likely to injure friends than foes. Fortunately, soon after this, the ammunition of the Third and Eighty-eighth becoming exhausted, the firing in the woods ceases, and. as the enemy has already abandoned the field, the affair ends. I try to find General Rousseau to report results, but can not; and so, worn out with fatigue and excitement, lie down for another night.

4. Every thing quiet in our front. It is reported that the enemy has disappeared. Investigation confirms the report, and the cavalry push into Murfreesboro and beyond.

During the forenoon the army crosses Stone River, and with music, banners, and rejoicings, takes possession of the old camps of the enemy. So the long and doubtful struggle ends.

5. I ride over the battle-field. In one place a caisson and five horses are lying, the latter killed in

harness, and all fallen together. Nationals and Confederates, young, middle-aged, and old, are scattered over the woods and fields for miles. Poor Wright, of my old company, lay at the barricade in the woods which we stormed on the night of the last day. Many others lay about him. Further on we find men with their legs shot off; one with brains scooped out with a cannon ball; another with half a face gone; another with entrails protruding; young Winnegard, of the Third, has one foot off and both legs pierced by grape at the thighs; another boy lies with his hands clasped above his head, indicating that his last words were a prayer. Many Confederate sharpshooters lay behind stumps, rails, and logs, shot in the head. A young boy, dressed in the Confederate uniform, lies with his face turned to the sky, and looks as if he might be sleeping. Poor boy! what thoughts of home, mother, death, and eternity, commingled in his brain as the life-blood ebbed away! Many wounded horses are limping over the field. One mule, I heard of, had a leg blown off on the first day's battle; next morning it was on the spot where first wounded; at night it was still standing there, not having moved an inch all day, patiently suffering, it knew not why nor for what. How many poor men moaned through the cold nights in the thick woods, where the first day's battle occurred, calling in vain to man for help, and finally making their last solemn petition to God!

In the evening I met Rousseau, McCook, and Crittenden. They had been imbibing freely. Rousseau insisted upon my turning back and going with them to his quarters. Crittenden was the merriest of the party. On the way he sang, in a voice far from melodious, a pastorial ditty with which childhood is familiar:

> " Mary had a little lamb,
>   His fleece was white as snow,
>   And every-where that Mary went
>   The lamb was sure to go."

Evidently the lion had left the chieftain's heart, and the lamb had entered and taken possession.

McCook complimented me by saying that my brigade fought well. He should know, for he sat behind it at the commencement of the second assault of the enemy in the cedars, on the first day; but very soon thereafter disappeared. Just when he left, and why he did so, I do not know.

At Rousseau's we found a large number of staff and line officers. The demijohn was introduced, and all paid their respects to it. The ludicrous incidents, of which there are more or less even in battles, of the last five days, were referred to, and much merriment prevailed.

6. The army is being reorganized, and we are busily engaged repairing the damages sustained in the battle.

Visited the hospitals, and, so far as possible, looked after the wounded of my brigade. To-morrow the chaplains will endeavor to hunt them all up, and report their whereabouts and condition.

7. I was called upon late in the evening to make a report of the operations of my brigade immediately, as General Rousseau intends to leave for Louisville in the morning. It is impossible to collect the information necessary in the short time allowed me. One of my regimental commanders, Colonel Foreman, was killed; another, Colonel Humphrey, was wounded, and is in hospital; another, Lieutenant-Colonel Shanklin, was captured, and is absent; but I gathered up hastily what facts I could obtain as to the casualties in the several regiments, and wrote my report in the few minutes which remained for me to do so, and sent it in. I have not had an opportunity to do justice either to my brigade or myself.

13. Move in the direction of Columbia, on a reconnoitering expedition. My brigade stops at Salem, and the cavalry pushes on.

14. Have been exposed to a drenching rain for thirty hours. The men are cold, hungry, and mutinous.

15. Ordered back to Murfreesboro, and march thither in a storm of snow and sleet. It is decidedly the coldest day we have experienced since last winter.

I find two numbers of Harper's Weekly on my return. They abound in war stories. The two heroes, of whom I read to-night, received saber cuts on the face and head, obtained leave of absence, returned home, and married forthwith. Saber cuts are very rare in the Army of the Cumberland, and if young officers were compelled to defer entering into wedlock until they got wounds of this kind, there would be precious few soldiers married. Bullet wounds are common enough; but the hand-to-hand encounters, knightly contests of swords, the cleaving of head-pieces and shattering of spears, are not incidents of modern warfare.

The long rain has completely saturated the ground. The floor of my tent is muddy; but my bed will be dry, and as I have not had my clothes off for three days, I look forward to a comfortable night's rest.

The picture in Harper, of "Christmas Eve," will bring tears to the eyes of many a poor fellow shivering over the camp-fire in this winter season. The children in the crib, the stockings in which Santa Claus deposits his treasures, recall the pleasantest night of the year.

Speaking of Christmas reminds me of the mistletoe bough. Mistletoe abounds here. Old, leafless trees are covered and green with it. It was in blossom a week or two ago, if we may call its white wax-like berries blossoms. They are known as Christmas blossoms. The vine takes root in the bark—in any crack, hole, or crevice of the tree—and continues green all winter. The berries grow in clusters.

16. I have as guests Mr. and Mrs. Johnson House, my old neighbors. They have come from their quiet home in Ohio to look over a battle-field, and I take pleasure in showing them the points of interest. Mr. House, with great frankness, tells me, in the presence of my staff, that he had been afraid I was not qualified for the high position I hold, and that I was getting along too fast; but he now feels

satisfied that I am capable and worthy, and would be well pleased to see me again promoted. I introduced my friends to Lieutenant Van Pelt, of Loomis' battery, and Mr. House asked : " Lieutenant, will these guns shoot with any kind of decision ?" " Precision," I suggested. " Yes," Van Pelt replied, " they will throw a ball pretty close to the mark."

17. Dr. Peck tells me that the wounded of the Third are doing well, and all comfortably quartered. He is an excellent physician and surgeon, and the boys are well pleased with him.

FEBRUARY, 1863.

3.   This has been the coldest day of the season in this latitude.   The ground is frozen hard.   I made the round of the picket line after dinner, and was thoroughly chilled.   Visited the hospital this evening.   Young Willets, of the Third, whom I thought getting along well before I left for home, died two days before my return.   Benedict is dead, and Glenn, poor fellow, will go next.   His leg is in a sling, and he is compelled to lie in one position all the time.   Mortification has set in, and he can not last more than a day or two.   Murfreesboro is one great hospital, filled with Nationals and Confederates.

4.   At noon cannonading began on our left and front, and continued with intervals until sunset.   I have heard no explanation of the firing, but think it probable our troops started up the Shelbyville road to reconnoiter, discovered the enemy, and a small fight ensued.

5.   It is said the enemy came within six miles of Murfreesboro yesterday, and attacked a forage train.

The weather has been somewhat undecided, and far from agreeable.

6.   A lot of rebel papers, dated January 31st, have

been brought in. They contain many extracts clipped from the Northern Democratic press, and the Southern soul is jubilant over the fact that a large party in Ohio and Indiana denounce President Lincoln. The rebels infer from this that the war must end soon, and the independence of the Southern States be acknowledged. Our friends at home should not give aid and comfort to the enemy. They may excite hopes which, in time, they will themselves be compelled to help crush.

7. Few of the men who started home when I did have returned. The General is becoming excited on the subject of absentees. From General Thomas' corps alone there are sixteen thousand men absent, sick, pretending to be sick, or otherwise. Of my brigade there are sixteen hundred men present for duty, and over thirteen hundred absent—nearly one-half away. The condition of other brigades is similar. If a man once gets away, either into hospital or on detached duty, it is almost impossible to get him back again to his regiment. A false excuse, backed up by the false statement of a family physician, has hitherto been accepted; but hereafter, I am told, it will not be. Uncle Sam can not much longer stand the drain upon his finances which these malingerers occasion, and his reputation suffers also, for he can not do with fifty thousand men what it requires one hundred thousand to accomplish.

People may say Rosecrans had at the battle of Murfreesboro nearly one hundred regiments. A reg-

19

iment should contain a thousand men; in a hundred regiments, therefore, there should have been one hundred thousand men. With this force he should have swallowed Bragg; but they must understand that the largest of these regiments did not contain over five hundred men fit for duty, and very many not over three hundred. The men in hospital, the skulkers at home, and the skedaddlers here, count only on the muster and pay-rolls; our friends at home should remember, therefore, that when they take a soldier by the hand who should be with his regiment, and say to him, " Poor fellow, you have seen hard times enough, stay a little longer, the army will not miss you," that some other poor fellow, too brave and manly to shirk, shivers through the long winter hours at his own post, and then through other long hours at the post of the absentee, thus doing double duty; and they should bear in mind, also, that in battle this same poor fellow has to fight for two, and that battles are lost, the war prolonged, and the National arms often disgraced, by reason of the absence of the men whom they encourage to remain at home a day or two longer. If every Northern soldier able to do duty would do it, Rosecrans could sweep to Mobile in ninety days; but with this skeleton of an army, we rest in doubt and idleness. There is a screw loose somewhere.

10. Fortifications are being constructed. My men are working on them.

Just now I heard the whistle of a locomotive, on the opposite side of the river. This is the first intimation we have had of the completion of the road to this point. The bridge will be finished in a day or two, and then the trains will arrive and depart from Murfreesboro regularly.

11. Called at Colonel Wilder's quarters, and while there met General J. J. Reynolds. He made a brief allusion to the Stalnaker times. On my return to camp, I stopped for a few minutes at Department head-quarters to see Garfield. General Rosecrans came into the room; but, as I was dressed in citizens' clothes, did not at first recognize me. Garfield said: "General Rosecrans, Colonel Beatty." The General took me by the hand, turned my face to the light, and said he did not have a fair view of me before. "Well," he continued, "you are a general now, are you?" I told him I was not sure yet, and he said: "Is it uncertainty or modesty that makes you doubt?" "Uncertainty." "Well," he replied, "you and Sam Beatty have both been recommended. I guess it will be all right." He invited me to remain for supper, but I declined.

16. To-day I rode over the battle-field, starting at the river and following the enemy's line off to their left, then crossing over on to the right of our line, and following it to the left. For miles through the woods evidences of the terrible conflict meet one at every step. Trees peppered with bullet and buckshot, and now and then one cut down by cannon ball; unexploded shell, solid shot, dead horses, broken caissons, haversacks, old shoes, hats, fragments of muskets, and unused cartridges, are to be seen every-

where. In an open space in the oak woods is a long
strip of fresh earth, in which forty-one sticks are
standing, with intervals between them of perhaps a
foot. Here forty-one poor fellows lie under the fresh
earth, with nothing but the forty-one little sticks
above to mark the spot. Just beyond this are twenty-
five sticks, to indicate the last resting-place of twenty-
five brave men; and so we found these graves in the
woods, meadows, corn-fields, cotton-fields, every-
where. We stumbled on one grave in a solitary spot
in the thick cedars, where the sunshine never pene-
trates. At the head of the little mound of fresh
earth a round stick was standing, and on the top of
this was an old felt hat; the hat still doing duty over
the head, if not on the head, of the dead soldier who
lay there. The rain and sun and growing vegetation
of one summer will render it impossible to find these
graves. The grass will cover the fresh earth, the
sticks will either rot or become displaced, and then
there will be nothing to indicate that—

" Perhaps in this neglected spot is laid
    Some heart once pregnant with celestial fire;
  Hands that the rod of empire might have swayed,
    Or waked to ecstasy the living lyre."

17. The army is turning its attention to politics
somewhat. Generals and colonels are ventilating
their opinions through the press. I think their letters may have good effect upon the people at home,
and prevent them from discouraging the army and
crippling the Administration. Surely the effort now

being put forth by a great party in the North to convince the troops in the field that this is an unjust war, an abolition or nigger war, must have a tendency to injure the army, and, if persisted in, may finally ruin it.

19. Work on the fortifications still continues. This is to be a depot of supplies, and there are provisions enough already here to subsist the army for a month. Now that the Cumberland is high, and the railroads in running order, any amount of supplies may be brought through.

Expeditions go out occasionally to different parts of the country, and slight affairs occur, which are magnified into serious engagements; but really nothing of any importance has transpired since we obtained possession of Murfreesboro. A day or two ago we had an account of an expedition into the enemy's country by the One Hundred and Twenty-third Illinois, Colonel Monroe commanding. According to this veracious report, the Colonel had a severe fight, killed a large number of the enemy, and captured three hundred stand of arms; but the truth is, that he did not take time to count the rebel dead, and the arms taken were one hundred old muskets found in a house by the roadside.

The expeditions sent out to capture John Morgan have all been failures. His own knowledge of the country is thorough, and besides, he has in his command men from every neighborhood, who know not only every road and cow-path in the locality, but every man, woman, and child. The people serve

222 THE CITIZEN SOLDIER; [FEBRUARY,

him also, by advising him of all our movements.
They guide him to our detachments when they are
weak, and warn him away from them when strong.
Were the rebel army in Ohio, and as bitterly hated
by the people of that State as the Nationals are by
those of Kentucky and Tennessee, it would be an
easy matter indeed to hang upon the skirts of that
army, pick up stragglers, burn bridges, attack wagon
trains, and now and then pounce down on an outlying
picket and take it in.

20. Colonel Lytle, my old brigade commander,
called on me to-day. He informed me that he had
not been assigned yet. I inferred from this that he
thought it utterly impossible for one so distinguished
as himself to come down to a regiment. His own
regiment, the Tenth Ohio, is here, and nominally a
part of my brigade, although it has not acted with it
since Rosecrans assumed command of the Army of
the Cumberland. Under Lieutenant-Colonel Burke,
it is doing guard duty at Department head-quarters.

MARCH, 1863.

1. There is talk of consolidation at Washington. This is a sensible idea, and should be carried into effect at once. There are too many officers and too few men. The regiments should be consolidated, and kept full by conscription, if it can not be done otherwise. The best officers should be retained, and the others sent home to stand their chances of the draft.

A major of the Fifteenth Kentucky sent in his resignation a few days ago, assigning as a reason for so doing that the object of the war was now the elevation of the negro. The concluding paragraph of his letter was in these words: "The service can not possibly suffer by my resignation." The document passed through my hands on its way to Department head-quarters, and I indorsed it as follows:

"Major H. F. Kalfus, Fifteenth Kentucky Volunteer Infantry, being 'painfully and reluctantly convinced' that the party in power is disposed to elevate the negro, desires to quit the service. I trust he will be allowed to do so, and cheerfully certify to the correctness of one statement which he makes herein, to-wit: The service can not possibly suffer by his resignation."

General Rosecrans has just sent me an order to arrest the Major, and send him under guard to the Provost-Marshal General. The arrest will be made in a few minutes, and may create some excitement among our Kentucky friends.

3. The fortifications are progressing. The men work four hours each day in the trenches. The remainder of the time they spend pretty much as they see fit.

General Garfield is now chief of staff. It is the first instance in the West of an officer of his rank being assigned to that position. It is an important place, however, and one too often held not merely by officers of inferior rank, but of decidedly inferior ability. General Buell had a colonel as chief of staff, and, until the appointment of Garfield, General Rosecrans had a lieutenant-colonel or major.

To-night an ugly and most singular specimen of the negro called to obtain employment. He was not over three feet and a half high, hump-backed, crooked-legged, and quite forty years old. Poking his head into my tent, and, taking off his hat, he said: "Is de Co'nel in?" "Yes." "Hurd you wants a boy, sah. Man tole me Co'nel Eighty-eighth Olehio wants a boy, sah." "What can you do? Can you cook?" "Yas, sah." "Where did you learn to cook?" "On de plantation, sah." "What is your master's name?" "Rucker, sah." "Is he a loyal man?" "No, sah, he not a lawyer; his brudder, de cussen one, is de lawyer." "Is he secesh?" "O, yas, sah; yas, he sesesh." "It is the Colonel of the

Eighty-eighth Indiana you should see;" and I directed him to the Colonel's tent. As he turned to leave, he muttered, "Man tole me Eighty-eighth Olehio;" but he went hobbling over to the Eighty-eighth, with fear, anxiety, and hope struggling in his old face.

4. Major Kalfus, Fifteenth Kentucky, arrested on Sunday, and since held in close confinement, was dishonorably dismissed from the service to-day for using treasonable language in tendering his resignation. He was escorted outside the lines and turned loose. The Major is a cross-roads politician, and will, I doubt not, be a lion among his half-loyal neighbors when he returns home.

5. Our picket on the Manchester pike was driven in to-day. The cavalry, under General Stanley, went to the rescue, when a fight occurred. No particulars.

9. T. Buchanan Reid, the poet, entertained us at the court-house this evening. The room had been trimmed up by the rebels for a ball. The words, "Shiloh," " Fort Donelson," "Hartsville," "Santa Rosa," " Pensacola," were surrounded with evergreens. The letter " B," painted on the walls in a dozen places, was encompassed by wreaths of flowers, now faded and yellow. My native modesty led me to conclude that the letter so highly honored stood for Bragg, and not for the commander of the Seventeenth Brigade, U. S. A.

General Garfield introduced Mr. Reid by a short speech, not delivered in his usual happy style. I was impressed with the idea all the time, that he had too many buttons on his coat—he certainly had a great many buttons—and the splendor of the double row possibly detracted somewhat from the splendor of his remarks.

Mr. Reid is a small man, and has not sufficient voice to make himself heard distinctly in so large a hall. In a parlor his recitations would be capital. He read from his own poem, "The Wagoner," a description of the battle of Brandywine. It is possibly a very good representation of that battle; but, if so, the battle of Brandywine was very unlike that of Stone river. At Brandywine, it appears, the generals slashed around among the enemy's infantry with drawn swords, doing most of the hard fighting and most of the killing themselves. I did not discover anything of that kind at Stone river. It is possible the style went out of fashion before the rebellion began. It would, however, be very satisfactory to the rank and file to see it restored. Mr. Reid said some good things in his lecture, and was well applauded; but, in the main, he was too ethereal, vapory, and fanciful for the most of us leather-heads. When he puts a soldier-boy on the top of a high mountain to sing patriotic songs, and bid defiance to King George because "Eagle is King," we are impressed with the idea that that soldier could have been put to better use; that, in fact, he is entirely out of the line of duty. The position assigned him is unnatural, and the modern soldier-boy will be apt to conclude that nobody but a simpleton would be likely to wander about in solitary places, extemporizing in measured sentences; besides it is hard work, as I know from experience. I tried my hand at it the other day until my head ached, and this is the best I could do:

O! Lord, when will this war end?
These days of marchings, nights of lonely guard?
This terrible expenditure of health and life?
Where is the glory? Where is the reward,
For sacrifice of comfort, quiet, peace?
For sacrifice of children, wife, and friends?
For sacrifice of firesides—genial homes?
What hour, what gift, will ever make amends
For broken health, for bruised flesh and bones,
For lives cut short by bullet, blade, disease?
Where balm to heal the widow's heart, or what
Shall soothe a mother's grief for woes like these?

   Hold, murmurer, hold! Is country naught to thee?
Is freedom nothing? Naught an honored name?
What though the days be cold, or the nights dark,
The brave heart kindles for itself a flame
That warms and lightens up the world!
Home! What's home, if in craven shame
We seek its hearthstone? Bitterest of cold.
Better creep thither bruised, and torn, and lame,
Than seek it in health when justice needs our aid.

   Where is the glory? Where is the reward?
Think of the generations that will come
To praise and bless the hero. Think of God,
Who in due time will call His soldiers home.
How comfort mother for the loss of son?
What balm to which her heaviest grief must yield?
Ah! the plain, simple, ever-glorious words:
" Your son died nobly on the battle-field!"

What balm to soothe a widow's aching heart?
The grand assurance that in the battle shock
Foremost her husband stood, defying all,
For freedom and truth, unyielding as the rock.
Then, courage, all, and when the strife is past,
And grief for lost ones takes a milder hue,
This thought shall crown the living and the dead:
" He lived, he died, to God and duty true."

10. Rain has been descending most of the day,
and just now is pouring down with great violence. A
happy party in the adjoining tent are exercising their
lungs on a negro melody, of which this is something
like the chorus:

" De massa run, ha, ha!
De nigger stay, ho, ho!
It mus' be now de kingdom comin',
And de year of jubelo."

I can not affirm that the music with which these
gentlemen so abound, on this rainy and dismal night,
has that soothing effect on the human heart ascribed
to music in general; but, however little I may feel
like rejoicing now, I am quite sure I shall feel happier when the concert ends. The singers have concluded the negro melody, and are breathing out
their souls in a sentimental piece. Now and then,
when more than ordinarily successful in the higher
strains, they nearly equal the most exalted efforts of
the tom-cat; and then, again, in the execution of the
lower notes and more pathetic passages, we are
brought nigh unto tears by an inimitable imita-

tion of the wailings of a very young and sick kitten.

"Do they miss me at home; do they miss me?"

I venture to say they do, and with much gratification if, when there, you favored them often with this infernal noise.

14. The weather is remarkably fine to-day. I saw Mrs. and Major-General McCook and Mrs. and Major-General Wood going out to the battle-field, on horseback, this morning. Mrs. General Rosecrans arrived last night on a special train.

16. The roads are becoming good, and every body is on horseback. Many officers have their wives here. On the way to Murfreesboro this morning, I met two ladies with an escort going to the battle-field. Returning I met General Rosecrans and wife. The General hallooed after me, "How d'ye do?" to which I shouted back, at the top of my voice, the very original reply, "Very well, thank you." From the number of ladies gathering in, one might very reasonably conclude that no advance was contemplated soon. Still all signs fail in war times, as they do in dry weather. As a rule, perhaps, when a movement appears most improbable, we should be on the lookout for orders to start.

The army, under Rosecrans' administration, looks better than it ever did before. He certainly enters into his work with his whole soul, and unless some unlucky mishap knocks his feet from under him, he will soon be recognized as the first general of the

Union. I account for his success thus far, in part at least, by the fact that he has been long enough away from West Point, mixing with the people, to get a little common sense rubbed into him.

While writing the last word above, the string band of the Third struck up at the door of my tent. Going out, I found all the commissioned officers of that regiment standing in line. Adjutant Wilson nudged me, and said they expected a speech. I asked if beer would not suit them better. He thought not. I have not attempted to make a speech for two years, and never made a successful attempt in my life; but I knocked the ashes out of my pipe and began :

" GENTLEMEN : I am informed that all the officers of the Third are here. I am certainly very glad to see you, and extremely sorry that I am not better prepared to receive and entertain you. The press informs us that I have been very highly honored. If the report that I have been promoted is true, I am indebted to your gallantry, and that of the brave men of the Third, for the honor. You gave me my first position, and then were kind enough to deem me worthy of a second; and if now I have obtained a third, and higher one, it is because I have had the good fortune to command good soldiers. The step upward in rank will simply increase my debt of gratitude to you."

The officers responded cordially, by assuring me that they rejoiced over my promotion, and were anxious that I should continue in command of the brigade to which the Third is attached.

Charlie Davison can sing as many songs as Mickey Free, of " Charles O'Malley," and sing them well. In Irish melodies he is especially happy.   Hark!

" Dear Erin, how sweetly thy green bosom rises,
      An emerald set in the ring of the sea;
   Each blade of thy meadows my faithful heart prizes,
      Thou Queen of the West, the world's cush la machree.
         *   *   *   *   *   *

   Thy sons they are brave; but the battle once over,
      In brotherly peace with their foes they agree,
   And the roseate cheeks of thy daughters discover,
      The soul-speaking blush that says cush la machree."

17.   Dined with General Wagner, and, in company with Wagner and General Palmer, witnessed an artillery review.

18.   My brigade is still at work on the fortifications.   They are, however, nearly completed.

Shelter tents were issued to our division to-day. We are still using the larger tent; but it is evidently the intention to leave these behind when we move. Last fall the shelter tents were used for a time by the Pioneer Brigade.   They are so small that a man can not stand up in them.   The boys were then very bitter in condemnation of them, and called them dog tents and dog pens.   Almost every one of these tents was marked in a way to indicate the unfavorable opinion which the boys entertained of them, and in riding through

the company quarters of the Pioneer Brigade, the
eye would fall on inscriptions of this sort:

PUPS FOR SALE—RAT TERRIERS—BULL PUPS HERE—
    DOG-HOLE NO. 1—SONS OF BITCHES WITHIN—
    DOGS—PURPS.

General Rosecrans and staff, while riding by one
day, were greeted with a tremendous bow-wow. The
boys were on their hands and knees, stretching their
heads out of the ends of the tents, barking furiously
at the passing cavalcade. The General laughed
heartily, and promised them better accommodations.

The news from Vicksburg is somewhat encouraging, but certainly very indefinite, and far from satisfactory.

19. Reviews are the order of the hour. All the
brigades of our division, except mine, were reviewed
by General Rosecrans this afternoon. It was a fine
display, but hard on the soldiers; they were kept so
long standing.

At Middletown, sixteen miles away, the rebels are
four thousand strong, and within a day or two they
have ventured to Salem, five miles distant.

20. Loomis, who has just returned from home,
called this evening, and we drank a bottle of wine
over the promotion. He is in trouble about his commission as colonel of artillery. Two months ago the
Governor of Michigan gave him the commission, and
since that time he has been wearing a colonel's uniform; but General Rosecrans has expressed doubts

about his right to assume the rank. Loomis is all right, doubtless, and to-morrow, when the matter is talked over between the General and himself, it will be settled satisfactorily.

21. I have been running over Russell's diary, "North and South," and must say the Yankee Nation, when looked at. through Mr. Russell's spectacles, does not appear enveloped in that star-spangled glory and super-celestial blue with which it is wont to loom up before patriotic eyes on Fourth of July occasions. He has treated us, however, fully as well as we have treated him. We became angry because he told unpleasant truths about us, and he became enraged because we abused him for it. He thanks God that he is not an American; and should not we, in a spirit of conciliation, meet him half way, and feel thankful that he is not?

Flaming dispatches will appear in the Northern papers to-morrow respecting the defeat of John Morgan, by a small brigade of our troops under Colonel Hall. The report will say that forty of the enemy were killed, one hundred and fifty wounded, and one hundred and twenty captured; loss on our side inconsiderable. The reporters have probably contributed largely to the brilliancy of this affair. It is always safe to accept with distrust all reports which affirm that a few men, with little loss, routed, slaughtered, or captured a large force.

Peach and cherry trees are in full bloom. The grass is beginning to creep out. Summer birds occa-

20

sionally sing around us. In a few weeks more the trees will be in full leaf again.

23. General Negley, who went home some time ago, returned to-day, and, I see, wears two stars.

General Brannan arrived a day or two ago. He was on the train captured by guerrillas, but was rescued a few minutes after.

The boys have a rumor that Bragg is near, and has sent General Rosecrans a very polite note requesting him to surrender Murfreesboro at once. If the latter refuses to accept this most gentlemanly invitation to deliver up all his forces, Bragg proposes to commence an assault upon our works at twelve M., and show us no mercy. This, of course, is reliable.

At sunset rain began to fall, and has continued to pour down steadily ever since. The night is gloomy. Adjutant Wilson, in the next tent, is endeavoring to lift himself from the slough of despond by humming a ditty of true love; but the effort is evidently a failure.

This morning I stood on the bank of the river and observed the pontoniers as they threw their bridge of boats across the stream. Twice each week they unload the pontoons from the wagons, run them into the water, put the scantling from boat to boat, lay down the plank, and thus make a good bridge on which men, horses, and wagons can cross. After completing the bridge, they immediately begin to take it up, load the lumber and pontoons on the wagons, and return to camp. They can bridge any stream between this and the Tennessee in an hour, and can put a bridge over that in probably three hours.

General Rosecrans makes a fine display in his visits about the camps. He is accompanied by his staff and a large and well-equipped escort, with outriders in front and rear. The National flag is borne at the head of the column.

Rosecrans is of medium height and stout, not quite so tall as McCook, and not nearly so heavy. McCook is young, and very fleshy. Rousseau is by far the handsomest man in the army; tall and well-proportioned, but possibly a little too bulky. R. S. Granger is a little man, with a heavy, light sandy mustache. Wood is a small man, short and slim, with dark complexion, and black whiskers. Crittenden, the major-general, is a spare man, medium height, lank, common sort of face, well whiskered. Major-General Stanley, the cavalryman, is of good size, gentlemanly in bearing, light complexion, brown hair. McCook and Wood swear like pirates, and affect the rough-and-ready style. Rousseau is given to profanity somewhat, and blusters occasionally. Rosecrans indulges in an oath now and then; but is a member of the Catholic Church in good standing. Crittenden, I doubt not, swears like a trooper, and yet I have never heard him do so. He is a good drinker; and the same can be said of Rousseau. Rosecrans is an educated officer, who has rubbed much against the world, and has experience. Rousseau is brave, but knows little of military science. McCook is a chucklehead. Wood and Crittenden know how to blow their own

horns exceedingly well. Major-General Thomas is
tall, heavy, sedate; whiskers and head grayish. Puts
on less style than any of those named, and is a gentlemanly, modest, reliable soldier. Rosecrans and
McCook shave clean; Crittenden and Wood go the
whole whisker; Thomas shaves the upper lip. Rosecrans' nose is large, and curves down; Rousseau's is
large, and curves up; McCook has a weak nose, that
would do no credit to a baby. Rosecrans' laugh is not
one of the free, open, hearty kind; Rousseau has a
good laugh, but shows poor teeth; McCook has a
grin, which excites the suspicion that he is either still
very green or deficient in the upper story.

22. Colonels Wilder and Funkhauser called. We
had just disposed of a bottle of wine, when Colonel
Harker made his appearance, and we entered forthwith upon another. Colonel Wilder expects to accomplish a great work with his mounted infantry.
He is endeavoring to arm them with the Henry rifle,
a gun which, with a slight twist of the wrist, will
throw sixteen bullets in almost that many seconds. I
have no doubt he will render his command very effi-
cient and useful, for he has wonderful energy and
nerve, and is, besides, sensible and practical. Colonel
Harker is greatly disappointed because he was not
confirmed as brigadier-general during the last session
of Congress. He is certainly young enough to afford
to wait; but he seems to fear that, after commanding
a brigade for nine months, he may have to go back to
a regiment. He feels, too, that, being a New Jersey
man, commanding Ohio troops, neither State will take

an interest in him, and render him that assistance which, under other circumstances, either of them might do. These gentlemen dined with me. Harker and Wilder expressed a high opinion of General Buell. Wilder says Gilbert is a d—d scoundrel, and responsible for the loss at Mumfordsville. Harker, however, defended Gilbert, and is the only man I have ever heard speak favorably of him.

The train coming from Nashville to-day was fired upon and four men wounded. Yesterday there was a force of the enemy along the whole south front of our picket line.

From the cook's tent, in the rear, comes a devotional refrain:

> " I 'm gui-en home, I 'm gui-en home,
>   To d-i-e no mo'."

24. We are still pursuing the even tenor of our way on the fortifications. There are no indications of an advance. The army, however, is well equipped, in good spirits, and prepared to move at an hour's notice. Its confidence in Rosecrans is boundless, and whatever it may be required to do, it will, I doubt not, do with a will.

The conscript law, and that clause especially which provides for the granting of a limited number of furloughs, gives great satisfaction to the men. They not only feel that they will soon have help, but that if their conduct be good, there will be a fair chance for them to see home before the expiration of their term of enlistment. Hitherto they have been something like prisoners without hope.

26. Another little misfortune has occurred to our arms at Brentwood. The Twenty-second Wisconsin, numbering four hundred men, was captured by General Forrest. The rebels succeed admirably in gathering up and consolidating our scattered troops.

The Adjutant and others are having a concert in the next tent, and certainly laugh more over their own performance than singers do generally. They have just executed

> " The foin ould Irish gintleman,"

And are at this present writing shouting

> " Vive l' America, home of the free."

I think it more than probable that as their enthusiasm increases, the punch in their punch-bowl diminishes.

27. A mule has just broken the stillness of the night by a most discordant bray, and I am reminded that all horses are to be turned over to the mounted infantry regiments, and mules used in the teams in their stead. Mules are far better for the wagons than horses. They require less food, are hardier, and stand up better under rough work and irregular feeding.

I catch the faintest possible sound of a violin Some indomitable spirit is enlivening the night, and trenching upon the Sabbath, by giving loose rein to his genius.

During the light baggage and rapid marches of the latter part of Buell's administration, together with the mishaps at Perryville, the string band of the Third was very considerably damaged; but the boys have recently resuscitated and revived it to all the glory and usefulness of former days. One of its sweetest singers, however, has either deserted or retired to hospital or barracks, where the duties are less onerous and life more safe. His greatest hit was a song known as " The Warble," in which the following lines occurred :

" Mein fadter, mein modter, mein sister, mein frau,
Und zwi glass of beer for meinself.
Dey called mein frau one blacksmit-schopt ;
Und such dings I never did see in my life."

When, at Shelbyville and Huntsville, this melody mingled with the moonlight of summer evenings, people generally were deluded into the supposition that an ethereal songster was on the wing, enrapturing them with harmonies of other spheres. But sutlers, it is well known, are men of little or no refinement, with ears for money rather than music. To their unappreciative and perverted senses the warble seemed simply a dolorous appeal for more whisky; and while delivering up their last bottle to get rid of the warbler and his friends, in order that they might get sleep themselves, they have been known to express the hope that both song and singers might, without unnecessary delay, go to that region which we are told is paved with good intentions.

The voice of a colored person in the rear breaks in upon my recollections of the warbler. The most interesting and ugliest negro now in camp, is known as Simon Bolivar Buckner. He is an animal that has been worth in his day eighteen hundred dollars, an estray from the estate of General S. B. Buckner. He manages, by blacking boots and baking leather pies, to make money. He deluded me into buying a second pie from him one day, by assuring me, "on honah, sah, dat de las pie was better'n de fus', case he hab strawberries in him." True, the pie had "strawberries in him," but not enough to pay one for chewing the whit-leather crust.

30. Read Judge Holt's review of the proceedings and findings in the case of Fitzjohn Porter. If the review presents the facts fairly, Porter should have been not only dismissed, but hung. An officer who, with thirteen thousand men, will remain idle when within sight of the dust and in hearing of the shouts of the enemy and the noise of battle, knowing that his friends are contending against superior numbers, and having good reason to believe that they are likely to be overwhelmed, deserves no mercy.

It is dull. I have hardly enough to do to keep me awake. The members of the staff each have their separate duties to perform, which keep them more or less engaged. The quartermaster issues clothing to the troops; the commissary of subsistence issues food; the inspector looks into the condition of each regiment as to clothing, arms, and camp equipage; the adjutant makes out the detail for guard and other duties, and transmits orders received from the division commander to the regiments. All of these officers have certain reports to make also, which consumes much of their time.

21

APRIL, 1863.

1. Adjutant Wilson received a letter to-day, written in a hand that bespoke the writer to be feminine. He looked at the name, but could not recollect having heard it before. The writer assured him, however, that she was an old friend, and said many tender and complimentary things of him. He tried to think; called the roll of his lady friends, but the advantage, as people say, which the writer had of him was entirely too great. If he had ever heard the name, he found it impossible now to recall it. Finally, as he was going to fold the letter and put it away, he noticed one line at the top, written upside down. On reading it the mystery was solved: " If this reaches you on the first day of April, a reply to it is not expected."

The colored gentlemen of the staff are in a great state of excitement. One of the number has been illustrating the truth of that maxim which affirms that a nigger will steal. The war of words is terrible. " Yer d—d ole nigger thief," says one. " Hush! I 'll break yer black jaw fer yer," says another. They say very few harder things of each other than " you dam nigger." One would think the pot in this instance would hardly take to calling the kettle black, but it does. They use the word nigger to express contempt, dislike, or defiance, as often and freely as the whites. Finally, the parties to this controversy agree to leave the matter to "de Co'nel." The accused was the first to thrust his head into my tent, and ask permission to enter. "Dey is a gwine to tell yer as I stole some money from ole Hason. I didn't done it, Co'nel; as sure as I'm a livin' I didn't done it." "Yaas, yer did, you lyin' nigger!" broke in old Hason. "Now, Co'nel, I want ter tell you the straight of it." I listened patiently to the old man's statement and to the evidence adduced, and as it was very clear that the accused was guilty, put him under guard.

The first day of April has been very pleasant, cool but clear. The night is beautiful; the moon is at its full almost, and its light falls mellow and soft on the scene around me. The redoubt is near, with its guns standing sentinel at each corner, the long line of earthworks stretches off to the right and left; the river gleams and sparkles as it flows between its rugged banks of stone; the shadowy flags rise and fall lazily; the sentinels walk to and fro on their beats with silvered bayonets, and the dull glare of the camp-fires, and the snow-white tents, are seen every-where.

Somebody, possibly the Adjutant, whose thoughts may be still running on the fair unknown, breaks forth:

> "O why did she flatter my boyish pride,
> She is going to leave me now;"

And then, with a vehemence which betokens desperation,

> " I'll hang my harp on a willow tree,
>   And off to the wars again."

From which I infer it would be highly satisfactory to the young man to be demolished at the enemy's earliest convenience.

A large amount of stores are accumulated here. Forty thousand boxes of hard bread are stacked in one pile at the depot, and greater quantities of flour, pork, vinegar, and molasses, than I have ever seen before.

3. An Indiana newspaper reached camp to-day containing an obituary notice of a lieutenant of the Eighty-eighth Indiana. It gives quite a lengthy biographical sketch of the deceased, and closes with a letter which purports to have been written on the battle-field by one Lieutenant John Thomas, in which Lieutenant Wildman, the subject of the sketch, is said to have been shot near Murfreesboro, and that his last words were : " Bury me where I have fallen, and do not allow my body to be removed." The letter is exceedingly complimentary to the said lamented young man, and affirms that " he was the hero of heroes, noted for his reckless daring, and universally beloved." The singular feature about this whole matter is that the letter was written by the lamented young officer himself to his own uncle. The deceased justifies his action by saying that he had expended two dollars for foolscap and one dollar for postage

stamps in writing to the d—d old fool, and never received a reply, and he concluded finally he would write a letter which would interest him. It appears by the paper referred to that the lieutenant succeeded. The uncle and his family are in mourning for another martyr gone—the hero of heroes and the universally beloved.

Lieutenant DuBarry, topographical engineer, has just been promenading the line of tents in his night-shirt, with a club, in search of some scoundrel, supposed to be the Adjutant, who has stuffed his bed with stove-wood and stones. Wilson, on seeing the ghostly apparition approach, breaks into song:

> " Meet me by moonlight alone,
> And there I will tell you a tale."

Lieutenant Orr, commissary of subsistence, coming up at this time, remarks to DuBarry that he " is surprised to see him take it so coolly," whereupon the latter, notwithstanding the chilliness of the atmosphere, and the extreme thinness of his dress, expresses himself with very considerable warmth. Patterson, a clerk, and as likely to be the offender as any one, now joins the party, and affirms, with great earnestness, that " this practical joke business must end, or somebody will get hurt."

4. Saw Major-General McCook, wife, and staff riding out this morning. General Rosecrans was out this afternoon, but I did not see him. At this hour the signal corps is communicating from the dome of the court-house with the forces at Triune, sixteen

miles away, and with the troops at Readyville and other points. In daylight this is done by flags, at night by torches.

5.   There are many fine residences in Murfreesboro and vicinity; but the trees and shrubbery, which contributed in a great degree to their beauty and comfort, have been cut or trampled down and destroyed. Many frame houses, and very good ones, too, have been torn down, and the lumber and timber used in the construction of hospitals.

There is a fearful stench in many places near here, arising from decaying horses and mules, which have not been properly buried, or probably not buried at all.   The camps, as a rule, are well policed and kept clean; but the country for miles around is strewn with dead animals, and the warm weather is beginning to tell on them.

6.   It is said that the Third Regiment, with others, is to leave to-morrow on an expedition which may keep it away for months.   No official notice of the matter has been given me, and I trust the report may be unfounded.   I should be sorry indeed to be separated from the regiment.   I have been with it now two years, and to lose it would be like losing the greater number of my army friends and acquaintances.

7.   The incident of the day, to me at least, is the departure of the Third.   It left on the two P. M. train for Nashville.   I do not think I have been properly treated.   They should at least have consulted me before detaching my old regiment.   I am

informed that Colonel Streight, who is in command of
the expedition, was permitted to select the regiments,
and the matter has been conducted so secretly that,
before I had an intimation of what was contemplated,
it was too late to take any steps to keep the Third.
I never expect to be in command of it again. It will
get into another current, and drift into other brigades, divisions, and army corps. The idea of being
mounted was very agreeable to both officers and men;
but a little experience in that branch of the service
will probably lead them to regret the choice they
have made. My best wishes go with them.

All are looking with eager eyes toward Vicksburg.
Its fall would send a thrill of joy through the loyal
heart of the country, especially if accompanied by
the capture of the Confederate troops now in possession.

8. Six months ago this night, parching with thirst
and pinched with hunger, we were lying on Chaplin
Hills, thinking over the terrible battle of the afternoon, expecting its renewal in the morning, listening to the shots on the picket line, and notified by
an occasional bullet that the enemy was occupying
the thick woods just in our front, and very near. A
little over three months ago we were in the hurry,
confusion, anxiety, and suspense of an undecided battle, surrounded by the dead and dying, with the enemy's long line of camp-fires before us. Since then
we have had a quiet time, each succeeding day seeming the dullest.

Rode into town this afternoon; invested twenty-five cents in two red apples; spoke to Captain Blair, of Reynolds' staff; exchanged nods with W. D. B., of the Commercial; saw a saddle horse run away with its rider; returned to camp; entertained Shanks, of the New York Herald, for ten minutes; drank a glass of wine with Colonel Taylor, Fifteenth Kentucky, and soon after dropped off to sleep.

A brass band is now playing, away over on the Lebanon pike. The pontoniers are singing a psalm, with a view, doubtless, to making the oaths with which they intend to close the night appear more forcible. The signal lights are waving to and fro from the dome of the court-house. The hungry mules of the Pioneer Corps are making the night hideous with howls. So, and amid such scenes, the tedious hours pass by.

10. A soldier of the Fortieth Indiana, who, during the battle of Stone river, abandoned his company and regiment, and remained away until the fight ended, was shot this afternoon. Another will be shot on the 14th instant for deserting last fall. A man in our division who was sentenced to be shot, made his escape.

It seems these cases were not affected by the new law, and the President's proclamation to deserters. Hitherto deserters have been seldom punished, and, as a rule, never as severely as the law allowed.

My parchment arrived to-day, and I have written the necessary letter of acceptance and taken the oath, and henceforth shall subscribe myself yours, very respectfully, B. G., which, in my case, will probably stand for big goose.

General Rosecrans halted a moment before my quarters this evening, shook hands with me very cordially, and introduced me to his brother, the Bishop, as a young general. The General asked why I had not called. I replied that I knew he must be busy, and did not care to intrude. "True," said he, "I am busy, but have always time to say how d'ye do." He promised me another regiment to replace the Third, and said my boys looked fat enough to kick up their heels. The General's popularity with the army is immense. On review, the other day, he saw a sergeant who had no haversack; calling the attention of the boys to it he said: "This sergeant is without a haversack; he depends on you for food; don't give him a bite; let him starve."

The General appears to be well pleased with his fortifications, and asked me if I did not think it looked like remaining. I replied that the works were strong, and a small force could hold them, and that I should be well pleased if the enemy would attack us here, instead of compelling us to go further south. "Yes," said he, "I wish they would."

General Lytle is to be assigned to Stanley Matthews' brigade. The latter was recently elected judge, and will resign and return to Cincinnati.

The anti-Copperhead resolution business of the army must be pretty well exhausted. All the resolutions and letters on this subject that may appear hereafter may be accepted as bids for office. They have.

however, done a great deal of good, and I trust the public will not be forced to swallow an overdose. I had a faint inclination, at one time, to follow the example of my brother officers, and write a patriotic letter, but concluded to reserve my fire, and have had reason to congratulate myself since that I did so, for these letters have been as plenty as blackberries, and many of them not half so good.

A Republican has not much need to write. His patriotism is taken for granted. He is understood to be willing to go the whole nigger, and, like the ogre of the story books, to whom the most delicious morsel was an old woman, lick his chops and ask for more.

Wilder came in yesterday, with his mounted infantry, from a scout of eight or ten days, bringing sixty or seventy prisoners and a large number of horses.

11. A railway train was destroyed by the rebels near Lavergne yesterday. One hundred officers fell into the hands of the enemy, and probably one hundred thousand dollars in money, on the way to soldiers' families, was taken. This feat was accomplished right under the nose of our troops.

To the uninitiated army life is very fascinating. The long marches, nights of picket, and ordeal of battle are so festooned by the imagination of the inexperienced with shoulder straps, glittering blades, music, banners, and glory, as to be irresistible; but when we sit down to the hard crackers and salt pork, with which the soldier is wont to regale himself, we can not avoid recurring to the loaded tables and delicious morsels of other days, and are likely at such times to put hard crackers and glory on one side, the good things of home and peace on the other and owing probably to the unsubstantial quality of glory, and the adamantine quality of the crackers, arrive at conclusions not at all favorable to army life.

A fellow claiming to have been sent here by the Governor of Maine to write songs for the army, and who wrote songs for quite a number of regiments, was arrested some days ago on the charge of being a spy. Last night he attempted to get away from the guard, and was shot. Drawings of our fortifications were found in his boots. He was quite well known throughout the army, and for a long time unsuspected.

12. Called on General Rousseau. He referred to his trip to Washington, and dwelt with great pleasure on the various efforts of the people along the route to do him honor. At Lancaster, Pennsylvania, they stood in the cold an hour and a half awaiting his appearance. Our division, he informs me, is understood to possess the chivalric and dashing qualities -which the people admire. With all due respect, I suggested that dash was a good thing, doubtless, but steady, obstinate, well-directed fighting was better, and, in the end, would always succeed.

W. D. B., of the Commercial, Major McDowell, of Rousseau's staff, and Lieutenant Porter, called this afternoon. My report of the operations of my brigade at Stone river was referred to. Bickham thought it did not do justice to my command, and I have no doubt it is a sorry affair, compared with the elaborate reports of many others. The historian who accepts these reports as reliable, and permits himself to be guided by them through all the windings of a five-days' battle, with the expectation of finally allotting to each one of forty brigades the proper credit, will probably not be successful. My report was called for late one evening, written hastily, without having before me the reports of my regimental commanders, and is incomplete, unsatisfactory to me, and unjust to my brigade.

13. General Thomas called for a moment this evening, to congratulate me on my promotion.

The practical-joke business is occasionally resumed. Quartermaster Wells was astonished to find that his stove would not draw, or, rather, that the smoke, contrary to rule, insisted upon coming down instead of going up. Examination led to the discovery that the pipe was stuffed with old newspapers. Their removal heated the stove and his temper at the same time, but produced a coolness elsewhere, which the practical joker affected to think quite unaccountable.

14. Colonel Dodge, commanding the Second Brigade of Johnson's division, called this afternoon. The Colonel is a very industrious talker, chewer, spitter, and drinker. He has been under some tremendous hot firing, I can tell you! Well, if he don't know what heavy firing is, and the d—dest hottest work, too, then there is no use for men to talk! The truth is, however much other men may try to conceal it, his command stood its ground at Shiloh, and never gave back an inch. No, sir! Every other brigade fal-

tered or fell back, damned if they didn't; but he drove the enemy, got 'em started, other brigades took courage and joined in the chase. At Stone river he drove the enemy again. Bullets came thicker'n hail; but his men stood up. He was with 'em. Damned hot, you better believe! Well, if he must say it himself, he knew what hard fighting was. Why, sir, one of his men has five bullets in him; dam' me if he hasn't five! Says he, Dick says he, how did they hit you so many times? The first time I fired, says Dick, I killed an officer; yes, sir, killed him dead; saw him fall, dam me, if he didn't, sir; and at the same time, says Dick, I got a ball in my leg; rose up to fire again, and got one in my other leg, and one in my thigh, and fell; got on my knees to fire the third time, says Dick, and received two more. Well, you see, the firing was hotter'n hell, and Colonel Dodge knows what hot firing is, sir!

15. Since the fight at Franklin, and the capture of the passenger train at Lavergne, nothing of interest has occurred. There were only fifteen or twenty officers on the captured train. A large amount of money, however, fell into rebel hands. The postmaster of our division was on the train, and the Confederates compelled him to accompany them ten miles. He says they could have been traced very easily by the letters which they opened and scattered along the road.

16. Morgan, with a considerable force, has taken possession of Lebanon, and troops are on the way thither to rout him. The tunnel near Gallatin has

been blown up, and in consequence trains on the Nashville and Louisville Railroad are not running.

17. Am member of a board whose duty it will be to inquire into the competency, qualifications, and conduct of volunteer officers. The other members are Colonels Scribner, Hambright, and Taylor. We called in a body on General Rousseau, and found him reading "Les Miserables." He apologized for his shabby appearance by saying that he had become interested in a foolish novel. Colonel Scribner expressed great admiration for the characters Jean Val Jean and Javort, when the General confessed to a very decided anxiety to have Javort's neck twisted. This is the feeling of the reader at first; but when he finds the old granite man taking his own life as punishment for swerving once from what he considered to be the line of duty, our admiration for him is scarcely less than that we entertain for Jean Val Jean.

18. The Columbus (Ohio) Journal, of late date, under the head of "Arrivals," says: "General John Beatty has just married one of Ohio's loveliest daughters, and is stopping at the Neil House. Good for the General." This is a slander. I trust the paper of the next day made proper correction, and laid the charge, where it belongs, to wit: on General Samuel. If General Sam continues to demean himself in this youthful manner, I shall have to beg him to change his name. My reputation can not stand many more such blows. What must those who know I have a wife and children think,

when they see it announced that I have married again, and am stopping at the Neil with "one of Ohio's loveliest daughters?" What a horrible reflection upon the character of a constant and faithful husband! (This last sentence is written for my wife.)

19. Colonel Taylor and I rode over to General Rousseau's this morning. Returning, we were joined by Colonel Nicholas, Second Kentucky; Colonel Hobart, Twenty-first Wisconsin, and Lieutenant-Colonel Bingham, First Wisconsin, all of whom took dinner with me. We had a right pleasant party, but rather boisterous, possibly, for the Sabbath day.

There is at this moment a lively discussion in progress in the cook's tent, between two African gentlemen, in regard to military affairs. Old Hason says: "Oh, hush, darkey!" Buckner replies: "Yer done no what'r talkin' about, nigger." "I'll bet yer a thousand dollars." "Hush! yer ain't got five cents." "Gor way, yer do n't no nuffin'." And so the debate continues; but, like many others, leads simply to confusion and bitterness.

20. This evening an order came transferring my brigade to Negley's division. It will be known hereafter as the Second Brigade, Second Division, Fourteenth Army Corps.

28. Late last Monday night an officer from Stokes' battery reported to me for duty. I told him I had received no orders, and knew of no reason why he should report to me, and that in all probability General Samuel Beatty, of Van Cleve's division, was the person to whom he should report. I regarded

the matter as simply one of the many blunders which
were occurring because there were two men of the
same name and rank commanding brigades in this
army; and so, soon after the officer left, I went to
bed. Before I had gotten fairly to sleep, some one
knocked again at my tent-door. While rising to
strike a light the person entered, and said that he
had been ordered to report to me. Supposing it to
be the officer of the battery persisting in his mistake,
I replied as before, and then turned over and went to
sleep. I thought no more of the matter until 11:30
A. M. next day, when an order came which should
have been delivered twenty-four hours before, requiring me to get my brigade in readiness, and with
one regiment of Colonel Harker's command and the
Chicago Board of Trade Battery, move toward Nashville at two o'clock Tuesday morning. Then, of
course, I knew why the two officers had reported to
me on the night previous, and saw that there had
been an inexcusable delay in the transmission of the
order to me. Giving the necessary directions to the
regimental commanders, and sending notice to Harker
and the battery, I proceeded with all dispatch direct
to Department head-quarters, whence the order had
issued, to explain the delay. When I entered General Rosecrans shook hands with me cordially, and
seemed pleased to see me; but I had no sooner announced my business, and informed him that the order had been delivered to me not ten minutes before,
than he flew into a violent passion, and asked if a
battery and regiment had not reported to me the night

before. I replied yes, and was proceeding to give my reasons for supposing that the officers reporting them were in error, when he shouted: " Why, in hell and damnation, did you not mount your horse and come to head-quarters to inquire what it meant?" I undertook again to tell him I had received no order, and as my brigade had been detailed to work on fortifications I was expecting none; that I had taken it for granted that it was another of the many mistakes occurring constantly because there were two officers of the same name and rank in the army, and had so told the parties reporting; but he would not listen to me. His face was inflamed with anger, his rage uncontrollable, his language most ungentlemanly, abusive, and insulting. Garfield and many officers, commissioned and non-commissioned, and possibly not a few civilians, were present to witness my humiliation. For an instant I was tempted to strike him; but my better sense checked me. I turned on my heel and left the room. Death would have had few terrors for me just then. I had never felt such bitter mortification before, and it seemed to me that I was utterly and irreparably disgraced. However, I had a duty to perform, and while in the execution of that I would have time to think.

My brigade, one regiment of Colonel Harker's brigade, and the Chicago Board of Trade Battery, were already on the road. We marched rapidly, and that night (Tuesday) encamped in the woods north of Lavergne. Rain fell most of the night; but the

22

men had shelter tents, and I passed the time comfortably in a wagon. The next morning at daylight we started again, and a little after sunrise arrived at Scrougeville. Here my orders directed me to halt and watch the movements of the enemy. The rebel cavalry, in pretty strong force, had been in the vicinity during the day and evening before; but on learning of our approach had galloped away. We were exceedingly active, and scoured the country for miles around, but did not succeed in getting sight of even one of these dashing cavaliers.

The sky cleared, the weather became delightful, and the five days spent in the neighborhood of Scrougeville were very agreeable. It was a pleasant change from the dull routine of camp duty, and my men were in exuberant spirits, excessively merry and gay. While there, a good-looking non-commissioned officer of the battery came up to me, and, extending his hand, said: "How do you do, General?" I shook him by the hand, but could not for the life of me recollect that I had ever seen him before. Seeing that I failed to recognize him, he said: "My name is Concklin. I knew you at Sandusky, and used to know your wife well." Still I could not remember him. "You knew General Patterson?" he asked. "Yes." "Mary Patterson?" "Yes; I shall never forget her." "Do you recollect a stroll down to the bay shore one moonlight night?" Of course I remembered it. This was John Concklin, Mary's cousin. I remembered very well how he devoted himself to one I felt considerable interest in, while his cousin Mary and I talked in a jocular way about the cost of housekeeping, both agreeing that it would require but a very small sum to set up such an establishment as our modest ambition demanded. I was heartily glad to meet the young man. He looks very different from the smooth-faced boy of ten years ago. I was slightly jealous of him then, and I do not know but I might have reason to be now, for he is a fine, manly fellow.

At Scrougeville—how softly the name ripples on the ear!—we were entertained magnificently. Above us was the azure canopy; around us a dense forest of cedars, and in a shady nook, a sylvan retreat as it were, a barrel of choice beer. The mocking-birds caroled from the evergreen boughs. The plaintive melody of the dove came to us from over the hills, and pies at a quarter each poured in upon us in profusion; and such pies! When night threw over us her shadowy mantle, and the crescent moon blessed us with her mellow light, the notes of the whip-poor-will mingling with the bark of watch-dogs and the barbaric melody of the Ethiopian, floated out on the genial air, and, as stretched on the green sward, we smoked our pipes and drank our beer, thoughts of fairy land possessed us, and we looked wonderingly around and inquired, is Scrougeville a reality or a vision? I fear we shall never see the like of Scrougeville again.

On the morning of the 26th instant I received a telegram ordering our immediate return, and we reached Murfreesboro at two o'clock P. M. same day.

I had not forgotten the terrible scolding received from the General just before starting on this expedition; in fact, I am not likely ever to forget it. It had now been a millstone on my heart for a week. I could not stand it. What could I do? At first I thought I would send in my resignation, but that I concluded would afford me no relief; on the contrary, it would look as if I had been driven out of the army. My next impulse was to ask to be relieved from duty in this department, and assigned elsewhere; but on second thought this did not seem desirable. It would appear as if I was running away from the displeasure of the commanding general, and would affect me unfavorably wherever I might go. I felt that if I was to blame at all in this matter, it was in a very slight degree. The General's language was utterly inexcusable. He was a man simply, and I concluded finally that I would not leave either the army or the department under a cloud. I, therefore, sat down and wrote the following letter:

"MURFREESBORO, *April* 27, 1863.
"MAJOR-GENERAL W. S. ROSECRANS,
    "*Commanding Department of the Cumberland:*

"SIR—Your attack upon me, on the morning of the 21st instant, has been the subject of thought since. I have been absent on duty five days, and, therefore, have not referred to it before. It is the first time since I entered the army, two years ago, as it is the first time in my life, that it has been my misfortune to listen to abuse so violent and unreasonable

as that with which you were pleased to favor me in
the presence of the aids, orderlies, officers, and visitors, at your quarters. While I am unwilling to rest
quietly under the disgrace and ridicule which at-
taches to the subject of such a tirade, I do not question your right to censure when there has been
remissness in the discharge of duties; and to such
reasonable admonition I am ever ready to yield respectful and earnest attention; but I know of no
rule, principle, or precedent, which confers upon the
General commanding this Department the right to
address language to an officer which, if used by a private soldier to his company officer, or by a company
officer to a private soldier, would be deemed disgraceful and lead to the punishment of the one or
the dismissal of the other. Insisting, therefore, upon
that right, which I conceive belongs to the private in
the ranks, as well at to every subordinate officer in
the army who has been aggrieved, I demand from
you an apology for the insulting language addressed
to me on the morning of the 21st instant.

"I am, sir, respectfully,
"Your obedient servant,
"JOHN BEATTY, Brig.-Gen'l."

I sent this. Would it be regarded as an act of
presumption and treated with ridicule and contempt?
I feared it might, and sat thinking anxiously over
the matter until my orderly returned, with the envelope marked " W. S. R.," the army mode of acknowl-

edging receipt of letter or order.   Fifteen minutes
later this reply came :

"HEAD-QUARTERS DEPARTMENT OF THE CUMBERLAND, }
            "MURFREESBORO, *April*, 1863.   }

"MY DEAR GENERAL—I have just received the
inclosed note, marked "Private," but addressed to
me as commanding the Department of the Cumberland.   It compromises you in so many ways that I
return it to you.   I am your friend, and regretted
that the circumstances of the case compelled me, as a
commanding officer, to express myself warmly about a
matter which might have cost us dearly, to one for
whom I felt so kindly.   You will report to me in
person, without delay.

W. S. ROSECRANS, Maj.-Gen'l.

"Brig.-Gen'l JOHN BEATTY, Fortifications, Stone
river.

"P. S.—It might be well to bring this inclosure
with you."

The inclosure referred to was, of course, my letter
to him.   The answer was not, by any means, an apology.   On the contrary, it assumed that he was justifiable in censuring me as he did, and yet it expressed
good feeling for me.   It was probably written in
haste, and without thought.   It was not satisfactory ;
but I was led by it to hope that I could reach a point
which would be.

I obeyed the order to report promptly.   He took
me into his private office, where we talked over the

whole affair together. He expressed regret that he
had not known all the circumstances before, and said,
in conclusion: "I am your friend. Some men I like
to scold, for I don't like them; but I have always
entertained the best of feeling for you." Taking me,
at the close of our interview, from his private office
into the public room, where General Garfield and
others were, he turned and asked if it was all right—
if I was satisfied. I expressed my thanks, shook
hands with him, and left, feeling a thousand times
more attached to him, and more respect for him than
I had ever felt before. He had the power to crush
me, for at this time he is almost omnipotent in this
department, and by a simple word he might have
driven me from the army, disgraced in the estimation
of both soldiers and citizens. His magnanimity and
kindness, however, lifted a great load from my spirits,
and made me feel like a new man; and I am very
sure that he felt better and happier also, for no man
does a generous act to one below him in rank or station, without being recompensed therefor by a feeling
of the liveliest satisfaction. I may have been too sen-
sitive, and may not, probably did not, realize fully
the necessity for prompt action, and the weight of re-
sponsibility which rested upon the General. There
are times when there is no time for explanation;
great exigencies, in the presence of which lives, fortunes, friendships, and all matters of lesser importance must give way; moments when men's thoughts
are so concentrated on a single object, and their whole

being so wrought up, that they can see nothing, know nothing, but the calamity they desire to avert, or the victory they desire to achieve. Nashville had been threatened. To have lost it, or allowed it to be gutted by the enemy, would have been a great misfortune to the army, and brought down upon Rosecrans not only the anathemas of the War Department, but would have gone far to lose him the confidence of the whole people. He supposed the enemy's movements had been checked, and was startled and thrown off his balance by discovering that they were still unopposed. The error was attributable in part possibly to me, in part to a series of blunders, which had resulted from the fact that there were two persons in the army of the same name and rank, but mainly to those who failed to transmit the order in proper time.

29. Our large tents have been taken away, and shelter tents substituted. This evening, when the boys crawled into the latter, they gave utterance, good-humoredly, to every variety of howl, bark, snap, whine, and growl of which the dog is supposed to be capable.

Colonel George Humphreys, Eighty-eighth Indiana, whom I supposed to be a full-blooded Hoosier, tells me he is a Scotchman, and was born in Ayrshire, in the same house in which Robert Burns had birth. His grandfather, James Humphreys, was the neighbor and companion of the poet. It was of him he wrote this epitaph, at an ale-house, in the way of pleasantry:

> " Below these stanes lie Jamie's banes.
> O ! Death, in my opinion,
> You ne'er took sic a blither'n bitch
> Into thy dark dominion."

30. This afternoon called on General Thomas;
met General R. S. Granger; paid my respects to
General Negley, and stopped for a moment at General
Rousseau's. The latter was about to take a horseback ride with his daughter, to whom I was introduced.

22

MAY, 1863.

1. The One Hundred and Thirteenth Ohio is at Franklin. Colonel Wilcox has resigned; Lieutenant-Colonel Mitchell will succeed to the colonelcy. I rode over the battle-field with the latter this afternoon.

4. Two men from Breckenridge's command strayed into our lines to-day.

7. Colonels Hobart, Taylor, Nicholas, and Captain Nevin spent the afternoon with me.

The intelligence from Hooker's army is contradictory and unintelligible. We hope it was successful, and yet find little beside the headlines in the telegraphic column to sustain that hope. The German regiments are said to have behaved badly. This is, probably, an error. Germans, as a rule, are reliable soldiers. This, I think, is Carl Schurz's first battle; an unfortunate beginning for him.

9. The arrest of Vallandingham, we learn from the newspapers, is creating a great deal of excitement in the North. I am pleased to see the authorities commencing at the root and not among the branches.

I have just read Consul Anderson's appeal to the people of the United States in favor of an extensive representation of American live stock, machinery, and manufactures, at the coming fair in Hamburg.   Friend James made a long letter of it; and, I doubt not, drank a gallon of good Dutch beer after each paragraph.

11.   The Confederate papers say Streight's command was surrendered to four hundred and fifty rebels.   I do not believe it.   The Third Ohio would have whipped that many of the enemy on any field and under any circumstances.   The expedition was a foolish one.   Colonel Harker, who knows Streight well, predicted the fate which has overtaken him. He is brave, but deficient in judgment.   The statement that his command surrendered to an inferior force is, doubtless, false.   Forrest had, I venture to say, nearer four thousand and fifty than four hundred and fifty.   The rebels always have a great many men before a battle, but not many after.   They profess still to believe in the one-rebel-to-three-Yankee theory, and make their statements to correspond.   The facts when ascertained will, I have no doubt, show that the Union brigade was pursued by an overwhelming force, and being exhausted by constant riding, repeated fights, want of food and sleep, surrendered after ammunition had given out and all possibility of escape gone.   The enemy is strong in cavalry, and it is not at all probable that he would have sent but four hundred and fifty men to look after a brigade, which had boldly ventured hundreds of miles inside his lines.   In fact, General Forrest seldom, if ever,

travels with so small a command as he is said to have had on this occasion.

13. An order has been issued prohibiting women from visiting the army. I infer from this that a movement is contemplated.

14. General Negley called to-day, and remained for half an hour. He is a large, rosy-cheeked, handsome, affable man, and a good disciplinarian.

I am going to have a horse-race in the morning with Major McDowell, of Rousseau's staff. Stakes two bottles of wine.

When we entered Murfreesboro, nearly a year ago, the boys brought in a lame horse, which they had picked up on the road. The horse hobbled along with difficulty, and for a long time was used to carry the knapsacks and guns of soldiers who were either too unwell or too lazy to transport these burdens themselves. The horse had belonged to a Texas cavalryman, and had been abandoned when so lame as to be unfit for service. Finally, when his shattered hoof got well, he was transferred from the hospital department to the quartermaster's, where he became a favorite. The quartermaster called my attention to the horse, and I had him appraised and took him for my own use. Under the skillful and attentive hands of my hostler he soon shook off his shaggy coat of ugly brown, and put on one of velvety black. After a few days of trial I discovered not only that he was an easy goer, but had the speed of the wind. When at his fastest pace he is liable to overreach; it was thus that his left fore hoof had been shattered. To prevent a recurrence of the accident, I keep his hoof protected by leathers. I believe he is the fastest horse in the Army of the Cumberland.

15. Major McDowell did not put in an appearance until after I had returned from my morning ride. He brought Colonel Loomis with him to witness the grand affair; but as it was late, we finally concluded to postpone the race until another morning.

Some one has been kind enough to lay on my table a handsome bunch of red pinks and yellow roses.

My staff has been increased, the late addition being "U. S.," a large and very lazy yellow dog. The two letters which give him his title are branded on his shoulder. He sticks very close to me, for the reason, possibly, that I do not kick him, and say "Get out," as most persons are tempted to do when they look upon his most unprepossessing visage. He is a solemn dog, and probably has had a rough row to hoe through life. At times, when I speak an encouraging word, he brightens up, and makes an effort to be playful; but cheerfulness is his forte no more than " fiten " was A. Ward's, and he soon relapses into the deepest melancholy.

16. Read Emil Schalk's article on Hooker. It is an easy matter for that gentleman to sit in his library, plan a campaign, and win a battle. I could do that myself; but when we undertake to make the campaign, fight the battle, and win the victory, we find it very much more difficult. Book farmers are wonderfully successful on paper, and show how fortunes may

be gathered in a single season, but when they come down to practical farming, they discover quite often that frost, or rain, or drouth, plays the mischief with their theories, and renders them bankrupt.

It can be demonstrated, doubtless, that a certain blow, delivered at a certain place and time, against a certain force, will crush it; but does it not require infinite skill and power to select the place and time with certainty? A broken bridge, swollen stream, or even the most trifling incident, which no man can foresee or overrule, may disarrange and render futile the best-laid plans, and lead to defeat and disaster. After a battle we can easily look back and see where mistakes have been made; but it is more difficult, if not impossible, to look forward and avoid them. War is a blind and uncertain game at best, and whoever plays it successfully must not only hold good cards, but play them discreetly, and under the most favorable circumstances.

17. Starkweather informs me that he has been urged to return to Wisconsin and become a candidate for governor, and for fear he might accede to the wishes of the people in this regard, the present governor was urging his promotion. He is still undecided whether to accept a brigadier's commission or the nomination for this high civil office. Wind.

18. Two deserters came into our lines to-day. They were members of a regiment in Cleburne's division, and left their command at Fosterville, ten or fifteen miles out. They represent the Southern army in our front as very strong, in good condition

and fine spirits. The rebel successes on the Rappahannock have inspired them with new life, and have, to some extent, dispirited us. We do not, however, build largely on the Eastern army. It is an excellent body of men, in good discipline, but for some reason it has been unfortunate. When we hear, therefore, that the Eastern army is going to fight, we make up our minds that it is going to be defeated, and when the result is announced we feel sad enough, but not disappointed.

19. Generals Rosecrans, Negley, and Garfield, with the staffs of the two former, appeared on the field where I was drilling the brigade. General Rosecrans greeted me very cordially. I am satisfied that those who allow themselves to be damned once without remonstrance are very likely to be damned always.

I am becoming quite an early riser; have seen the sun rise every morning for two weeks. Saw the moon over my right shoulder. Lucky month ahead. Am devoting a little more time than usual to my military books.

Colonel Moody, Seventy-fourth Ohio, has resigned.

20. This afternoon I received orders to be in readiness to move at a moment's notice.

21. The days now give us a specimen of the four seasons. At sunrise it is pretty fair winter for this latitude. An hour after, good spring; at noon, midsummer; at sunset, fall. Flies are too numerous to mention even by the million. They come on drill at 8 A. M., and continue their evolutions until sundown.

Wilson, Orr, and DuBarry are indisposed. My cast-

iron constitution holds good.   As a rule, I take no
medicine or medical advice.   In a few instances I
have acceded to the wishes of my friends, and applied
to the doctors; but have been careful not to allow
their prescriptions to get further than my vest
pocket.

The colt has just whinnied in response to another
horse.   He is in fine condition; coat as sleek and
glossy as that of a bridegroom.   Yesterday I rode
him on drill, and the little scamp got into a quarrel
with another horse, reared up, and made a plunge
that came near unseating me.   He agrees with Wilson's horse very well, but seems to think it his duty
to exercise a sort of paternal care over him; and so
on all occasions when possible he takes the reins of
Wilson's bridle between his teeth and holds it tightly,
as if determined that the speed of the Adjutant's
horse should be regulated by his own.   My black is
also in excellent condition, and certainly very fast.
My race has not yet come off.

23.   Received a box of catawba wine and pawpaw
brandy from Colonel James G. Jones, half of which
I was requested to deliver to General Rosecrans, and
the other half keep to drink to the Colonel's health,
which at present is very poor.

Colonel Gus Wood called this afternoon.   He is
one of those who were captured on the railroad train
near Lavergne, 10th of last April, and has returned
to camp via Tullahoma, Chattanooga, and Richmond.
He says the rebel troops are in good condition and
good spirits; thinks there is an immense force in

our front, and that it would not be advisable to advance.

The enlisted men of the Third are at Annapolis, Maryland, and will soon be at Camp Chase, Ohio. The officers are in Libby.

The box of cigars presented to me by my old friend, W. H. Marvin, still holds out. Whenever I am in a great straight for a smoke I try one; but I have not yet succeeded in finding a good one. I affect to be very liberal, and pass the box around freely; but all who have tried the cigars once insist that they do not smoke. They will probably last to the end of the war.

26. The privates of the Eighty-eighth Indiana presented a two-hundred-dollar sword to Colonel Humphreys, and the Colonel felt it to be his duty to invest the price of the sword in beer for the boys.

Lieutenant Orr was kind enough to give me a field glass.

Hewitt's Kentucky battery has been assigned to me. Colonel Loomis has assumed command of his battery again. His commission as colonel was simply a complimentary one, conferred by the Governor of Michigan. He should be recognized by the War Department as colonel. No man in the army is better entitled to the position. His services at Perryville and Stone river, to say nothing of those in West Virginia and North Alabama, would be but poorly requited by promotion.

Hewitt's battery has not been fortunate in the past. It was captured at this place last summer, when General T. T. Crittenden was taken, and lost quite a number of men, horses, and one gun, in the battle of Stone river.

28. At midnight orderlies went clattering around the camps with orders for the troops to be supplied with five days' provisions, and in readiness to march at a moment's notice. We expected to be sent away this morning, but no orders have yet come to move.

Mrs. Colonel B. F. Scribner sent me a very handsome bouquet with her compliments.

Mr. Furay accompanied Vallandigham outside the Federal lines, and received from him a parting declaration, written in pencil and signed by himself, wherein he claimed that he was a citizen of Ohio and of the United States, brought there by force and against his will, and that he delivered himself up as a prisoner of war.

30. Captain Gilbert E. Winters, A. C. S., took tea with me. He is as jovial as the most successful man in the world, and overruns with small jokes and stories, many of which he claims were told him by President Lincoln. From this we might infer that the President has very little to do but entertain and amuse gentlemen, who apply to him for appointments, with conversation so coarse that it would be discreditable to a stable boy.

31. Received a letter from daughter Nellie, a little school girl. She "wishes the war was out." So do I.

JUNE, 1863.

1. By invitation, the mounted officers of our brigade accompanied General Negley to witness the review of Rousseau's division. There were quite a large number of spectators, including a few ladies. I was introduced to General Wood for the first time, although I have known him by sight, and known of him well, for months. Many officers of Wood's and Negley's divisions were present. After the review, and while the troops were leaving the field, Colonel Ducat, Inspector-General on General Rose-crans' staff, and Colonel Harker, challenged me for a race. Soon after, Major McDowell, of Rousseau's staff, joined the party; and, while we were getting into position for the start, General Wagner, who has a long-legged white horse, which, he insisted, could beat any thing on the ground, took place in the line. McCook, Wood, Loomis, and many others, stopped to witness the race. The horses were all pacers; it was, in fact, a gathering of the best horses in the army, and each man felt confident. I was absolutely sure my black would win, and the result proved that I was correct.

The only time during the race that I was honored with the company of my competitors, was at the starting; then, I observed, they were all up; but a half a minute later the black took the lead. The old fellow had evidently been on the track before, and felt as much interest in the contest as his owner. He knew what was expected of him, and as he went flying over the ground astonished me, as he did every body else. Loomis, who professes to know much about horses, said to me before the race took place, " Your's is a good-looking horse, but he can't beat McDowell's." Before leaving the field, however, he admitted that he had been mistaken. My horse was quicker of foot than he supposed.

2. Called on Colonel Scribner and wife, where I met also Colonel Griffin and wife; had a long conversation about spiritualism, mesmerism, clair-voyance, and subjects of that ilk. At night there was a fearful thunder-storm. The rain descended in torrents, and the peals of thunder were, I think, louder and more frequent than I ever heard before.

Met Loomis; he had accompanied General Rose-crans and others to witness the trial of a machine, invented by Wilder, for tearing up railroad tracks and injuring the rails in such a manner as to render them worthless. Hitherto the rebels, when they have torn up our railroads, have placed the bars crosswise on a pile of ties, set fire to the latter, and so heated and bent the rails; but by heating them again they could be easily straightened and made good.   Wilder's instrument twists them so they can not be used again.

The New York Herald, I observe, refers with great severity to General Hascall's administration of affairs in Indiana; saying that "to place such a brainless fool in a military command is not simply an error, it is a crime." This is grossly unjust. Hascall is not only a gallant soldier, but a man of education and excellent sense. He has been active, and possibly severe, in his opposition to treasonable organizations and notoriously disloyal men, whose influence was exerted to discourage enlistments and retard the enforcement of the draft.   Unfortunately, in time of civil war, besides the great exigencies which arise to threaten the commonwealth, innumerable lesser evils gather like flies about an open wound, to annoy, irritate, and kill.   Against these the law has made no adequate provision.   The military must, therefore, often interpose for the public good, without waiting for legislative authority, or the slow processes of the civil law, just as the fireman must proceed to batter down the doors of a burning edifice, without stopping to obtain the owner's permission to enter and subdue the flames.

3. Our division was reviewed to-day.   The spectators were numerous, numbering among other distinguished personages Generals Rosecrans, Thomas, Crittenden, Rousseau, Sheridan, and Wood.   The weather was favorable, and the review a success. In the evening, a large party gathered at Negley's

quarters, where lunch and punch were provided in abundance.

Generals Wood and Crittenden, of the Twenty-first Army Corps, claimed that I did not beat Wagner fairly in the horse-race the other day. I expressed a willingness to satisfy them that I could do so any day; and, further, that my horse could out-go any thing in the Twenty-first Corps. The upshot of the matter is that we have a race arranged for Friday afternoon at four o'clock.

The party was a merry one; gentlemen imbibed freely. General Rosecrans' face was as red as a beet; he had, however, been talking with ladies, and being a diffident man, was possibly blushing. Wood persisted that the Twenty-first Corps could not be beaten in a horse-race, and that Wagner's long-legged white was the most wonderful pacer he ever saw. Negley seemed possessed with the idea that every body was trying to escape, and that it was necessary for him to seize them by the arm and haul them back to the table; he seemed also to be laboring under the delusion that his guests would not drink unless he kept his eye on them, and forced them to do so. Lieutenant-Colonel Ducat, an Irishman of the Charles O'Malley school, insisted upon introducing me to the ladies, but fortunately I was sober enough to decline the invitation. Harker, late in the evening, thought he discovered a disposition on the part of others to play off on him; he felt in duty bound to empty a full tumbler, while they shirked by taking only half of one, which he affirmed was unfair and inexcusable. General Thomas, after sitting at his wine an hour, conversing the while with a lady, arose from the table evidently very much refreshed, and proceeded to make himself exceedingly agreeable. I never knew the old gentleman to be so affable, cordial, and complimentary before.

4. The guns have been reverberating in our front all day. I am told that Sheridan's division advanced on the Shelbyville road. It is probable that a part, if not the whole, of the firing is in his front.

5. Read the Autobiography of Peter Cartright. It is written in the language of the frontier, and presents a rough, strong, uneducated man, full of vanity, courage, and religious zeal. He never reached the full measure of dignity requisite to a minister of the Gospel. There are many amusing incidents in the volume, and many tales of adventures with sinners, in the cabin, on the road, and at camp meeting, in all of which Cartright gets the better of the sons of Belial, and triumphs in the Lord.

8. The One Hundred and Fourth Illinois, Colonel Moore, reported to me for duty, so that I have now four regiments and a battery. This Colonel Moore is the same who was in command at Hartsville, and whose regiment and brigade were captured by the ubiquitous John Morgan last winter. He has but recently returned from the South, where, for a time, he was confined in Libby prison.

The rebels are still prowling about our lines, but making no great demonstrations of power.

9. Governor (?) Billy Williams, of Indiana, dined

with me to-day; he resides in Warsaw, is a politician, a fair speaker, and an inveterate story teller.

Wilson has been appointed Assistant Adjutant-General, with the rank of captain.

13. Had brigade drill in a large clover field, just outside the picket line. The men were in fine condition, well dressed, and well equipped. I kept them on the jump for two hours. Generals Thomas and Negley were present, and were well pleased. I doubt if any brigade in the army can execute a greater variety of movements than mine, or go through them in better style. My voice is excellent, I can make myself heard distinctly by a whole brigade, without becoming hoarse by hours of exertion. Starkweather has the best voice in the army; he can be heard a mile away.

Our division and brigade flags have been changed from light to dark blue. They look almost like a black no-quarter flag.

We have one solitary rooster: he crows early in the morning, all day, and through the night if it be moonlight. He mounted a stump near my door this morning, stood between the tent and the sun, so that his shadow fell on the canvas, and crowed for half an hour at the top of his voice. I think the scamp knew I was lying abed longer than usual, and was determined to make me get up. He is on the most intimate terms with the soldiers, and struts about the camp with an air of as much importance as if he wore shoulder-straps, and had been reared at West Point. He enters the boys' tents, and inspects their quarters with all the freedom and independence of a regularly detailed inspecting officer. He is a fine type of the soldier, proud and vain, with a tremendous opinion of his own fighting qualities.

16. Had a grand corps drill. The line of troops, when stretched out, was over a mile in length. The Corps was like a clumsy giant, and hours were required to execute the simplest movement. When, for instance, we changed front, my brigade marched nearly, if not quite, a mile to take position in the new line. The waving of banners, the flashing of sabers and bayonets, the clattering to and fro of muddle-headed aids-de-camp on impatient steeds, the heavy rumble of artillery wagons, the blue coats of the soldiers, the golden trappings of the field and staff, made a grand scene for the disinterested spectator to look upon; but with the thermometer ranging from eighty-five to one hundred, it was hard work for the soldier who bore knapsack, haversack, and gun, and calculated to produce an unusual amount of perspiration, and not a little profanity. Major-General Thomas guided the immense mass of men, while the operations of the divisions were superintended by their respective commanders. I fear the brigade and regimental commanders profited little by the drill, but I hope the major-generals learned something. The latter, in their devotion to strategy, have evidently neglected tactics, and failed to unravel the mysteries of the school of the battalion.

In the morning, with my division commander, I

24

called on General Thomas, at his quarters, and had the honor to accept from his hands the most abominable cigar it has ever been my misfortune to attempt to smoke.

19. The army has been lying here now nearly six months. It has of late been kept pretty busy. Sunday morning inspections, monthly inspections of troops, frequent inspections of arms and ammunition, innumerable drills, and constant picketing.

Colonel Miller assumes command of a brigade in Johnson's division. Since the troops were at Nashville he has been commanding what was known as the Second Brigade of Negley's division; but the colonels of the brigade objected to having an imported colonel placed over them, and so Miller takes command of the brigade to which his regiment is attached. He is a brave man and a good officer. Colonel Harker's brigade has been relieved from duty at the fortifications, and is now encamped near us, on the Liberty road.

21. Mrs. Colonel Scribner and Mrs. Colonel Griffin stopped at my tent-door for a moment this morning. They were on horseback, and each had a child on the saddle. They were giving Mrs. Scribner's children a little ride.

Attended divine service in the camp of the Eighty-eighth Indiana, and afterward called for a few minutes on Colonel Moore, of the One Hundred and Fourth Illinois. On returning to my quarters I found Colonels Hobart and Taylor awaiting me. They were about to visit Colonel T. P. Nicholas, of the Second

Kentucky Cavalry, and desired me to accompany them. We dined with Colonel Nicholas, and, as is the custom, observed the apostolic injunction of taking something for the stomach's sake. Toward evening we visited the field hospital, and paid our respects to Surgeon Finley and lady. Here, much against our wills, we were compelled to empty a bottle of sherry. On the way to our own quarters Colonel Taylor insisted upon our calling with him to see a friend, with whom we were obliged to take a glass of ale. So that it was about dark when we three sober gentlemen drew near to our respective quarters. We had become immensely eloquent on the conduct of the war, and with great unanimity concluded that if Grant were to take Vicksburg he would be entitled to our profoundest admiration and respect. Hobart, as usual, spoke of his State as if it were a separate and independent nation, whose sons, in imitation of LaFayette, Kosciusko and DeKalb, were devoting their best blood to the maintenance of free government in a foreign land; while Taylor, incited thereto by this eulogy on Wisconsin, took up the cudgel for Kentucky, and dwelt enthusiastically on the gallantry of her men and the unrivaled beauty of her women.

When I dismounted and turned my horse over to the servant, I caught a glimpse of the signal lights on the dome of the court-house, and was astonished to find just double the usual number, in the act of performing a Dutch waltz. I concluded that the Signal Corps must be drunk. Saddened by the reflection that those occupying high places, whose duty it was to let their light shine before men, should be found in this condition of hopeless inebriety, I heaved a sigh which might have been mistaken by the uncharitable for a hic-cough, and lay down to rest.

23. My colt had a sore eye a day or two ago, but it is now getting well. The boys pet him, and by pinching him have taught him to bite. I fear they will spoil him. I have not ridden him much of late. He has a way of walking on his hind legs, for which the saddles in use are not calculated, and there is, consequently, a constant tendency, on the part of the rider, to slip over his tail.

Captain Wells sent a colored teamster, who had just come in, tired and hungry, to his quarters for dinner. Simon Bolivar Buckner, who now has charge of the commissary and culinary branch of the Captain's establishment, was in the act of dining when the teamster entered the tent and seated himself at the table. Buckner, astonished at this unceremonious intrusion, exclaimed : " What you doin' har, sah ?" " De Capin tole me fer to come and get my dinnah." "Hell," shouted Buckner, " does de Capin 'spose I 'm guiane to eat wid a d—n common nigger? Git out'er har, till I 'm done got through."

Buckner gets married every time we move camp. On last Sunday Captain Wells found him dressed very elaborately, in white vest and clean linen, and said to him : " What 's in the wind, Buckner ?" " Gwine to be married dis ebening, sah." " What time ?" " Five o'clock, sah." " Can 't spare you, Buckner. Expect friends here to dine at six, and want a good dinner

gotten up." "Berry well, sah; can pos'pone de
wedin', sah. Dis'pintment to lady, sah; but it'll be
all right."

24. The note of preparation for a general advance
sounded late last night. Reynolds moved at 4 A. M.;
Rousseau at 7; our division will leave at 10. A long
line of cavalry is at this moment going out on the
Manchester pike.   *   *   *   *

Rain commenced falling soon after we left Mur-
freesboro, and continued the remainder of the day.
The roads were sloppy, and marching disagreeable.
Encamped at Big creek for the night; Rousseau and
Reynolds in advance.

Before leaving Murfreesboro I handed John what I
supposed to be a package of tea, and told him to fill
my canteen with cold tea. On the road I took two
or three drinks, and thought it tasted strongly of tobacco; but I accounted for it on the supposition that
I had been smoking too much, and that the tobacco
taste was in my mouth, and not in the tea. After getting into camp I drank of it again, when it occurred
to me that John had neglected to cleanse the canteen
before putting the tea in, and so I began to scold him.
" I did clean it, sah," retorted John. "Well, this
tea," I replied, "tastes very much like tobacco juice."
"It is terbacker juice, sah." "Why, how is that?"
" You gib me paper terbacker, an' tole me hab some
tea made, sah, and I done jes as you tole me, sah."
" Why you are a fool, John; did you suppose I
wanted you to make me tea out of tobacco?" "Don

know, sah ; dat's what you tole me, sah ; done jes as you tole me, sah."

25. Marched to Hoover's Gap. Heavy skirmishing in front during the day. Reynolds lost fifteen killed, and quite a number wounded. A stubborn fight was expected, and our division moved up to take part in it; but the enemy fell back. Rain has been falling most of the day. A pain in my side admonishes me that I should have worn heavier boots.

26. Moved to Beech Grove. Cannonading in front during the whole day; but we have now become so accustomed to the noise of the guns that it hardly excites remark. The sky is still cloudy, and I fear we shall have more rain to-night. The boys are busy gathering leaves and twigs to keep them from the damp ground. General Negley's quarters are a few rods to my left, and General Thomas' just below us, at the bottom of the hill. Reynolds is four miles in advance.

27. We left Beech Grove, or Jacob's Store, this morning, at five o'clock, and conducted the wagon train of our division through to Manchester. Rosecrans and Reynolds are here. The latter took possession of the place two or three hours before my brigade reached it, and the former came up three hours after we had gone into camp. We are now twelve miles from Tullahoma. The guns are thundering off in the direction of Wartrace. Hardie's corps was driven from Fairfield this morning.

My baggage has not come, and I am compelled to sleep on the wet ground in a still wetter overcoat.

28. My baggage arrived during the night, and this morning I changed my clothes and expected to spend the Sabbath quietly; but about 10 A. M. I was ordered to proceed to Hillsboro, a place eight miles from Manchester, on the old stage road to Chattanooga. When we were moving out I met Durbin Ward, who asked me where I was going. I told him. "Why," said he, "I thought, from the rose in your button-hole, that you were going to a wedding." "No," I replied; "but I hope we are going to nothing more serious."

29. My position is one of great danger, being so far from support and so near the enemy. Last night my pickets on the Tullahoma road were driven in, after a sharp fight, and my command was put in line of battle, and so remained for an hour or more; but we were not again disturbed. No fires were built, and the darkness was impenetrable.

At noon I received orders to proceed to Bobo's Cross-roads, and reach that point before nightfall. There were two ways of going there: the one via Manchester was comparatively safe, although considerably out of the direct line; the other was direct, but somewhat unsafe, because it would take me near the enemy's front. The distance by this shorter route was eleven miles. I chose the latter. It led through a sparsely settled, open oak country. Two regiments of Wheeler's cavalry had been hovering about Hillsboro during the day, evidently watching our movements.   After proceeding about three miles, a dash was made upon my skirmish line, which resulted in the killing of a lieutenant, the capture of one man, and the wounding of several others.   I instantly formed line of battle, and pushed forward as rapidly as the nature of the ground would admit; but the enemy fell back.

About five o'clock, as we drew near Bobo's, two cannon shots and quite a brisk fire of musketry advised us that the rebels were either still in possession of the Cross-roads or our friends were mistaking us for the enemy.   I formed line of battle, and ordered the few cavalrymen who accompanied me to make a detour to the right and rear, and ascertain, if possible, who were in our front.   The videttes soon after reported the enemy advancing, with a squadron of cavalry in the lead, and I put my artillery in position to give them a raking fire when they should reach a bend of the road.   At this moment when life and death seemed to hang in the balance, and when we supposed we were in the presence of a very considerable, if not an overwhelming, force of the enemy, a half-grown hog emerged from the woods, and ran across the road. Fifty men sprang from the ranks and gave it chase, and before order was fully restored, and the line readjusted, my cavalry returned with the information that the troops in front were our own.

The incidents of the last six days would fill a volume; but I have been on horseback so much, and otherwise so thoroughly engaged, that I have been, and am now, too weary to note them down, even if I had the conveniences at hand for so doing.

25

JULY, 1863.

1. My brigade, with a battalion of cavalry attached, started from Bobo's Cross-roads in the direction of Winchester. When one mile out we picked up three deserters, who reported that the rebels had evacuated Tullahoma, and were in full retreat. Half a mile further along I overtook the enemy's rear guard, when a sharp fight occurred between the cavalry, resulting, I think, in very little injury to either party. The enemy fell back a mile or more, when he opened on us with artillery, and a sharp artillery fight took place, which lasted for perhaps thirty minutes. Several men on both sides were killed and wounded. The enemy finally retired, and taking a second position awaited our arrival, and opened on us again. I pushed forward in the thick woods, and drove him from point to point for seven miles. Negley followed with the other brigades of the division, ready to support me in case the enemy proved too strong, but I did not need assistance. The force opposed to us simply desired to retard pursuit; and whenever we pushed against it vigorously fell back.

2. This morning we discover that we bivouacked during the night within half a mile of a large force

of rebel cavalry and infantry. After proceeding a little way, we found the enemy in position on the bluffs on the opposite side of Elk river, with his artillery planted so as to sweep the road leading to the bridge. Halting my infantry and cavalry under the cover of the hill, I sent to the rear for an additional battery, and, before the enemy seemed to be aware of what we were doing, I got ten guns in position on the crest of the hill and commenced firing. The enemy's cavalry and infantry, which up to this time had lined the opposite hills, began to scatter in great confusion; but we did not have it all our own way by any means. The rebels replied with shot and shell very vigorously, and for half an hour the fight was very interesting; at the end of that time, however, their batteries limbered up and left on the double quick. In the meantime, I had sent a detachment of infantry to occupy a stockade which the enemy had constructed near the bridge, and from this position good work was done by driving off his sharpshooters. We found the bridge partially burned, and the river too much swollen for either the men or trains to ford it. Rousseau and Brannan, I understand, succeeded in crossing at an upper ford, and are in hot pursuit.

3. Repaired the bridge, and crossed the river this morning; and are now bivouacking on the ground over which the cavalry fought yesterday afternoon—quite a number of the dead were discovered in the woods and fields. We picked up, at Elk river, an order of Brigadier-General Wharton, commanding

the troops which have been serving as the rear guard of the enemy's column.   It reads as follows:

"COLONEL HAMAR: Retire the artillery when you think best.   Hold the position as long as you can with your sharpshooters; when forced back, write to Crew to that effect.   Anderson is on your right.   Report all movements to me on this road.

"JNO. A. WHARTON, Brigadier-General.
"July 2d, 1863."

I have been almost constantly in the saddle, and have hardly slept a quiet three hours since we started on this expedition.   My brigade has picked up probably a hundred prisoners.

4.   At twelve o'clock, noon, my brigade was ordered to take the advance, and make the top of the Cumberland before nightfall; proceeding four miles, we reached the base of the mountain, and began the ascent.   The road was exceedingly rough, and the rebels had made it impassable, for artillery, by rolling great rocks into it and felling trees across it.   The axmen were ordered up, and while they were clearing away the obstructions I rode ahead with the cavalry to the summit, and some four miles on the ridge beyond.   In the meantime, General Negley ordered the artillery and infantry to return to the foot of the mountain, where we are now encamped.

5.   Since we left Murfreesboro (June 24) rain has been falling almost constantly; to-day it has been coming down in torrents, and the low grounds around us are overflowed.

Rousseau's division is encamped near us on the left, Reynolds in the rear.

The other day, while sitting on the fence by the roadside smoking my pipe, waiting for my troops to get in readiness to march, some one cried out, " Here is a philosopher," and General Reynolds rode up and shook my hand very cordially.

My brigade has been so fortunate, thus far, as to win the confidence of the commanding generals. It has, during the last week, served as a sort of a cow-catcher for Negley's division. At Elk river General Thomas rode up, while I was making my dispositions to attack the enemy, and approved what I had done and was doing.

We hear that the Army of the East has won a decisive victory in Pennsylvania. This is grand! It will show the rebels that it will not do to put their feet on free soil. Now if Grant succeeds in taking Vicksburg, and Rosecrans drives Bragg beyond the Tennessee, the country will have reason to rejoice with exceeding great joy.

6. An old lady, whose home is on the side of the mountain, called on me to-day and said she had not had a cup of coffee since the war commenced. She was evidently very poor; and, although we had no coffee to spare, I gave her enough to remind her again of the taste.

Our soldiers have been making a clean sweep of the hogs, sheep, and poultry on the route. For the rich rebels I have no sympathy, but the poor we must pity. The war cuts off from them entirely the food which, in the best of times, they acquire with great labor and difficulty. The forage for the army horses and mules, and we have an immense number, consists almost wholly of wheat in the sheaf—wheat that has been selling for ten dollars per bushel in Confederate money. I have seen hundreds of acres of wheat in the sheaf disappear in an hour. Rails have been burned without stint, and numberless fields of growing corn left unprotected. However much suffering this destruction of property may entail on the people of this section, I am inclined to think the effect will be good. It will bring them to a realizing sense of the loss sustained when they threw aside the protecting shield of the old Constitution, and the security which they enjoyed in the Union.

The season's crop of wheat, corn, oats, and hogs would have been of the utmost value to the Confederate army; when destroyed, there will be nothing in middle Tennessee to tempt it back.

7. Hundreds, perhaps thousands, of Tennesseeans have deserted from the Southern army and are now wandering about in the mountains, endeavoring to get to their homes. They are mostly conscripted men. My command has gathered up hundreds, and the mountains and coves in this vicinity are said to be full of them.

It rains incessantly. We moved to Decherd and encamped on a ridge, but are now knee-deep in mud and surrounded by water.

This morning a hundred guns echoed among the mountain gorges over the glad intelligence from the

East and South : Meade has won a famous victory, and Grant has taken Vicksburg.

Stragglers and deserters from Bragg's army continue to come in. It is doubtless unfortunate for the country that rain and bad roads prevented our following up Bragg closely and forcing him to fight in the present demoralized condition of his army. We would have been certain of a decisive victory.

9. Dined with General Negley. Colonels Stoughton and Surwell, brigade commanders, were present. The dinner was excellent; soups, punch, wine, blackberries were on the table; and, to men who for a fortnight had been feeding on hard crackers and salt pork, seemed delicious. The General got his face poisoned while riding through the woods on the 2d instant, and he now looks like an old bruiser.

McCook, whose corps lies near Winchester, called while we were at Negley's; he looks, if possible, more like a blockhead than ever, and it is astonishing to me that he should be permitted to retain command of a corps for a single hour. He brought us cheering information, however. The intelligence received from the East and South a few days ago has been confirmed, and the success of our armies even greater than first reports led us to believe.

10. We have a cow at brigade head-quarters. Blackberries are very abundant. The sky has cleared, but the Cumberland mountains are this morning covered by a thin veil of mist. Supply trains arrived last night.

11. We hear nothing of the rebel army. Rose-

crans, doubtless, knows its whereabouts, but his subordinates do not. A few of the enemy may be lingering in the vicinity of Stevenson and Bridgeport, but the main body is, doubtless, beyond the Tennessee. The rebel sympathizers here acknowledge that Bragg has been outgeneraled. Our cavalry started on the 9th instant for Huntsville, Athens, and Decatur, and I have no doubt these places were re-occupied without opposition.

The rebel cavalry is said to be utterly worn out, and for this reason has performed a very insignificant part in recent operations.

The fall of Vicksburg, defeat of Lee, and retreat of Bragg, will, doubtless, render the adoption of an entirely new plan necessary. How long it will take to perfect this, and get ready for a concerted movement, I have no idea.

12.   Our soldiers, I am told, have been entering the houses of private citizens, taking whatever they saw fit, and committing many outrages. I trust, however, they have not been doing so badly as the people would have us believe. The latter are all disposed to grumble; and if a hungry soldier squints wistfully at a chicken, some one is ready to complain that the fowls are in danger, and that they are the property of a lone woman, a widow, with nothing under the sun to eat but chickens. In nine cases out of ten the husbands of these lone women are in the Confederate army; but still they are women, and should be treated well.

14.   The brigade baker has come up, and will have

his oven in operation this afternoon; so we shall have fresh bread again.

General Rosecrans will allow no ladies to come to the front. This would seem to be conclusive that no gentlemen will be permitted to go to the rear.

16. We have blackberries and milk for breakfast, dinner, and supper. To-night we had hot ginger-bread also. I have eaten too much, and feel uncomfortable.

Meade's victory has been growing small by degrees and beautifully less; but the success of Grant has improved sufficiently on first reports to make it all up. Our success in this department, although attended with little loss of life, has been very gratifying. We have extended our lines over the most productive region of Tennessee, and have possession also of all North Alabama, a rich tract of country, the loss of which must be sorely felt by the rebels.

18. To-night I received a bundle of Northern papers, and among others the Union (?) Register. While reading it I felt almost glad that I was not at home, for certainly I should be very uncomfortable if compelled to listen every day to such treasonable attacks upon the Administration, sugar-coated though they be with hypocritical professions of devotion to the Union, the Constitution, and the soldier. How supremely wicked these men are, who, for their own personal advantage, or for party success, use every possible means to bring the Administration into dis-respect, and withhold from it what, at this time, it so greatly needs, the hearty support and co-operation of

the people. The simple fact that abuse of the party in power encourages the rebels, not only by evincing disaffection and division in the North, but by leading them to believe, also, that their conduct is justifiable, should, of itself, be sufficient to deter honest and patriotic men from using such language as may be found in the opposition press. The blood of many thousand soldiers will rest upon the peace party, and certainly the blood of many misguided people at the North must be charged to the same account. The draft riots of New York and elsewhere these croakers and libelers are alone responsible for. After the war has ended there will be abundant time to discuss the manner in which it has been conducted. Certainly quarreling over it now can only tend to the defeat and disgrace of our arms.

We hardly hear of politics in the army, and I certainly did not dream before that there was so much bitterness of feeling among the people in the North. Republicans, Democrats, and every body else think nearly alike here. I know of none who sympathize with the so-called peace party. It is universally damned, for there is no soldier so ignorant that he does not know and feel that this party is prolonging the war by stimulating his enemies. A child can see this. The rebel papers, which every soldier occasionally obtains, prove it beyond a peradventure.

20. Mrs. General Negley, it appears, has been allowed to visit her husband. Mrs. General McCook is said to be coming.

Received a public document, in which I find all the

reports of the battle of Stone river, and, I am sorry
to say, my report is the poorest and most unsatisfactory of the whole lot.   The printer, as if for the purpose of aggravating me beyond endurance, has, by an
error of punctuation, transformed what I considered a
very considerable and creditable action, into an inconsiderable skirmish.   The report should read :

"On the second and third days my brigade was in
front, a portion of the time skirmishing.   On the
night of January 3d, two regiments, led by myself,
drove the enemy from their breastworks in the edge
of the woods."

This appears in the volume as follows :

"On the second and third days my brigade was in
front a portion of the time.   Skirmishing on the
night of January 3d, two regiments, led my myself,
drove the enemy from the breastworks in the edge
of the woods."

Thus, by taking the last word of one sentence and
making it the first word of another, the intelligent
compositor belittles a night fight for which I thought
my command deserved no inconsiderable credit.   I
regret now that I did not take the time to make an
elaborate report of the operations of my brigade, de-
scribing all the terrible situations in which it had
been placed, and dwelling with special emphasis
on the courage and splendid fighting of the men.   In
contrast with my stupidly modest report, is that of
Brigadier-General Spears.   He does not hesitate to

claim for his troops all the credit of the night engagement referred to; and yet while my men stormed the barricade of logs, and cleaned out the woods, his were lying on their faces fully two hundred yards in the rear, and I should never have known that they were even that near the enemy if his raw soldiers had not fired an occasional shot into us from behind. If General Spears was with his men, he must have known that his report of their action on that occasion was utterly untruthful. If, however, as I apprehend, he was behind the rifle pits, six hundred yards in the rear, he might, like thousands of others, who were distant spectators of the scene, have honestly conceived that his troops were doing the fighting. General Rousseau's report contradicts his statements, and in a meager way accords the credit to my regiments.

Officers are more selfish, dishonest, and grasping in their struggle for notoriety than the miser for gold. They lay claim to every thing within reach, whether it belongs to them or not. I know absolutely that many of the reports in the volume before me are base exaggerations—romances, founded upon the smallest conceivable amount of fact. They are simply elaborate essays, which seek to show that the author was a little braver, a little more skillful in the management of his men, and a little worthier than anybody else. I know of one officer who has great credit, in official reports and in the newspapers, for a battle in which he did not participate at all. In fact, he did not reach the field until after the enemy had not only been repulsed, but retired out of sight; and yet he has not the manliness to correct the error, and give the honor to whom it is due.

21. The day has been a pleasant one. The night is delightful. The new moon favors us with just sufficient light to reveal fully the great oaks, the white tents, and the shadowy outline of the Cumberland mountains. The pious few of the Eighty-eighth Indiana, assembled in a booth constructed of branches, are breathing out their devotional inspirations and aspirations, in an old hymn which carries us back to the churches and homes of the civilized world, or, as the boys term it, "God's country."

Katydids from a hundred trees are vigorous and relentless in their accusations against poor Katy. That was a pleasant conceit of Holmes, "What did poor Katy do?" I never appreciated it fully until I came into the country of the katydids.

Two trains, laden with forage, commissary, and quartermaster stores, are puffing away at the depot.

General Rosecrans will move to Winchester, two miles from us, to-morrow.

No one ever more desired to look again on his wife and babies than I; but, alack and alas! I am bound with a chain which seems to tighten more and more each day, and draw me further and further from where I desire to be. But I trust the time will soon come when I shall be free again.

Morgan's command has come to grief in Ohio. I trust he may be captured himself. The papers say Basil Duke is a prisoner. If so, the spirit of the great raider is in our hands, and it matters but little, perhaps, what becomes of the carcass.

A soldier of the Forty-second Indiana, who ran away from the battle of Stone river, had his head shaved and was drummed out of camp to-day. David Walker, Paul Long, and Charley Hiskett, of the Third Ohio, go with him to Nashville, where he is to be confined in military prison until the end of the war.

Shaving the head and drumming out of camp is a fearful punishment. I could not help pitying the poor fellow, as with carpet-sack in one hand and hat in the other he marched crest-fallen through the camps, to the music of the " Rogue's March." Death and oblivion would have been less severe and infinitely more desirable.

25. General Rosecrans, although generally supposed to be here, has been, it is said, absent for some days. It is intimated that he has gone to Washington. If it be true, he has flanked the newspaper men by a wonderful burst of strategy. He must have gone through disguised as an old woman—a very ugly old woman with a tremendous nose—otherwise these newspaper pickets would have arrested and put him in the papers forthwith. They are more vigilant than the rebels, and terribly intent upon finding somebody to talk about, to laud to the skies, or abuse in the most fearful manner, for they seldom do things by halves, unless it be telling the truth. They have a marvelous distaste for facts, and use no more of them

than are absolutely necessary to string their guesses and imaginings upon.

My colt has just whinnied. He is gay as a lark, and puts Davy, the hostler, through many evolutions unknown to the cavalry service. The other day Davy had him out for exercise, and when he came rearing and charging back, I said : " How does he behave to-day, Davy?" " Mighty rambunctious, sah ; he's gettin' bad, sah."

Major James Connelly, One Hundred and Twenty-third Illinois, called. His regiment is mounted and in Wilder's brigade. It participated in the engagement at Hoover's Gap. When my brigade was at Hillsboro, Connelly's regiment accompanied Wilder to to this place (Decherd). The veracious correspondent reported that Wilder, on that expedition, had destroyed the bridge here and done great injury to the railroad, permanently interrupting communication between Bridgeport and Tullahoma; but, in fact, the bridge was not destroyed, and trains on the railroad were only delayed two hours. The expedition succeeded, however, in picking up a few stragglers and horses.

26.   General Stanley has returned from Huntsville, bringing with him about one thousand North Alabama negroes. This is a blow at the enemy in the right place. Deprived of slave labor, the whites will be compelled to send home, or leave at home, white men enough to cultivate the land and keep their families from starving.

27.   Adjutant Wilson visited Rousseau's division

at Cowan, and reports the return of Starkweather from Wisconsin, with the stars. This gentleman has been mourning over the ingratitude of Republics ever since the battle of Perryville; but henceforth he will, doubtless, feel better.

A court-martial has been called for the trial of Colonel A. B. Moore, One Hundred and Fourth Illinois. Some ill-feeling in his regiment has led one of his officers to prefer charges against him.

28. General Thomas is an officer of the regular army; the field is his home; the tent his house, and war his business. He regards rather coolly, therefore, the applications of volunteer officers for leaves of absence. Why should they not be as contented as himself? He does not seem to consider that they suddenly dropped business, every thing, in fact, to hasten to the field. But, then, on second thought, I incline to the opinion that the old man is right. Half the army would be at home if leaves and furloughs could be had for the asking.

29. Lieutenant Orr received notice yesterday of his appointment as captain in the subsistence department, and last night opened a barrel of beer and stood treat. I did not join the party until about ten o'clock, and then Captain Hewitt, of the battery, the story-teller of the brigade, was in full blast, and the applause was uproarious. He was telling of a militia captain of Fentress county, Tennessee, who called out his company upon the supposition that we were again at war with Great Britain; that Washington had been captured by the invaders, and the arch-iv-es destroyed.

A bystander questioned the correctness of the Captain's information, when he became very angry, and, producing a newspaper, said: " D—n you, sir, do you think *I* can 't read, sir?" The man thus interrogated looked over the paper, saw that it announced the occupation of Washington by the British, but called the attention of the excited militiaman to the fact that the date was 1812. "So it is," said the old captain; " I did not notice the date. But, d—n me, sir, the paper just come. Go on with the drill, boys." This story was told to illustrate the fact that the people of many counties in Tennessee were behind the times.

It would take too much time to refer, even briefly, to all the stories related, and I will allude simply to a LONDON GHOST STORY, which Captain Halpin, an Irishman, of the Fifteenth Kentucky, undertook to tell. The gallant Captain was in the last stages of inebriety, and laid the scene of his London ghost story in Ireland. Steadying himself in his seat with both hands, and with a tongue rather too thick to articulate clearly, he introduced us to his ancestors for twenty generations back. It was a famous old Irish family, and among the collateral branches were the O'Tooles, O'Rourkes, and O'Flahertys. They had in them the blood of the Irish kings, and accomplished marvelous feats in the wars of those times. And so we staggered with the Captain from Dublin to Belfast, and thence made sorties into all the provinces on chase of the London ghost, until finally our leader wound up with a yawn

26

and went to sleep. The party, disappointed at this sudden and unsatisfactory termination of the London ghost story, took a mug of beer all around, and then one gentleman, drunker probably than the others, or possibly unwilling, after all the time spent, to allow the ghost to escape, punched the Captain in the ribs and shouted: "Captain—Captain Halpin, you said it was a London ghost story; maybe you'll find the ghost in London, for I'll be d—d if it's in Ireland!" The Captain was too far gone to profit by the suggestion.

30. This evening General Rosecrans, on his way to Winchester, stopped for a few minutes at the station. He shook hands with me, and asked how I liked the water at the foot of the mountains, and about the health of my troops. I told him the water was good, and that the boys were encamped on high ground and healthy. "Yes," he replied, "and we'll take higher ground in a few days."

On the march to Tullahoma I had my brigade stretched along a ridge to guard against an attack from the direction of Wartrace. General Rosecrans passed through my lines, and was making some inquiries, when I stepped out: "Hello," said he, "here is the young General himself. You've got a good ridge. Who lives in that house? Find a place for Negley on your right or left. Send me a map of this ridge. How do ye do?"

31. Met General Turchin for the first time since he was before our court-martial at Huntsville. He appeared to be considerably cast down in spirit. He

had just been relieved from his cavalry command, and was on his way to General Reynolds to take command of a brigade of infantry. General Crook, hitherto in command of a brigade, succeeds Turchin as commander of a division. In short, Crook and Turchin just exchange places. The former is a graduate of the West Point Military Academy, and is an Ohio man, who has not, I think, greatly distinguished himself thus far. He has been in Western Virginia most of the time, and came to Murfreesboro after the battle of Stone river.

General R. B. Mitchell is, with his command, in camp a little over a mile from us. He is in good spirits, and dwells with emphasis on the length and arduousness of the marches made by his troops since he left Murfreesboro. The labor devolving upon him as the commander of a division of cavalry is tremendous; and yet I was rejoiced to find his physical system had stood the strain well. The wear and tear upon his intellect, however, must have been very great.

AUGUST, 1863.

2. Rode with Colonel Taylor to Cowan; dined with Colonel Hobart, and spent the day very agreeably. Returning we called on Colonel Scribner, remained an hour, and reached Decherd after nightfall. My request for leave of absence was lying on the table approved and recommended by Negley and Thomas, but indorsed not granted by Rosecrans.

General Rousseau has left, and probably will not return. The best of feeling has not existed between him and the commanding general for some time past. Rousseau has had a good division, but probably thought he should have a corps. This, however, is not the cause of the breach. It has grown out of small matters—things too trifling to talk over, think of, or explain, and yet important enough to create a coldness, if not an open rupture. Rosecrans is marvelously popular with the men.

3. The papers state that General R. B. Mitchell has gone home on sick leave. Poor fellow! he must have been taken suddenly, for when I saw him, a day or two ago, he was the picture of health. It is wonderful to me how a fellow as fat as Bob can come the

sick dodge so successfully. He can get sick at a moment's notice.

4. Called on General Thomas; then rode over to Winchester. Saw Garfield at department head-quarters. He said he regretted very much being compelled to refuse my application for a leave. Told him I expected to command this department soon, and when I got him and a few others, including Rosecrans and Thomas, under my thumb, they would obtain no favors. I should insist not only upon their remaining in camp, but upon their wives remaining out.

In company with Colonel Mihalotzy I called on Colonel Burke, Tenth Ohio, and drank a couple of bottles of wine with him and his spiritual adviser, Father O'Higgin. Had a very agreeable time. The Colonel pressed us to remain for dinner; but we pleaded an engagement, and afterward obtained a very poor meal at the hotel for one dollar each.

The Board for the examination of applicants for commissions in colored regiments, of which I have the honor to be Chairman, met, organized, and adjourned to convene at nine o'clock to-morrow. Colonel Parkhurst, Ninth Michigan, and Colonel Stanley, Eighteenth Ohio, are members.

I am anxious to go home; but it is not possible for me to get away. Almost every officer in the army desires to go, and every conceivable excuse and argument are urged. This man is sick; another's house has burned, and he desires to provide for his family; another has lawsuits coming off involving large sums, and his presence during the trial is necessary to save him from great loss; still another has deeds to make out, and an immense property interest to look after.

6. This is the day appointed by the President for thanksgiving and prayer. The shops in Winchester are closed.

Colonel Parkhurst has obtained a leave, and will go home on Monday.

7. Captain Wilson and Lieutenant Ellsworth arose rather late this morning, and found a beer barrel protruding from the door of their tent, properly set up on benches, with a flaming placard over it:

> "New Grocery!!
> Wilson & Ellsworth.
> Fresh Beer, 3c. a Glass.
> Give us a call."

Later in the day a grand presentation ceremony took place. All the members of the staff and hangers-on about head-quarters were gathered under the oaks; Lieutenant Calkins, One Hundred and Fourth Illinois, was sent for, and, when he appeared, Lieutenant Ellsworth proceeded to read to him the following letter:

> "Ottowa, Illinois, *July* 20, 1863.

"Lieutenant W. W. Calkins—*Sir:* Your old friends of Ottowa, as a slight testimonial of their respect for you, and admiration for those chivalrous instincts which, when the banner of beauty and glory was assailed by traitorous legions, induced you to spring unhesitatingly to its defense, have the honor to present you a beautiful field-glass. Trusting that, by its assistance, you will be able to see through your enemies, and ultimately find your way to the arms of your admiring fellow-citizens, we have the honor to subscribe ourselves,

"Your most obedient servants,
"Peter Brown,
"John Smith,
"Thomas Jones, and others."

The box containing the gift was carefully opened, and the necks and upper parts of two whisky bottles, fastened together by a piece of wood, taken out and delivered in due form to the Lieutenant. He seemed greatly surprised, and for a few minutes addressed the donors in a very emphatic and uncomplimentary way; but finding this only added to the merriment of the party, he finally cooled down, and, lifting the field-glass to his eyes, leveled it upon the staff, and remarked that they appeared to be thirsty. This, of course, was hailed as undeniable evidence that the glass was perfect, and Lieutenant Calkins was heartily congratulated on his good luck, and on the proof which the testimonial afforded of the high estimation in which he was held by the people of his native town. Many of his brother officers, in their friendly ardor, shook him warmly by the hand.

8. Hewitt's battery has been transferred to the Corps of Engineers and Mechanics, and Bridges' battery, six guns, assigned to me. I gain two guns and many men by the exchange.

Our Board grinds away eight or nine hours a day, and turns out about the usual proportion of wheat and chaff. The time was when we thought it would be impossible to obtain good officers for colored regiments. Now we feel assured that they will have as good, if not better, officers than the white regiments. From sergeants applying for commissions we are able to select splendid men; strong, healthy, well informed, and of considerable military experience. In fact, we occasionally find a non-commissioned officer who is better qualified to command a regiment than nine-tenths of the colonels. I certainly know colonels who could not obtain a recommendation from this Board for a second lieutenancy.

Saw General Garfield yesterday; he was in bed sick. I have no fears of his immediate dissolution; in fact, I think he could avail himself of a twenty-day leave. I know if I were no worse than he appears to be, I would, with the permission of the general commanding, undertake to ride the whole distance home on horseback, and swim the rivers. In a little over a week I think my wife would see me, and the black horse, followed by the pepper-and-salt colt, charging up to the front door in such style as would remind her of the days of chivalry and the knights of the olden time. I should cry out in thunder tones, "Ho! within! Unbar the door!" The colt would kick up his heels with joy at sight of the grass in the yard, while the black would champ his bit with impatience to get into a comfortable stall once more.

Altogether the sight would be worth seeing; but it will not be seen.

The Board holds its sessions in the office of an honorable Mr. Turney, who left on our approach for a more congenial clime, and left suddenly. His letters and papers are lying around us in great confusion and profusion. Among these we have discovered a document bearing the signatures of Jeff. Davis, John Mason, Pierre Soule, and others, pledging themselves to resist, by any and every means, the admission of California, unless it came in with certain boundaries which they prescribed. The document was gotten up in Washington, and Colonel Parkhurst says it is the original contract.

Dined with Colonel D. H. Gilmer, Thirty-eighth Illinois. Dinner splendid; corn, cabbage, beans; peach, apple, and blackberry pie; with buttermilk and sweetmilk. It was a grand dinner, served on a snow-white table-cloth. Where the Colonel obtained all these delicacies I can not imagine. He is an out-and-out Abolitionist, and possibly the negroes had favored him somewhat.

Colonel Gilmer is delighted to find the country coming around to his ideas. He believes the Lord, who superintends the affairs of nations, will give us peace in good time, and *that time* will be when the institution of slavery has been rooted up and destroyed. He is a Kentuckian by birth, and says he has kinfolks every-where. He is the only man he knows of who can find a cousin in every town he goes to.

27

9. Dined with Colonel Taylor. Colonels Hobart, Nicholas, and Major Craddock were present. After dinner we adjourned to my quarters, where we spent the afternoon. Hobart dilated upon his adventures at New Orleans and elsewhere, under Abou Ben Butler. He says Butler is a great man, but a d—d scoundrel. I have heard Hobart say something like this at least a thousand times, and am pleased to know that his testimony on this point is always clear, decisive, and uncontradictory.

My visitors are gone. The cars are bunting against each other at the depot. The katydids are piping away on the old, old story. The trees look like great shadows, and unlike the substantial oaks they really are. The camps are dark and quiet. This is all I can say of the night without.

In a little booth made of cedar boughs is a table, on which sputters a solitary tallow candle, in a stick not remarkable for polish. This light illuminates the booth, and reveals to the observer—if there be one, which is very unlikely, for those who usually observe have in all probability retired—a wash basin, a newspaper, a penknife, which originally had two blades, but at present has but one, and that one very dull, a gentleman of say thirty, possibly thirty-five, two steel pens, rusty with age, an inkstand, and one miller, which miller has repeatedly dashed his head against the wick of the candle and discovered that the operation led to unsatisfactory results. Wearied, disappointed, and disheartened, the miller now sits quietly on the table, mourning, doubtless, over the

unpleasant lesson which experience has taught him.
His head is now wiser; but, alas! his wings are
shorter than they were, and of what use is his head
without wings? He feels very like the man who made
a dash for fame, and fell wounded and bleeding on
the field, or the child who, for the first time, discovers that all is not gold that glitters. The gentleman
referred to—and I trust it may be no stretch of the
verities to call him a gentleman—leans over the table
writing. He has an abundant crop of dark hair on
his head, under his chin, and on his upper lip. He
is not just now troubled with a superabundance of
flesh, or, in other words, no one would suspect him of
being fat. On the contrary, he might remind one
of the lean kine, or the prodigal son who had been
feeding on husks. He is wide awake at this late hour
of the night, from which I conclude he has slept more
or less during the day. No one, to look at this gentleman, would take him to be a remarkable man; in
fact, his most intimate friends could not find it in
their hearts to bring such an accusation against him.
His face is browned by exposure, and his blue eyes
look quite dark, or would do so if there were sufficient light to see them. When he straightens up—
and he generally straightens when up at all—he is
five feet eleven, or thereabouts. His appetite is good,
and his education is of that superior kind which ena-
bles him, without apparent effort, to misspell three-
fourths of the words in the English language; in
fact, at this present moment he is holding an imaginary discussion with his wife, who has written him

that the underclothing for gentlemen's feet should be spelled *s-o-c-k-s*, and not "s-o-x." He begs leave to differ with her, which he would probably not dare to do were she not hundreds of miles away; and he argues the matter in this way: S-o-x, o-x, f-o-x—the termination sounds alike in all. Now how absurd it would be to insist that ox should be spelled o-c-k-s, or fox f-o-c-k-s. The commonest kind of sense teaches one that the old lady is in error, and "sox" clearly correct. Much learning hath evidently made her mad. Having satisfied himself about this matter, he takes a photograph from an inside pocket; it is that of his wife. He makes another dive, and brings out one of his children; then he lights a laurel-wood pipe, and, as the white smoke curls about his head and vanishes, his thoughts skip off five hundred miles or less, to a community of sensible, industrious, quiet folks, and when he finally awakes from the reverie and looks about him upon the beggarly surroundings—he does not swear, for he bethinks him in time that swearing would do no good.

10. Colonel Hobart, Twenty-first Wisconsin, and Colonel Hays, Tenth Kentucky, have been added to the Board—the former at my request.

11. To-day I dined with a Wisconsin friend of Colonel Hobart's; had a good dinner, Scotch ale and champagne, and a very agreeable time. Colonel Hegg, the dispenser of hospitalities, is a Norwegian by birth, a Republican, a gentleman who has held important public positions in Wisconsin, and who stands well with the people. In the course of the table talk I

learned something of the history of my friend Hobart. He is an old wheel-horse of the Democratic
party of his State; was a candidate for governor a
few years ago, and held joint debates with Randall
and Carl Schurz. He is the father of the Homestead
Law, which has been adopted by so many States, and
was for many years the leader of the House of Rep-
resentatives of Wisconsin. All this I gathered from
Colonel Hegg, for Hobart seldom, if ever, talks about
himself. I imagine that even the most polished
orator would obtain but little, if any, advantage over
Hobart in a discussion before the people. He has the
imagination, the information, and the oratorical fury
in discussion which are likely to captivate the masses.
He was at one time opposed to arming the negroes;
but now that he is satisfied they will fight, he is in
favor of using them.

To-night Colonels Hays and Hobart held quite an
interesting debate on the policy of arming colored
men, and emancipating those belonging to rebels.
Hays, who, by the way, is an honest man and a gallant soldier, presented the Kentucky view of the matter, and his arguments, evidently very weak, were
thoroughly demolished by Hobart. I think Colonel
Hays felt, as the controversy progressed, that his
position was untenable, and that his hostility to the
President's proclamation sprang from the prejudice in
which he had been educated, rather than from reason
and justice.

12. Old Tom, known in camp as the veracious
nigger, because of a "turkle" story which he tells, is

just coming along as I wait a moment for the breakfast bell. The "turkle," which Tom caught in some creek in Alabama, had two hundred and fifty eggs in "him." "Yas, sah, two hunder an' fifty."

Tom has peculiar notions about certain matters, and they are not, by any means, complimentary to the white man. He says: "It jus' 'pears to me dat Adam was a black man, sah, an' de Lord he scar him till he got white, cos he was a sinner, sah."

"Tom, you scoundrel, how dare you slander the white man in that way?"

"'Pears to me dat way; hab to tell de truf, sah; dat's my min'. Men was 'riginally black; but de Lord he scare Adam till he got white; dat's de reasonable supposition, sah. Do a man's har git black when he scared, sah? No, sah, it gits white. Did you ebber know a man ter get black when he's scard, sah? No, sah, he gits white."

"That does seem to be a knock-down argument, Tom."

"Yas, sah, I've argied with mor'n a hunder white men, sah, an' they can't never git aroun dat pint. When yer strip dis subjec ob prejdice, an' fetch to bar on it de light o' reason, sah, yer can 'rive at but one 'clusion, sah. De Lord he rode into de garden in chariot of fire, sah, robed wid de lightnin', sah, thunder bolt in his han', an' he cried ADAM, in de voice of a airthquake, sah, an' de 'fec on Adam was powerful, sah. Dat's my min', sah." And so Tom goes on his way, confident that the first man was black, and that another white man has been vanquished in argument.

13.   The weather continues oppressively hot.   The names of candidates for admission to the corps *d'Afrique* continue to pour in.   The number has swelled to eight hundred.   We begin our labors at nine, adjourn a few minutes for lunch, and then continue our work until nearly six.

16.   We move at ten o'clock A. M.   Had a heavy rain yesterday and a fearful wind.   The morning, however, is clear, and atmosphere delightful.

Our Board has examined one hundred and twenty men.   Perhaps forty have been recommended for commissions.

The present movement will, doubtless, be a very interesting one.   A few days will take us to the Tennessee, and thereafter we shall operate on new ground. Georgia will be within a few miles of us, the long-suffering and long-coveted East Tennessee on our left, Central Alabama to our front and right.   A great struggle will undoubtedly soon take place, for it is not possible that the rebels will give us a foothold south of the Tennessee until compelled to do it.

21.   We are encamped on the banks of Crow creek, three miles northerly from Stevenson.   The table on which I write is under the great beech trees.   Colonel Hobart is sitting near studying Casey.   The light of the new moon is entirely excluded by foliage. On the right and left the valley is bounded by ranges of mountains eight hundred or a thousand feet high. Crow creek is within a few feet of me; in fact, the sand under my feet was deposited by its waters.   The army extends along the Tennessee, from opposite

Chattanooga to Bellefonte. Before us, and just beyond the river, rises a green-mountain wall, whose summit, apparently as uniform as a garden hedge, seems to mingle with the clouds. Beyond this are the legions of the enemy, whose signal lights we see nightly.

22. Our Board has resumed its sessions at the Alabama House, Stevenson. The weather is intensely hot. Father Stanley stripped off his coat and groaned. Hobart's face was red as the rising sun, and the anxious candidates for commissions did not certainly resemble cucumbers for coolness.

Hobart rides a very poor horse—poor in flesh, I mean; but he entertains the most exalted opinion of the beast. This morning, as we rode from camp, I thought I would please him by referring to his horse in a complimentary way. Said I: "Colonel, your horse holds his own mighty well." His face brightened, and I continued: "He hasn't lost a bone since I have known him." This nettled him, and he began to badger me about an unsuccessful attempt which I made some time ago to get him to taste a green persimmon. Hobart has a good education, is fluent in conversation, and in discussion gets the better of me without difficulty. All I can do, therefore, is to watch my opportunity to give him an occasional thrust as best I can. Father Stanley is slow, destitute of either education or wit, and examines applicants like a demagogue fishes for votes.

Brigadier-General Jeff. C. Davis and Colonel Hegg called to-day. Davis is, I think, not quite so tall as I am, but a shade heavier. Met Captain Gaunther. He has been relieved from duty here, and ordered to Washington. He is an excellent officer, and deserves a higher position than he holds at present. I thought, from the very affectionate manner with which he clung to my hand and squeezed it, that possibly, in taking leave of his friends, he had burdened himself with that "oat" which is said to be one too many Hobart says that Scribner calls him Hobart up to two glasses, and further on in his cups ycleps him Hogan.

Wood had a bout with the enemy at Chattanooga yesterday; he on the north side and they on the south side of the river. Johnson is said to have reinforced Bragg, and the enemy is supposed to be strong in our front. Rosecrans was at Bridgeport yesterday looking over the ground, when a sharpshooter blazed away at him, and put a bullet in a tree near which the General and his son were standing.

24. Deserters are coming in almost every day. They report that secret societies exist in the rebel army whose object is the promotion of desertion. Eleven men from one company arrived yesterday. Not many days ago a Confederate officer swam the river and gave himself up. For some time past the pickets of the two armies have not been firing at each other; but yesterday the rebels gave notice that they should commence again, as the "Yanks were becoming too d—n thick."

26. To-day we were examining a German who desired to be recommended for a field officer. "How

do you form an oblique square, sir?"   "Black square? Black square?" exclaimed the Dutchman; "I dush not know vot you means by de black square."

As I write the moon shines down upon me through an opening in the branches of the beech forest in which we are encamped, and the objects about me, half seen and half hidden, in some way suggest the half-remembered and half-forgotten incidents of childhood.

How often, when a boy, have I dreamed of scenes similar to those through which I have passed in the last two years! Knightly warriors, great armies on the march and in camp, the skirmish, the tumult and thunder of battle, were then things of the imagination; but now they have become familiar items of daily life. Then a single tap of the drum or note of the bugle awakened thoughts of the old times of chivalry, and regrets that the days of glory had passed away. Now we have martial strains almost every hour, and are reminded only of the various duties of our every-day life.

As we went to Stevenson this morning, Hobart caught a glimpse of a colored man coming toward us. It suggested to him a hobby which he rides now every day, and he commenced his oration by saying, in his declamatory way: "The negro is the coming man." "Yes," I interrupted, "so I see, and he appears to have his hat full of peaches;" and so the coming man had.

28. Rode to the river with Hobart and Stanley. The rebel pickets were lying about in plain view on

the other side   Just before our arrival quite a number of them had been bathing. The outposts of the two armies appear still to be on friendly terms. " Yesterday," a soldier said to me, " one of our boys crossed the river, talked with the rebs for some time, and returned."

29.   The band is playing " Yankee Doodle," and the boys break into an occasional cheer by way of indorsement. There is something defiant in the air of " Doodle " as he blows away on the soil of the cavliers, which strikes a noisy chord in the breast of Uncle Sam's nephews, and the demonstrations which follow are equivalent to " Let 'er rip," " Go in old boy."

Colonel Hobart's emphatic expression is " egad." He told me to-day of a favorite horse at home, which would follow him from place to place as he worked in the garden, keeping his nose as near to him as possible. His wife remarked to him one day : " Egad, husband, if you loved me as well as you do that horse, I should be perfectly happy."

" Are you quite sure sure Mrs. Hobart said ' egad,' Colonel ?"

" Well, no, I would n't like to swear to that."

This afternoon Colonels Stanley, Hobart, and I rode down to the Tennessee to look at the pontoon bridge which has been thrown across the river.   On the way we met Generals Rosecrans, McCook, Negley, and Garfield.   The former checked up, shook hands, and said : " How d' ye do ?"   Garfield gave us a grip which suggested "vote right, vote early." Negley smiled affably, and the cavalcade moved on. We crossed the Tennessee on the bridge of boats, and rode a few miles into the country beyond. Not a gun was fired as the bridge was being laid. Davis' division is on the south side of the river.

The Tennessee at this place is beautiful. The bridge looks like a ribbon stretched across it. The island below, the heavily-wooded banks, the bluffs and mountain, present a scene which would delight the soul of the artist. A hundred boys were frolicking in the water near the pontoons, tumbling into the stream in all sorts of ways, kicking up their heels, ducking and splashing each other, and having a glorious time generally.

30. (Sunday.) The brigade moved into Stevenson.

31. It crossed the Tennessee.

In one of the classes for examination to-day was a sergeant, fifty years old at least, but still sprightly and active; not very well posted in the infantry tactics now in use, but of more than ordinary intelligence. The class had not impressed the Board favorably. This Sergeant we thought rather too old, and the others entirely too ignorant. When the class was told to retire, this old Sergeant, who, by the way, belongs to a Michigan regiment, came up to me and asked: "Was John Beatty, of Sandusky, a relative of yours?" "He was my grandfather." "Yes, you resemble your mother. You are the son of James Beatty. I have carried you in my arms many a time. My mother saved your life more than once. Thirty years ago your father and mine were neighbors. I recollect the cabin where you were born as well as if I had seen it but yesterday." "I am heartily glad to see you, my old friend," said I, taking his hand. "You must stay with me to-night, and we will talk over the old times together."

When the Sergeant retired, Hobart, with a twinkle in his eye, said he did not think much of that fellow; his early associations had evidently been bad; he was entirely too old, anyway. What the army needed, above all things, were young, vigorous, dashing officers; but he supposed, notwithstanding all this, that we should have to do something for the Sergeant. He had rendered important service to the country by carrying the honored President of our Board in his arms, and but for the timely doses of catnip tea, administered by the Sergeant's mother, the gallant knight of the black horse and pepper-and-salt colt would have been unknown. "What do you say, gentlemen, to a second lieutancy for General Beatty's friend?"

"I shall vote for it," replied Stanley.

"Recommend him for a first lieutenancy," I suggested; and they did.

In the evening I had a long and very pleasant conversation with the Sergeant. He had fought under Bradley in the Patriot war at Point au Pelee; served five years in the regular army during the

Florida war, and two years in the Mexican war. His name is Daniel Rodabaugh. He has been in the United States service as a soldier for nine years, and richly deserves the position for which we recommended him.

SEPTEMBER, 1863.

1. Closed up the business of the Board, and at seven o'clock in the evening (Tuesday) left Stevenson to rejoin the brigade. On the way to the river I passed Colonel Stanley's brigade of our division. The air was thick with dust. It was quite dark when I crossed the bridge. The brigade had started on the march hours before, but I thought best to push on and overtake it. After getting on the wrong road and riding considerably out of my way, I finally found the right one, and about ten o'clock overtook the rear of the column. The two armies will face each other before the end of the week. General Lytle's brigade is bivouacking near me. I have a bad cold, but otherwise am in good health.

3. We moved from Moore's Spring, on the Tennessee, in the morning, and after laboring all day advanced less than one mile and a quarter. We were ascending Sand mountain; many of our wagons did not reach the summit.

4. With two regiments I descended into Lookout valley and bivouacked at Brown's Springs about dark. Our transportation, owing to the darkness and extreme badness of the roads, remained on the top of

the mountain. I have no blankets, and nothing to eat except one ear of corn which one of the colored boys roasted for me. Wrapped in my overcoat, about nine o'clock, I lay down on the ground to sleep; but a terrible toothache took hold of me, and I was compelled to get up and find such relief as I could in walking up and down the road. The moon shone brightly, and many camp-fires glimmered in the valley and along the side of the mountain. It was three o'clock in the morning before gentle sleep made me oblivious to aching teeth and head, and all the other aches which had possession of me.

5. A few deserters come in to us, but they bring little information of the enemy. We are now in Georgia, twenty miles from Chattanooga by the direct road, which, like all roads here, is very crooked, and difficult to travel. The enemy is, doubtless, in force very near, but he makes no demonstrations and retires his pickets without firing a gun. The developments of the next week or two will be matters for the historian.

Sheridan's division is just coming into the valley; what other troops are to cross the mountain by this road I do not know. As I write, heavy guns are heard off in the direction of Chattanooga. The roads are extremely dusty. This morning I consigned to the flames all letters which have come to me during the last two months.

I have just returned from a ride up the valley to the site of the proposed iron works of Georgia. Work on the railroad, on the mountain roads, and on the furnaces, was suspended on our approach. The negroes and white laborers were run off to get them beyond our reach. The hills in the vicinity of the proposed works are undoubtedly full of iron; the ore crops out so plainly that it is visible to all passers. Here the Confederacy proposed to supply its railroads with iron rail, an article at present very nearly exhausted in the South. Had the Georgians possessed common business sense and common energy, extensive furnaces would have been in operation in this valley years ago; and now, instead of a few poorly cultivated corn-fields, with here and there a cabin, the valley and hillsides would be overflowing with population and wealth.

We returned from the site of the iron works by way of Trenton, the seat of justice of Dade county. Reynolds and Sheridan are encamped near Trenton. I feel better since my ride.

6. (Sunday.) Marched to Johnson's Crook, and bivouacked, at nightfall, at McKay's Spring, on the north side of Lookout mountain; here my advance regiment, the Forty-second Indiana, had a slight skirmish with the enemy, in which one man was wounded.

7. We gained the summit of Lookout mountain, and the enemy retired to the gaps on the south side.

8. Started at four o'clock in the morning and pushed for Cooper's Gap. Surprised a cavalry picket at the foot of the mountain, in McLemore's Cove, Chattanooga valley. In this little affair we captured

28

five sabers, one revolver, one carbine, one prisoner, and seriously wounded one man.

While standing on a peak of Lookout, we saw far off to the east long lines of dust trending slowly to the south, and inferred from this that Bragg had abandoned Chattanooga, and was either retiring before us or making preparations to check the center and right of our line.

9. Marched up the valley to Stephen's Gap and rejoined the division.

10. Our division marched across McLemore's Cove to Pigeon mountain, found Dug Gap obstructed, and the enemy in force on the right, left, and front. The skirmishers of the advance brigade, Colonel Surwell's, were engaged somewhat, and during the night information poured in upon us, from all quarters, that the enemy, in strength, was making dispositions to surround and cut us off before reinforcements could arrive.

11. Two brigades of Baird's division joined us about 10 A. M. Five thousand of the enemy's cavalry were reported to be moving to our left and rear; soon after, his infantry appeared on our right and left, and, a little later, in our front. From the summit of Pigeon mountain, the rebels could observe all our movements, and form a good estimate of our entire force. Our immense train, swelled now by the transportation of Baird's division to near four hundred wagons, compelled us to select such positions as would enable us to protect the train, and not such as were most favorable for making an offensive or defensive fight.

It was now impossible for Brannan and Reynolds to reach us in time to render assistance. General Negley concluded, therefore, to fall back, and ordered me to move to Bailey's Cross-roads, and await the passage of the wagon train to the rear. The enemy attacked soon after, but were held in check until the transportation had time to return to Stephens' Gap.

12. We expected an attack this morning, but, reinforcements arriving, the enemy retired. This afternoon Brannan made a reconnoissance, but the result I have not ascertained; there was, however, no fighting.

I am writing this in the woods, where we are bivouacking for the night. For nearly two weeks, now, I have not had my clothes off; and for perhaps not more than two nights of the time have I had my boots and spurs off. I have arisen at three o'clock in the morning and not lain down until ten or eleven at night. My appetite is good and health excellent. Last night my horse fell down with me, and on me, but strange to say only injured himself.

We find great numbers of men in these mountains who profess to be loyal. Our army is divided—Crittenden on the left, our corps (Thomas) in the center, and McCook far to the right. The greatest danger we need apprehend is that the enemy may concentrate rapidly and fight our widely separated corps in detail. Our transportation, necessarily large in any case, but unnecessarily large in this, impedes us very much. The roads up and down the mountains are extremely bad; our progress has therefore been slow, and the march hither a tedious one. The brigade lies in the open field before me in battle line. The boys have had no time to rest during the day, and have done much night work, but they hold up well. A katydid has been very friendly with me to-night, and is now sitting on the paper as if to read what I have written.

17. Marched from Bailey's Cross-roads to Owensford on the Chickamauga.

18. Ordered to relieve General Hazen, who held position on the road to Crawfish Springs; but as he had received no orders, and as mine were but verbal, he declined to move, and I therefore continued my march and bivouacked at the springs.

About midnight I was ordered to proceed to a ford of the Chickamauga and relieve a brigade of Palmer's division, commanded by Colonel Grose. The night was dark and the road crooked. About two in the morning I reached the place; and as Colonel Grose's pickets were being relieved and mine substituted, occasional shots along the line indicated that the enemy was in our immediate front.

CHICKAMAUGA.

19. At an early hour in the morning the enemy's pickets made their appearance on the east side of the Chickamauga and engaged my skirmishers. Some hours later he opened on us with two batteries, and a sharp artillery fight ensued. During this engagement, the Fifteenth Kentucky, Colonel Taylor, occupied an advanced position in the woods on the low ground, and the shots of the artillery passed immedi-

ately over it. I rode down to this regiment to see that
the men were not disturbed by the furious cannonading, and to obtain at the same time a better view of the
enemy. While thus absent, Captain Bridges, concluding
that the Confederate guns were too heavy for him, limbered up and fell back.   Hastening to the hill, I sent
Captain Wilson with an order to Bridges to return ;
and, being reinforced soon after by three pieces of
Shultz's First Ohio Battery, we opened again on the
advancing columns of the enemy, when they fell back
precipitately, evidently concluding that the lull in
our firing and withdrawal of our artillery were simply
devices to draw them on.

In this affair eight men of the infantry were
wounded; and Captain Bridges had two men killed,
nine wounded, and lost twelve horses.

About five o'clock in the afternoon I was directed
to withdraw my picket line—which had been greatly
extended in order to connect with troops on the left—
as silently and carefully as possible, and return to
Crawfish Springs.   Arriving at the springs, the boys
were allowed time to fill their canteens with water,
when we pushed forward on the Chattanooga road to
a ridge near Osbern's, where we bivouacked for the
night.

There had been heavy fighting on our left during
the whole afternoon; and while the boys were preparing supper, a very considerable engagement was occurring not far distant to the east and south of us.
Elsewhere an occasional volley of musketry, and
boom of artillery, with scattered firing along an

extended line indicated that the two grand armies were concentrating for battle, and that the morrow would give us hot and dangerous work.

20. (Sunday.)   At an early hour in the morning I was directed to move northward on the Chattanooga road and report to General Thomas. He ordered me to go to the extreme left of our line, form perpendicularly to the rear of Baird's division, connecting with his left. I disposed of my brigade as directed. Baird's line appeared to run parallel with the road, and mine running to the rear crossed the road. On this road and near it I posted my artillery, and advanced my skirmishers to the edge of the open field in front of the left and center of my line. The position was a good one, and my brigade and the one on Baird's left could have co-operated and assisted each other in maintaining it. Fifteen minutes after this line was formed, Captain Gaw, of General Thomas' staff, brought me a verbal order to advance my line to a ridge or low hill (McDaniel's house), fully one-fourth of a mile distant. I represented to him that in advancing I would necessarily leave a long interval between my right and Baird's left, and also that I was already in the position which General Thomas himself told me to occupy. He replied that the order to move forward was imperative, and that I was to be supported by Negley with the other two brigades of his division. I could object no further, although the movement seemed exceedingly unwise, and, therefore, pushed forward my men as rapidly as possible to the point indicated. The Eighty-eighth Indiana (Colonel

Humphreys), on the left, moved into position without difficulty. The Forty-second Indiana (Lieutenant-Colonel McIntyre), on its right, met with considerable opposition in advancing through the woods, but finally reached the ridge. The One Hundred and Fourth Illinois (Lieutenant-Colonel Hapeman), and Fifteenth Kentucky (Colonel Taylor), on the right, became engaged almost immediately and advanced slowly. The enemy in strong force pressed them heavily in front and on the right flank.

At this time I sent an aid to request General Baird or General King to throw a force in the interval between my right and their left, and dispatched Captain Wilson to the rear to hasten forward General Negley to my support. My regiment on the right was confronted by so large a force that it was compelled to fall back, which it did in good order, contesting the ground stoutly. About this time a column of the enemy, *en masse*, on the double quick, pressed into the interval between the One Hundred and Fourth Illinois and Forty-second Indiana, and turned with the evident intention of capturing the latter, which was then busily engaged with the rebels in its front; but Captain Bridges opened on it with grape and canister, when it broke and fell back in disorder to the shelter of the woods. The Forty-second Indiana, but a moment before almost surrounded, was thus enabled to fight its way to the left and unite with the Eighty-eighth. Soon after this the enemy made another and more furious assault upon the One Hundred and Fourth Illinois and Fifteenth Kentucky, and, driving them back, advanced to within fifty yards of my battery, and poured into it a heavy fire, killing Lieutenant Bishop, and killing or wounding all the men and horses belonging to his section, which consequently fell into rebel hands. Captain Bridges and his officers, by the exercise of great courage and coolness, succeeded in saving the remainder of the battery. It was in this encounter that Captain LeFevre, of my staff, was killed, and Lieutenant Calkins, also of the staff, was wounded.

The enemy having now gained the woods south of the open field and west of the road, I opposed his further progress as well as I could with the Fifteenth Kentucky and One Hundred and Fourth Illinois; but as he had two full brigades, the struggle on our part seemed a hopeless one. Fortunately, at this juncture, I discovered a battery on the road in our rear (I think it was Captain Goodspeed's), and at my request the Captain ordered it to change front and open fire. This additional opposition served for a time to entirely check the enemy.

The Eighty-eighth and Forty-second Indiana, compelled, as their officers claim, to make a detour to the left and rear, in order to escape capture or utter annihilation, found General Negley, and were ordered to remain with him, and finally to retire with him in the direction of Rossville. This, however, I did not ascertain until ten hours later in the day.

Firing having now ceased in my front, and being the only mounted officer or mounted man present, I

left the Fifteenth Kentucky and One Hundred and
Fourth Illinois temporarily in charge of Colonel
Taylor, and hurried back to see General Thomas or
Negley, and urge the necessity for more troops to enable me to re-establish the line.   On the way, and before proceeding far, I met the Second Brigade of our
division, Colonel Stanley, advancing to my support.
Had it reached me an hour earlier, I feel assured that
I would have been able to maintain the position
which I had just been compelled to abandon.   I
directed Colonel Stanley to form line of battle at
once, at right angles with the road and on its left,
facing north.   Returning to Colonel Taylor, I ordered him to fall back with the Fifteenth Kentucky
and One Hundred and Fourth Illinois, and form in
rear of the left of Stanley's line, as a support to it.
Soon after we had got our lines adjusted, the enemy
pressed back the skirmishers of the Fifteenth Kentucky and One Hundred and Fourth Illinois, who
had not been retired with the regiments, and, following them up, drove in also the skirmish line of
Stanley's brigade, whereupon the Eleventh Michigan
(Colonel Stoughton), and the Eighteenth Ohio (Lieutenant-Colonel Grosvenor), gave him a well-directed
volley, which brought him to a halt.   Our whole line
then opened at short range, and he wavered.   I gave
the order to advance, then to charge, and the brigade
rushed forward with a yell, drove the enemy fully
one-fourth of a mile, strewing the ground with his
dead and wounded, and capturing many prisoners.

29

Among the latter was General Adams, the commander of a Louisiana brigade.

Finding now that Colonel Taylor had not followed the movement with his regiment and the One Hundred and Fourth Illinois, and seeing the necessity for some support for a single line so extended, I hastened to the rear, and, being unable to find Taylor where I had left him, I induced four regiments, of I know not what command, which I found idle in the woods, to move forward and form a second line.

At this time Captain Wilson, whom I had sent to General Negley some time before the Second Brigade reached me, to inform him of my position and need of assistance, returned, and brought from him a verbal order to retire to the hill in the rear and join him. Convinced that the withdrawal of the troops at this time from the position occupied might endanger the whole left wing of the army, I thought best to defer the execution of this order until I could see General Negley and explain to him the necessity of maintaining and reinforcing it with the other brigade of our division. But before Captain Wilson could find either Colonel Taylor, who had in charge the Fifteenth Kentucky and One Hundred and Fourth Illinois, or General Negley, the enemy made a fierce attack on Stanley's brigade and forced it back. The unknown brigade which I had posted in the rear to support it retired with unseemly haste, and without firing a shot.

At this juncture frightened soldiers and occasional shots were coming from the right and rear of our line, indicating that the right wing of the army had either been thrown back or changed position. Stanley's brigade, considerably scattered and shattered by the last furious assault of the enemy, was gathered up by its officers and retired to the ridge on the right and to the rear of the original line of battle. Wilson and I made diligent efforts to find Taylor, but were unable to do so. I was greatly provoked at his retirement without consulting me, and at a time, too, when his presence was so greatly needed to support Stanley. But later in the day I ascertained from him that he had been ordered by Major Lowrie, General Negley's chief of staff, to join Negley and retire with him to Rossville. He also had much to say about saving many pieces of artillery; but it occurred to me that his presence on the field was of much more importance than a few pieces of trumpery artillery off the field. Why, at any rate, did he not notify me of the order which he had received from the division commander? The charge of Stanley's brigade had not occupied to exceed thirty minutes, and as soon as it was ended I had returned to find him gone. The Colonel, however, did, doubtless, what he conceived to be his duty, and for the best. His courage had been tested on too many occasions to allow me to think that anything but an error of judgment, or possibly the belief that under any circumstances he was bound to obey the order of the major-general commanding the division, could have induced him to abandon me.

Supposing my regiments and General Negley to be

still on the field, I again dispatched Captain Wilson in search of them, and in the meantime stationed myself near a fragment of the Second Brigade of our division, and gave such general directions to the troops about me as under the circumstances I felt warranted in doing. I found abundant opportunity to make myself useful. Gathering up scattered detachments of a dozen different commands, I filled up an unoccupied space on the ridge between Harker, of Wood's division, on the left, and Brannan, on the right, and this point we held obstinately until sunset. Colonel Stoughton, Eleventh Michigan; Lieutenant-Colonel Rappin, Nineteenth Illinois; Lieutenant-Colonel Grosvenor, Eighteenth Ohio; Colonel Hunter, Eighty-second Indiana; Colonel Hays and Lieutenant-Colonel Wharton, Tenth Kentucky; Captain Stinchcomb, Seventeenth Ohio, and Captain Kendrick, Seventy-ninth Pennsylvania, were there, each having a few men of their respective commands; and they and their men fought and struggled and clung to that ridge with an obstinate, persistent, desperate courage, unsurpassed, I believe, on any field. I robbed the dead of cartridges and distributed them to the men; and once when, after a desperate struggle, our troops were driven from the crest, and the enemy's flag waved above it, the men were rallied, and I rode up the hill with them, waving my hat, and shouting like a madman. Thus we charged, and the enemy only saved his colors by throwing them down the hill. However much we may say of those who held command, justice compels the acknowl-

edgment that no officer exhibited more courage
on that occasion than the humblest private in the
ranks.

About four o'clock we saw away off to our rear the
banners and glittering guns of a division coming toward us, and we became agitated by doubt and hope.
Are they friends or foes? The thunder, as of a thousand anvils, still goes on in our front. Men fall
around us like leaves in autumn. Thomas, Garfield,
Wood, and others are in consultation below the hill
just in rear of Harker. The approaching troops are
said to be ours, and we feel a throb of exultation.
Before they arrive we ascertain that the division is
Steedman's; and finally, as they come up, I recognize
my old friend, Colonel Mitchell, of the One Hundred
and Thirteenth. They go into action on our right,
and as they press forward the roar of the musketry
redoubles; the battle seems to be working off in that
direction. There is now a comparative lull in our
front, and I ride over to the right, and become
involved in a regiment which has been thrown
out of line and into confusion by another regiment that retreated through it in disorder. I assist
Colonel Mitchell in rallying it, and it goes into the
fight again. Returning to my old place, I find that
disorganized bodies of men are coming rapidly from
the left, in regiments, companies, squads, and singly.
I meet General Wood, and ask if I shall not
halt and reorganize them. He tells me to do so; but
I find the task impossible. They do not recognize
me as their commander, and most of them will not

obey my orders. Some few, indeed, I manage to hold together; but the great mass drift by me to the woods in the rear. The dead are lying every-where; the wounded are continually passing to the rear; the thunder of the guns and roll of musketry are unceasing and unabated until night-fall. Then the fury of the battle gradually dies away, and finally we have a silence, broken only by a cheer here and there along the enemy's line.

Wilson and I are together near the ridge, where we have been all the afternoon. We have heard nothing of Negley nor of my regiments. We take it for granted, however, that they are somewhere on the field. As the night darkens we discover a line of fires off to our left and rear, toward McDaniels' house. That is the place where Negley should have been in the morning, and we conclude he must be there now.

We have been badly used during the day; but it does not occur to us that our army has been whipped. We start together to find Negley. We have had nothing to eat since early morning, and so, passing a corn-field, we stop for a moment to fill our pockets with corn; then, proceeding on our way, we pass through an unused field, grown up with brush, and here meet a man coming toward us on horseback. I said to him, "Are those our troops?" pointing in the direction of the line of fires. He answered, "Yes; our troops are on the road and just beyond it." Pretty soon we emerged from the brushy woods and entered an open field; just before us was a long line of fires, and soldiers busily engaged preparing supper. We had approached to within two hundred feet of them, and could hear the soldiers talk and laugh, as soldiers will, over the incidents of the day, when we discerned that we were riding straight into the enemy's line. Instantly wheeling our horses, we drove the spurs into them and lay down on their backs. We had been discovered, and a dozen or more shots were sent after us; but we escaped unharmed. The man we met in the unused field had mistaken us for Confederate officers. Two or three shots were fired at us as we approached our own line, but the darkness saved us.

Near eight o'clock in the evening I ascertained, from General Wood, that the army had been ordered to fall back to Rossville, and I started at once to inform Colonel Stoughton and others on the ridge; but I found that they had been apprised of the movement, and were then on the road to the rear.

The march to Rossville was a melancholy one. All along the road, for miles, wounded men were lying. They had crawled or hobbled slowly away from the fury of the battle, become exhausted, and lay down by the roadside to die. Some were calling the names and numbers of their regiments, but many had become too weak to do this; by midnight the column had passed by. What must have been their agony, mental and physical, as they lay in the dreary woods, sensible that there was no one to comfort or to care for them, and that in a few hours more their career on earth would be ended.

At a little brook, which crossed the road, Wilson

and I stopped to water our horses. The remains of a fire, which some soldiers had kindled, were raked together, and laying a couple of ears of corn on the coals for our own use, we gave the remainder of what we had in our pockets to the poor beasts; they, also, had fasted since early morning.

How many terrible scenes of the day's battle recur to us as we ride on in the darkness. We see again the soldier whose bowels were protruding, and hear him cry, "Jesus, have mercy on my soul!" What multitudes of thought were then crowding into the narrow half hour which he had yet to live—what regrets, what hopes, what fears! The sky was darkening, earth fading; wealth, power, fame, the prizes most esteemed of men, were as nothing. His only hope lay in the Saviour of whom his mother had taught him. I doubt not his earnest, agonizing prayer was heard. Nay, to doubt would be to question the mercy of God!

A Confederate boy, who should have been at home with his mother, and whose leg had been fearfully torn by a minnie ball, hailed me as I was galloping by early in the day. He was bleeding to death, and crying bitterly. I gave him my handkerchief, and shouted back to him, as I hurried on, "Bind up the leg tight!"

The adjutant of the rebel General Adams called to me as I passed him. He wanted help, but I could not help him—could not even help our own poor boys who lay bleeding near him.

Sammy Snyder lay on the field wounded; as I

handed him my canteen he said, " General, I did my duty." " I know that, Sammy; I never doubted that you would do your duty." The most painful recollection to one who has gone through a battle, is that of the friends lying wounded and dying and who needed help so much when you were utterly powerless to aid them.

Between ten and eleven o'clock, at night, I reached Rossville, and found one of my regiments, the Forty-second Indiana, on picket one mile south of that place, and the other regiments encamped near the town. My men were surprised and rejoiced to see me. It had been currently reported that I was killed. One fellow claimed to know the exact spot on my body where the ball hit me; while another, not willing to be outdone, had given a minute description of the locality where I fell. General Negley rendered me good service by giving me something to eat and drink, for I was hungry as a wolf.

At this hour of the night (eleven to twelve o'clock) the army is simply a mob. There appears to be neither organization nor discipline. The various commands are mixed up in what seems to be inextricable confusion. Were a division of the enemy to pounce down upon us between this and morning, I fear the Army of the Cumberland would be blotted out.

21.   Early this morning the army was again got into order. Officers and soldiers found their regiments, regiments their brigades, and brigades their divisions. My brigade was posted on a high ridge,

east of Rossville and near it. About ten o'clock A. M it was attacked by a brigade of mounted infantry, a part of Forrest's command, under Colonel Dibble. After a sharp fight of half an hour, in which the Fifteenth Kentucky, Colonel Taylor, and the Forty-second Indiana, Lieutenant-Colonel McIntyre, were principally engaged, the enemy was repulsed, and retired leaving his dead and a portion of his wounded on the field. Of his dead, one officer and eight men were left within a few rods of our line. One little boy, so badly wounded they could not carry him off, said, with tears and sobs, "They have run off and left me in the woods to die." I directed the boys to carry him into our lines and care for him.

At midnight, the Fifteenth Kentucky was deployed on the skirmish line; the other regiments of the brigade withdrawn, and started on the way to Chattanooga. A little later the Fifteenth Kentucky quietly retired and proceeded to the same place.

22. We are at Chattanooga.

With the exception of a cold, great exhaustion, and extreme hoarseness, occasioned by much hallooing, I am in good condition. The rebels have followed us and are taking position in our front.

24. At midnight the enemy attempted to drive in our pickets, and an engagement ensued, which lasted an hour or more, and was quite brisk.

26. This morning another furious assault was made on our picket line; but, after a short time, the rebels retired and permitted us to remain quiet for the remainder of the day.

Their pickets are plainly seen from our lines, and their signal flags are discernable on Mission ridge. Occasionally we see their columns moving. Our army is busily engaged fortifying.

27. (Sunday.) Had a good night's rest, and am feeling very well. The day is a quiet one.

OCTOBER, 1863.

1. Have been trying to persuade myself that I am unwell enough to ask for a leave, but it will not work. The moment after I come to the conclusion that I am really sick, and can not stand it longer, I begin to feel better. The very thought of getting home, and seeing wife and children, cures me at once.

3. The two armies are lying face to face. The Federal and Confederate sentinels walk their beats in sight of each other. The quarters of the rebel generals may be seen from our camps with the naked eye. The tents of their troops dot the hillsides. To-night we see their signal lights off to the right on the summit of Lookout mountain, and off to the left on the knobs of Mission ridge. Their long lines of camp fires almost encompass us. But the camp fires of the Army of the Cumberland are burning also. Bruised and torn by a two days' unequal contest, its flags are still up, and its men still unwhipped. It has taken its position here, and here, by God's help, it will remain.

Colonel Hobart was captured at Chickamauga, and a fear is entertained that he may have been wounded.

4. This is a pleasant October morning, rather windy and cool, but not at all uncomfortable. The

bands are mingling with the autumn breezes such
martial airs as are common in camps, with now and
then a sentimental strain, which awakens recollections
of other days, when we were younger—thought
more of sweethearts than of war, when, in fact, we
did not think of war at all except as something
of the past.

Sitting at my tent door, with a field glass, I can
see away off to the right, on the highest peak of
Lookout mountain, a man waving a red flag to and
fro. He is a rebel officer, signaling to the Confederate generals what he observes of importance
in the valley. From his position he can look down
into our camp, see every rifle pit, and almost count
the pieces of artillery in our fortifications.

Captain Johnson, of General Negley's staff, has
just been in, and tells me the pickets of the two
armies are growing quite intimate, sitting about on
logs together, talking over the great battle, and
exchanging views as to the results of a future
engagement.

General Negley called a few minutes ago and invited me to dine with him at five o'clock. The General looks demoralized, and, I think, regrets somewhat the part he took, or rather the part he failed to
take, in the battle of Chickamauga. Remarks are
made in reference to his conduct on that occasion
which are other than complimentary. The General
doubtless did what he thought was best, and probably
had orders which will justify his action. After a
battle there is always more or less bad feeling, regi-

ments, brigades, and corps claiming that other regiments, brigades, and corps failed to do their whole
duty, and should therefore be held responsible for
this or that misfortune.

There was a rumor, for some days before the battle
of Chickamauga, that Burnside was on the way to
join us, and we shouted Burnside to the boys, on the
day of the battle, until we became hoarse. Did the
line stagger and show a disposition to retire: "Stand
up, boys, reinforcements are coming; Burnside is
near." Once, when Palmer's division was falling
back through a corn-field, our line was hotly pressed.
Pointing to Palmer's columns, which were coming
from the left toward the right, the officers shouted,
"Give it to 'em, boys, Burnside is here," and the boys
went in with renewed confidence. But, alas, at nightfall Burnside had played out, and the hearts of our
brave fellows went down with the sun. Burnside is
now regarded as a myth, a fictitious warrior, who is
said to be coming to the rescue of men sorely pressed,
but who never comes. When an improbable story is
told to the boys, now, they express their unbelief by
the simple word "Burnside," sometimes adding, "O
yes, we know him."

5. The enemy opened on us, at 11 A. M., from
batteries located on the point of Lookout mountain,
and continued to favor us with cast-iron in the shape
of shell and solid shot until sunset. He did little
damage, however, three men only were wounded, and
these but slightly. A shell entered the door of a dog
tent, near which two soldiers of the Eighteenth Ohio

were standing, and buried itself in the ground, when one of the soldiers turned very coolly to the other and said, " There, you d—d fool, you see what you get by leaving your door open."

6. The enemy unusually silent.

7. Visited the picket line this afternoon. A rebel line officer came to within a few rods of our picket station, to exchange papers, and stood and chatted for some time with the Federal officer. There appears to be a perfect understanding that neither party shall fire unless an advance is made in force.

NOVEMBER, 1863.

11. My new brigade consists of the following regiments:

One Hundred and Thirteenth Ohio Infantry, Colonel John G. Mitchell.

One Hundred and Twenty-first Ohio Infantry, Colonel H. B. Banning.

One Hundred and Eighth Ohio Infantry, Lieutenant-Colonel Piepho.

Ninety-eighth Ohio Infantry, Major Shane.

Third Ohio Infantry, Captain Leroy S. Bell.

Seventy-eighth Illinois Infantry, Colonel Van Vleck.

Thirty-fourth Illinois Infantry, Colonel Van Tassell.

There has been much suffering among the men. They have for weeks been reduced to quarter rations, and at times so eager for food that the commissary store-rooms would be thronged, and the few crumbs which fell from broken boxes of hard-bread carefully gathered up and eaten. Men have followed the forage wagons and picked up the grains of corn which fell from them, and in some instances they have picked up the grains of corn from the mud where mules have been fed. The suffering among the animals has been intense. Hundreds of mules and horses have died of starvation. Now, however, that we have possession of the river, the men are fully supplied, but the poor horses and mules are still suffering. A day or two more will, I trust, enable us to provide well for them also. Two steamboats are plying between this and Chattanooga, and one immense wagon train is also busy. Supplies are coming forward with a reasonable degree of rapidity. The men appear to be in good health and excellent spirits.

12. We are encamped on Stringer's ridge, on the north side of the Tennessee, immediately opposite Chattanooga. This morning Colonel Mitchell and I rode to the picket line of the brigade. The line runs along the river, opposite and to the north of the point of Lookout mountain. At the time, a heavy fog rising from the water veiled somewhat the gigantic proportions of Lookout point, or the nose of Lookout, as it is sometimes designated. While standing on the bank, at the water's edge, peering through the mist, to get a better view of two Confederate soldiers, on the opposite shore, a heavy sound broke from the summit of Lookout mountain, and a shell went whizzing over into Hooker's camps. Pretty soon a battery opened on what is called Moccasin point, on the north side of the river, and replied to Lookout. Later in the day Moccasin and Lookout got into an angry discussion which lasted two hours. These two batteries have a special spite at each other, and almost every day

30

thunder away in the most terrible manner. Lookout throws his missiles too high and Moccasin too low, so that usually the only loss sustained by either is in ammunition. Moccasin, however, makes the biggest noise. The sound of his guns goes crashing and echoing along the sides of Lookout in a way that must be particularly gratifying to Moccasin's soul. I fear, however, that both these gigantic gentlemen are deaf as adders, or they would not so delight in kicking up such a hellebaloo.

This afternoon I rode over to Chattanooga. Called at the quarters of my division commander, General Jeff. C. Davis, but found him absent; stopped at Department Head-quarters and saw General Reynolds, chief of staff; caught sight of Generals Hooker, Howard, and Gordon Granger. Soon General Thomas entered the room and shook hands with me. On my way back to camp I called on General Rousseau; had a long and pleasant conversation with him. He goes to Nashville to-morrow to assume command of the District of Tennessee. He does not like the way in which he has been treated; thinks there is a disposition on the part of those in authority to shelve him, and that his assignment to Nashville is for the purpose of letting him down easily. Palmer, who has been assigned to the command of the Fourteenth Corps, is Rousseau's junior in rank, and this grinds him. He referred very kindly to the old Third Division, and said it won him his stars. I told him I was exceedingly anxious to get home; that it seemed almost impossible for me to remain longer. He said that I must continue until they made me a major-general. I replied that I neither expected nor desired promotion.

At the river I met Father Stanley, of the Eighteenth Ohio. He presides over the swing ferry, in which he takes especial delight. A long rope, fastened to a stake in the middle of the river, is attached to the boat, and the current is made to swing it from one shore to the other.

14. My fleet-footed black horse is dead. Did the new moon, which I saw so squarely over my left shoulder when riding him over Waldron's ridge, augur this?

The rebel journals are expressing great dissatisfaction at Bragg's failure to take Chattanooga, and insist upon his doing so without further delay. On the other hand, the authorities at Washington are probably urging Grant to move, fearing if he does not that Burnside will be overwhelmed. Thus both generals must do something soon in order to satisfy their respective masters. There will be a battle or a foot-race within a week or two.

15. Have read Whitelaw Reid's statement of the causes of Rosecrans' removal. He is, I presume, in the main correct. Investigation will show that the army could have gotten into Chattanooga without a battle on the Chickamauga. There would have been a battle here, doubtless, and defeat would have resulted probably in our destruction; yet it seems reasonable to suppose that, if able to hold Chattanooga after defeat, we would have been able to do so before.

MISSION RIDGE.

20. Orders have been issued, and to morrow a great battle will be fought. May God be with our army and favor us with a substantial victory! My brigade will move at daylight. It is now getting ready.

Order to move countermanded at midnight.

22. The day is delightful. Lookout and Moccasin are furious. The Eleventh Corps (Howard's) is now crossing the pontoon bridge, just below and before us, to take position for to-morrow's engagement. Sherman is also moving up the river on the north side, with a view to getting at the enemy's right flank. My brigade will be under arms at daylight, and ready to move. Our division will operate with Sherman on the left. Hitherto I have gone into battle almost without knowing it; now we are about to bring on a terrible conflict, and have abundant time for reflection. I can not affirm that the prospect has a tendency to elevate one's spirits. There are men, doubtless, who enjoy having their legs sawed off, their heads trepanned, and their ribs reset, but I am not one of them. I am disposed to think of home and family—of the great suffering which results from engagements between immense armies. Somebody—Wellington, I guess—said there was nothing worse than a great victory except a great defeat.

Rode with Colonel Mitchell four miles up the river to General Davis' quarters; met there General Morgan, commanding First Brigade of our division; Colonel Dan McCook, commanding Third Brigade, and Mr. Dana, Assistant Secretary of War.

23. It is now half-past five o'clock in the morning. The moon has gone down, and it is that darkest hour which is said to precede the dawn. My troops have been up since three o'clock busily engaged making preparation for the day's work. Judging from the almost continuous whistling of the cars off beyond Mission Ridge, the rebels have an intimation of the attack to be made, and are busy either bringing reinforcements or preparing to evacuate.

Noon. There has been a hitch in affairs, and I am still in my tent at the old place.

About 2 P. M. a division or more was sent out to reconnoiter the enemy's front. The movement resulted in a sharp fight, which lasted until after sunset. Both artillery and infantry were engaged. As night grew on we could see the flash of the enemy's guns all along the crest of Mission Ridge, and then hear the report, and the prolonged reverberations as the sound went crashing among ridges, hills, and mountains. Rumor says that our troops captured five hundred prisoners.

24. Moved to Caldwell's, four miles up the river. A pontoon bridge was thrown across the stream; but there were many troops in advance of us, and my brigade did not reach the south side until after one o'clock. Our division was held in reserve; so we stacked arms and lay upon the grass midway between the river and the foot of Mission Ridge, and listened

to the preliminary music of the guns as the National line was being adjusted for to-morrow's battle.

25.   During the day, as we listened to the roar of the conflict, I thought I detected in the management what I had never discovered before on the battle-field, a little common sense.   Dash is handsome, genius glorious; but modest, old-fashioned, practical, every-day sense is the trump, after all, and the only thing one can securely rely upon for permanent success in any line, either civil or military.   This element evidently dominated in this battle.   The struggle along Mission Ridge seemed more like a series of independent battles than one grand conflict.   There were few times during the day when the engagement appeared to be heavy and continuous along the whole line.   There certainly was not an extended and unceasing roll, as at Chickamauga and Stone river, but rather a succession of heavy blows.   Now it would thunder furiously on the extreme right; then the left would take up the sledge, and finally the center would begin to pound; and so the National giant appeared to skip from point to point along the ridge, striking rapid and thundering blows here and there, as if seeking the weak place in his antagonist's armor.   The enemy, thoroughly bewildered, finally became most fearful of Sherman, who was raising a perfect pandemonium on his flank, and so strengthened his right at the expense of other portions of his line, when Thomas struck him in the center, and he abandoned the field.   The loss must be comparatively small, but

the victory is all the more glorious for this very reason.

26. At one o'clock in the morning we crossed the Chickamauga in pursuit of the retreating enemy. The First Brigade of our division having the lead, I had nothing to do but follow it. At Chickamauga depot we came in sight of the rebels, and formed line of battle to attack; but they retired, leaving the warehouses containing their supplies in flames. At 3 P. M. my brigade was ordered to head the column, and we drove the enemy's rear guard before us without meeting with any serious opposition until night-fall, when, on arriving at Mrs. Sheppard's spring branch, near Graysville, a brigade of Confederate troops, with a battery, under command of Brigadier-General Manny, opened on us with considerable violence. A sharp encounter ensued of about an hour's duration, resulting in the defeat of the enemy and the wounding of the rebel general. My brigade behaved well, did most of the fighting, and, owing to the darkness, probably, sustained but little loss. When General Davis came up I asked permission to make a detour through the woods to the right, for the purpose of overtaking and cutting off the enemy's train; but he thought it not advisable to attempt it.

DECEMBER, 1863.

I will not undertake to give a detailed account of our march to Knoxville, for the relief of Burnside, and the return to Chattanooga. We were gone three weeks, and during that time had no change of clothing, and were compelled to obtain our food from the corn-cribs, hen-roosts, sheep-pens, and smoke-houses on the way. The incidents of this trip, through the valleys of East Tennessee, where the waters of the Hiawasse, and the Chetowa, and the Ocoee, and the Estonola ripple through corn-fields and meadows, and beneath shadows of evergreen ridges, will be laid aside for a more convenient season. I append simply a letter of General Sherman :

"HEAD-QUARTERS DEPARTMENT OF THE TENNESSEE,
"CHATTANOOGA, *December* 18, 1863.

"GENERAL JEFF. C. DAVIS, *Chattanooga.*

"DEAR GENERAL—In our recent short but most useful campaign it was my good fortune to have attached to me the corps of General Howard, and the division commanded by yourself. I now desire to thank you personally and officially for the handsome manner in which you and your command have borne themselves throughout. You led in the pursuit of Bragg's army on the route designated for my command, and I admired the skill with which you handled the division at Chickamauga, and more especially in the short and sharp encounter, at night-fall, near Graysville.

" When General Grant called on us, unexpectedly and without due preparation, to march to Knoxville for the relief of General Burnside, you and your officers devoted yourselves to the work like soldiers and patriots, marching through cold and mud without a murmur, trusting to accidents for shelter and subsistence.

" During the whole march, whenever I encountered your command, I found all the officers at their proper places and the men in admirable order. This is the true test, and I pronounce your division one of the best ordered in the service. I wish you all honor and success in your career, and shall deem myself most fortunate if the incidents of war bring us together again.

" Be kind enough to say to General Morgan, General Beatty, and Colonel McCook, your brigade commanders, that I have publicly and privately commended their brigades, and that I stand prepared, at all times, to assist them in whatever way lies in my power.

" I again thank you personally, and beg to subscribe myself,   Your sincere friend,

" W. T. SHERMAN, Major-General."

31

Colonel Van Vleck, Seventy-eight Illinois, was kind enough in his report to say:

" In behalf of the entire regiment I tender to the general commanding the brigade, my sincere thanks for his uniform kindness, and for his solicitude for the men during all their hardships and suffering, as well as for his undaunted courage, self-possession, and military skill in time of danger."

26. Moved to McAffee's Springs, six miles from Chattanooga, and two miles from the battle-field of Chickamauga. My quarters are in the State of Tennessee, those of my troops in Georgia. The line between the states is about forty yards from where I sit. On our way hither, we saw many things to remind us of the Confederate army — villages of log huts, chimneys, old clothing, and miles of rifle pits.

27. Just a moment ago I asked Wilson the day of the week, and he astonished me by saying it was Sunday. It is the first time I ever passed a Sabbath, from daylight to dark, without knowing it.

Wilson lies on his cot to-night a disappointed man. His application for a leave was disapproved.

I am quartered in a log hut; a blanket over the doorway excludes the damp air and the cold blasts. The immense chinks, or rather lack of immense chinks, in various parts of the edifice, leave abundance of room for the admission of light. There are no windows, but this is fortunate, for if there were, they, like the door, would need covering, and blankets are scarce. The fire-place, however, is grand, and would be creditable to a castle.

The forest in which we are encamped, was, in former times, a rendezvous for the blacklegs, thieves, murderers, and outlaws, generally of two States, Tennessee and Georgia. An old inhabitant informs me he has seen hundreds of these persecuted and proscribed gentry encamped about this spring. When an officer of Tennessee came with a writ to arrest them, they would step a few yards into the State of Georgia and laugh at him. So, when Georgia sought to lay its official clutches on an offending Georgian, the latter would walk over into Tennessee and argue the case across the line. It was a very convenient spot for law-breakers. To reach across this imaginary line, and draw a man from Tennessee, would be kidnapping, an insult to a sovereign State, and in a States'-rights country such a procedure could not be tolerated. Requisitions from the governors of Tennessee and Georgia might, of course, be procured, but this would take time, and in this time the offender could walk leisurely into Alabama or North Carolina, neither of which States is very far away. In fact, the presence of large numbers of these desperados, in this locality, at all seasons of the year, has prevented its settlement by good men, and, in consequence, there are thousands of acres on which there has scarcely been a field cleared, or even a tree cut.

The somber forest, with its peculiar history, suggests to our minds the green woods of old England, where Robin Hood and his merry men were wont to pass their idle time ; or the Black Forest of Germany, where thieves and highwaymen found concealment in days of old.

What a country for the romancer! Here is the dense wilderness, the Tennessee and Chickamauga, the precipitous Lookout with his foot-hills, spurs, coves, and water-falls. Here are cosy little valleys from which the world, with its noise, bustle, confusions, and cares, is excluded. Here have congregated the bloody villains and sneaking thieves; the plumed knights, dashing horsemen, and stubborn infantry. Here are the two great battle-fields of Chickamauga and Mission Ridge. Here neighbors have divided, and families separated to fight on questions of National policy. Here, in short, every thing is supplied to the poet but the invention to construct the plot of his tale, and the genius to breathe life into the characters.

It may be possible, however, that the country is yet too young, and its incidents too new, to make it a fertile field for the novelist. The imagination works best amid scenes half known and half forgotten. When time shall have thrown its shadows over the events of the last century, and the real and unreal become so intermingled in the minds of men as to become indistinguishable, imaginary Robin Hoods will find hiding places in the caves; innocent men, in deadly peril, will seek safety in the mountain fastnesses until the danger be past; conspirators will meet in the shadowy recesses to concoct their hellish plots, over which truth, courage, and honesty will finally triumph. Here the blue and the gray will meet to fight, and to be reconciled; and there will not be wanting the Helen McGregors and Die Vernons to give color and interest to the scene.

27.   Our horses are on quarter feed.

Some benevolent gentleman should suggest a sanitary fair for the benefit of the disabled horses and mules of the Federal army.   There is no suffering so intense as theirs.   They are driven, with whip and spur, on half and quarter food, until they drop from exhaustion, and then abandoned to die in the mud-hole where they fall.   At Parker's Gap, on our return from Tennessee, I saw a poor white horse that had been rolled down the hill to get it out of the road. It had lodged against a fallen tree, feet uppermost; to get up the hill was impossible, and to roll down certain destruction.   So the poor brute lay there, looking pitiful enough, his big frame trembling with fright, his great eyes looking anxiously, imploringly for help. A man can give vent to his sufferings, he can ask for assistance, he can find some relief either in crying, praying, or cursing; but for the poor exhausted and abandoned beast there is no help, no relief, no hope.

To day we picked up, on the battle-field of Chicka-mauga, the skull of a man who had been shot in the head.   It was smooth, white, and glossy.   A little over three months ago this skull was full of life, hope, and ambition.   He who carried it into battle had, doubt-less, mother, sisters, friends, whose happiness was, to some extent, dependent upon him.   They mourn for him now, unless, possibly, they hope still to hear that he is safe and well.   Vain hope.   Sun, rain, and crows have united in the work of stripping the flesh from his bones, and while the greater part of these lay whitening where they fell, the skull has been rolling about the field the sport and plaything of the winds. This is war, and amid such scenes we are supposed to think of the amount of our salary, and of what the newspapers may say of us.

28. One of my orderlies approached me on my weak side to-day, by presenting me four cigars. Cigars are now rarely seen in camp. Sutlers have not been permitted to come further south than Bridgeport; and had it not been for the trip into East Tennessee the brigade would have been utterly destitute of tobacco.

While bivouacking on the Hiawasse, a citizen named Trotter, came into camp. He was an old, man, and professed to be loyal. I interrogated him on the tobacco question. He replied, " The crap has been mitey poor fur a year or two. I don't use terbacker myself, but my wife used to chaw it; but the frost has been a nippen of it fur a year or two, and it is so poor she has quit chawen ontirely."

· When returning from Knoxville, we passed a farm house which stood near the roadside. Three young women were standing at the gate, and appeared to be in excellent spirits. Captain Wager inquired if they had heard from Knoxville. "O yes," they answered, " General Longstreet has captured Knoxville and all of General Burnside's men." " Indeed," said the Captain; "what about Chattanooga?" "Well, we heard that Bragg had moved back to Dalton." "You have not heard, then, that Bragg was whipped; lost

sixty pieces of artillery and many thousand men?"
"O no!" "You have not heard that Longstreet was
defeated at Knoxville, and compelled to fall back with
heavy loss?" "No, no; we don't believe a word of it.
A man, who came from Knoxville and knows all about
it, says that you uns are retreating now as fast as you
can. You can't whip our fellers." "Well, ladies,"
said the Captain, "I am glad to see you feeling so
well under adverse circumstances. Good-by."

The girls were evidently determined that the Yank
should not deceive them.

At another place quite a number of women and
children were standing by the roadside. As the column approached, said one of the women to a soldier:
"Is these uns Yankees?" "Yes, madam," replied
the boy, "regular blue-bellied Yankees." "We never
seed any you uns before." "Well, keep a sharp
lookout and you'll see they all have horns on."

One day, while I was at Davis' quarters, near
Columbus, a preacher came in and said he wanted to
sell all the property he could to the army and get
greenbacks, as he desired to move to Illinois, where
his brother-in-law resided, and his Confederate notes
would not be worth a dime there. "How is that,
Parson," said Davis, affecting to misunderstand him;
"not worth a damn there?" "No, sir, no, sir; not
worth a dime, sir. You misunderstood me, sir. I
said not worth a dime there." "I beg your pardon,
Parson," responded Davis; "I thought you said not
worth a damn there, and was surprised to hear you
say so."

While we were encamped on the banks of the Hiawasse, a Union man, near seventy years old, was murdered by guerrillas. Not long before, a young lady,
the daughter of a Methodist minister, was robbed and
murdered near the same place. Murders and rob-
beries are as common occurrences in that portion of
Tennessee as marriages in Ohio, and excite about as
little attention. Horse stealing is not considered an
offense.

29. Nothing of interest has transpired to-day.
Bugles, drums, drills, parades—the old story over
and over again; the usual number of corn-cakes eaten,
of pipes smoked, of papers respectfully forwarded, of
how-do-ye-do's to colonels, captains, lieutenants, and
soldiers. You put on your hat and take a short walk.
It does you no good. Returning you lie down on
the cot, and undertake to sleep; but you have already
slept too much, and you get up and smoke again,
look over an old paper, yawn, throw the paper down,
and conclude it is confoundedly dull. Jack brings
in dinner. You see somebody passing; it is Captain
Clayson, the Judge-Advocate, and you cry out: " Hold
on, Captain; come in and have a bite of dinner."
He concludes to do so. Being a judge-advocate he
talks law, and impresses you with the idea that every
other judge-advocate has in some respects been faulty;
but he has taken pains to master his duties perfectly, and makes no mistakes. Pretty soon Major
Shane drops in, and you ask him to dine; but he has
just been to dinner, and thanks you. Observing Captain Clayson, he asks how the business of the court-

martial progresses, and says: "By the way, Captain, the sentence in that quarter-master's case was disapproved because the record was defective." The Captain blushes. He made up the record, and it strikes him the Major's remark is very untimely.

It is dull!

30. Took a ten-mile ride this afternoon. Two miles from camp I met Lieutenant Platt, one of my aids. He had asked permission in the morning to go into the country to secure a lady for a dance, which is to take place a night or two hence. I asked: "Where have you been, Lieutenant?" "At Mrs. Calisspe's, the house on the left, yonder." I did not, of course, ask if he had been successful in his mission; but as I approached the little frame in which Mrs. Calisspe resided, I thought I would drop in and see what sort of a woman had drawn the Lieutenant so far from camp. Knocking at the door, a feminine voice said "Come in," and I entered. There were three females. The elder I took to be Mrs. Calisspe. A handsome, neatly-dressed young lady I concluded was the one the Lieutenant sought. A heavy and rather dull woman, who stood leaning against the wall, I set down as a dependent or servant in the family. "Beg pardon, madam, is this the direct road to Shallow Ford?" "Yes, sir, the straight road. Won't you take a seat?" "Thank you, no. Good evening." Trotting along over the road which Mrs. Calisspe said was straight, but which, in fact, was exceedingly crooked, we came finally to the camp of

the Thirteenth Michigan, a regiment which General Thomas supposes to be engaged in cutting saw-logs, when, in truth, its principal business is strolling about the country stealing chickens. It is, however, known as the saw-log regiment.

On our return from Shallow Ford, as we approached Mrs. Calisspe's, we saw her handsome daughter on the porch inspecting a side-saddle, and concluded from this that the gallant Lieutenant's application had been successful, and that she proposed to accompany him to the ball on horseback. As we galloped by the house, a little flaxen-haired, chubby boy, who had climbed the fence, extended his head over the top rail and jabbered at us at the top of his voice; but the handsome young lady did not favor us with even a glance.

31. It is late. Hours ago the bugles notified the boys that it was time to retire to their dens. I have been reading Thackeray's "Lovell, the Widower," and as I sat alone in the silence of the middle night, the scenes depicted grew distinct and life-like; the characters encompassed me about real living men and women; the drawing-rooms, dining-halls, parlors, opened out before me; the streets, walks, drives, were all visible, and I became a spectator instead of a reader. Suddenly a low, unearthly wail broke the stillness, and my hair stiffened somewhat at the roots, as the fancy struck me that I heard the voice of the defunct Mrs. Lovell. A moment's reflection, however, dispelled this disagreeable

thought. Looking toward the corner of the cabin whence the ghostly sound emanated, I discovered a strange cat. My long-legged boots followed each other in quick succession toward the unhappy kitten, and I yelled "scat" in a very vindictive way.

JANUARY 1, 1864.

Standing on a peak of Mission Ridge to-day, we had spread out before us one of the grandest prospects which ever delighted the eye of man. Northward Waldron's Ridge and Lookout mountain rose massive and precipitous, and seemed the boundary wall of the world. Below them was the Tennessee, like a ribbon of silver; Chattanooga, with its thousands of white tents and miles of fortifications. Southward was the Chickamauga, and beyond a succession of ridges, rising higher and higher, until the eye rested upon the blue tops of the great mountains of North Carolina. The fact that a hundred and fifty thousand men, with all the appliances of war, have struggled for the possession of these mountains, rivers, and ridges, gives a solemn interest to the scene, and renders it one of the most interesting, as it is one of the grandest, in the world.

When history shall have recorded the thrilling tragedies enacted here; when poets shall have illuminated every hill-top and mountain peak with the glow of their imagination; when the novelist shall have given it a population from his fertile brain, what place can be more attractive to the traveler?

Looking on this panorama of mountains, ridges, rivers, and valleys, one has a juster conception of the power of God. Reflecting upon the deeds that have been done here, he obtains a truer knowledge of the character of man, and the incontestable evidences of his nobility.

Standing here to-day, I take off my hat to the reader, if by possibility there be one who has had the patience to follow me thus far, and as I bid him good-by, wish him " A Happy New Year."

CAPTURE, IMPRISONMENT,

AND

ESCAPE,

BY

GENERAL HARRISON C. HOBART,

OF MILWAUKEE, WISCONSIN.

EXPLANATORY.

AMONG the Union officers who escaped from Libby Prison at Richmond, on the night of the 9th of February, 1864, was my esteemed friend, General Harrison C. Hobart, then Colonel of the Twenty-first Wisconsin Volunteer Infantry. His name is mentioned quite frequently in the preceding pages. Ten years after the war closed, he spent a few days at my house, and while there was requested to tell the story of his capture, imprisonment, and escape. My children gathered about him, and listened to his narrative with an intensity of interest which I am very sure they never exhibited when receiving words of admonition and advice from their father.

While my manuscript was in the hands of the publishers, it occurred to me that General Hobart's story would be as interesting to others as it had been to my own family, and so I wrote, urging him to furnish it to me for publication. He finally consented to do so, and I have the pleasure now of presenting it to the reader. It bears upon its face the evidence of its entire truthfulness, and yet is as interesting as a romance.

32   JOHN BEATTY.

.

GENERAL HOBART'S NARRATIVE.

THE battles of Chickamauga were fought on the 19th and 20th of September, 1863. The Twenty-first Wisconsin, which I then commanded, formed a part of Thomas' memorable line, and fought through the battles of Saturday and Sunday. At the close of the second day, Thomas' Corps still maintained its position, and presented an unbroken front to the enemy, but the right of our army having fallen back, the tide of battle was turning against us.

To avoid a flank movement, our brigade was ordered to leave the breastworks, which they had held against the severest fire of the enemy during the day, and fall back to a second position. Here only a portion of the men, with three regimental standards, were rallied. A rebel battery was instantly placed in position on our right, and rebel cavalry swept between us and the retreating army.

Being the ranking officer among those who rallied, I directed the men to cut their way through to our retreating line. I was on the left of this movement to the rear, and, to avoid the approach of horsemen, rapidly passed to the left through a dense cluster of

(379)

small pines, and instantly found myself in the immediate front of a rebel line of infantry. I halted,
being dismounted, and an officer advanced and offered
his hand, saying that he was glad to see me, and proposed to introduce me to his commander, General
Cleburne. I replied, that I was not particularly
pleased to see him, but, under the circumstances,
should not decline his invitation.

I met the General, who was mounted and being
cheered by his men, and surrendered to him my
sword. He inquired where I had been fighting. I
said, "Right there," pointing to the line of Thomas'
Corps. He replied, "This line has given us our chief
trouble, sir; your soldiers have fought like brave
men; come with me and I will see that no one insults
or interferes with you."

It was now after sun-down, and the last guns of the
terrible battle of Chicamauga were dying away along
the hillsides of Mission Ridge. A large number of
prisoners of war were soon gathered, and marched to
the enemy's rear across the Chickamauga. Here we
witnessed the fearful results of the battle. The ground
strewed with the dead and wounded, the shattered fragments of transportation, and a general demoralization
among the forces, told the fearful price which the
enemy had paid for their victory. More than fifteen
hundred soldiers, prisoners of war, camped by a large
spring to pass the remainder of a cold night; some
without blankets or overcoats, and all without provisions.

The next day we were marched about thirty miles

to Tunnel Hill, where we received our first rations
from the enemy. On this march, the only food we
obtained was from a field of green sorghum. Here
we were placed in box cars and taken to Atlanta.
On arriving at this place, we were first marched to an
open field outside of the city, near a fountain of water,
and surrounded by a guard. Kind-hearted people
came out of the city, bringing bread with them, which
they threw to us across the guard line. Immediately
a second line was established, distant several rods
outside of the first, to prevent them from giving us
food.

From this place we were marched to the old slave-
pen, and every man, as he entered the narrow gate,
was compelled to give up his overcoat and blanket.
I remonstrated with the officers for stripping the soldiers of their necessary clothing, as an act in violation
of civilized warfare and inhuman. The men who
were executing this infamous duty, did not deny these
charges, but excused themselves on the ground that
they were simply obeying an order of General Bragg
from the front. That night I saw seventeen hundred
Union soldiers lie down upon the ground, without an
overcoat or blanket to protect them from the cold
earth, or shield them from the heavy Southern dew.

The next morning we were ordered to take the cars,
and proceed on our way to Richmond. These men
arose from the ground, cold and wet with dew, and
under my command organized and formed in column
by companies, and marched to the depot through one
of the main streets of Atlanta, singing in full chorus

the Star Spangled Banner. Crowds gathered around us as we entered the cars. A guard with muskets accompanied the train.

I will here relate an incident which occurred on our way. We overtook a train of open cars, filled with Confederate wounded from the battle-field. The two trains stopped for some time alongside and in close proximity. It was a spectacle to see the men of the two armies intently observe each other. On the one side was the calm, pale face of the wounded; on the other, the earnest, deep sympathy of the captive. No unkind look or word passed between them. Of the seventeen hundred prisoners, there was not one who would not have given his coat, or reached for his last cent, to help his wounded brother.

On the last day of September, after traveling more than eight hundred miles from the battle-field of Chickamauga, we arrived at Richmond, and the officers of the Cumberland Army, to the number of about two hundred and fifty, were marched to Libby Prison.

This building has a front of about one hundred and forty feet, with a depth of about one hundred and five. There are nine rooms, each one hundred and two feet long, by forty-five wide. The height of ceilings from the floor is about seven feet. The building is also divided into three apartments by brick walls, and there is a basement below.

On entering the prison, we were severally searched, and every thing of value taken from us. Some of us saved our money by putting it into the seams of our garments before we arrived at Richmond. The officers of the Army of the Cumberland were assigned to the middle rooms of the second and third stories. The lower middle room was used as a general kitchen, and the basement immediately below was fitted up with cells for the confinement and punishment of offenders. These rooms received the *sobriquet* of Chickamauga.

The whole number of officers of the army and navy in prison at this time was about eleven hundred—all having access to each other, except those in the hospital. There were no beds or chairs, and all slept on the floor. I shared a horse blanket with Surgeon Dixon, of Wisconsin, which was the only bedding we had for some time. Our bread was made of unbolted corn, and was cold and clammy. We were sometimes furnished with fresh beef, corn beef, and sometimes with rice and vegetable soup. The men formed themselves into messes, and each took his turn in preparing such food as we could get.

At one time, no meat was furnished for about nine days, and the reason given was, that their soldiers at the front required all they could obtain. During this period, we received nothing but corn bread. Kind friends sent us boxes of provisions from the North, which were opened and examined by the Confederates, and if nothing objectionable was found, and it pleased them, the party to whom a box was sent was directed to come down and get it. Many of these were never delivered. Every generous soul shared the contents of his box with his more unfortunate companions. Had it not been for this provision, our life in Libby would have been intolerable.

There was no glass in the windows, and for some time no fire in the rooms. An application for window glass, made during the severest cold weather, was answered by the assurance that the Confederates had none to furnish. The worst affliction, however, was the vermin, which invaded every department.

Each officer was permitted to write home the amount of three lines per week; but even these brief messages were not always allowed to leave Richmond.

A variety of schemes were adopted to improve or kill time. We played chess, cards, opened a theater, organized a band of minstrels, delivered lectures, established schools for teaching dancing, singing, the French language, and military tactics, read books, published a manuscript newspaper, held debates, and by these means rendered life tolerable, though by no means agreeable.

An incident occurred, after we had been in prison some time, which made a deep impression upon every one. Some of our men had been confined in a block not far from Libby, called the Pemberton Building. An order had been issued to remove them to North Carolina. When they left, their line of march was along the street in our front, and when they passed under our windows, we threw out drawers, shirts, stockings, etc., which they gathered up; and when they raised their pale and emaciated faces to greet their old commanders, there were but few dry eyes in Libby. Many of them were making their last march.

Our sick were removed to the room set apart, on the ground floor, for a hospital; and, when one died, he was put in a box of rough boards, placed in an open wagon, and rapidly driven away over the stony streets. There were no flowers from loving hands, and no mourning pageant, but a thousand hearts in Libby followed the gallant dead to his place of rest.

We were seldom visited by any person. The only call I received was from General Breckenridge, of Kentucky; I had known him before the war. During our interview, I referred to the resources of the North and South, and asked him upon what ground he hoped the Confederacy could succeed. His only reply was, that, " five millions of people, determined to be free, could not be conquered."

There being no exchange of prisoners at this time, projects of escape were discussed from the beginning. One scheme was, for a few persons at a time to put on the dress of a citizen, and attempt to pass the guard as visitors. A few actually recovered their liberty in this manner. Another plan was, to dig a tunnel to the city sewer, which was understood to pass under the street in front of the prison, and escape through that to the river. This project might have succeeded had not the water interfered. The final and successful plan was as follows:

On the ground floor of the building, on a level with the street, was a kitchen containing a fire-place, at a

33

stove connected with which the prisoners inhabiting the rooms above did their cooking. Beneath this floor was a basement, one of the rooms in which was used as a store-room. This store-room was under the hospital and next to the street, and though not directly under the kitchen, was so located that it was possible to reach it by digging downward and rearward through the masonry work of the chimney. From this basement room it was proposed to construct a tunnel under the street to a point beneath a shed, connected with a brick block upon the opposite side, and from this place to pass into the street in the guise of citizens. A knowledge of this plan was confided to about twenty-five, and nothing was known of the proceedings by the others until two or three days before the escape. A table knife, chisel, and spittoon were secured for working tools, when operations commenced. Sufficient of the masonry was removed from the fire-place to admit the passage of a man through a diagonal cut to the store-room below ; and an excavation was then made through the foundation wall toward the street, and the construction of the tunnel proceeded night by night. But two persons could work at the same time. One would enter the hole with his tools and a small tallow candle, dragging the spittoon after him attached to a string. The other would fan air into the passage with his hat, and with another string would draw out the novel dirt car when loaded, concealing its contents beneath the straw and rubbish of the cellar. Each morning before daylight the working party returned to their rooms, after carefully closing the mouth of the tunnel, and skillfully replacing the bricks in the chimney.

An error occurred during the prosecution of this work that nearly proved fatal to the enterprise. After a sufficient distance was supposed to have been made, an excavation was commenced to reach the top of the ground. The person working, carefully felt his way upward, when suddenly a small amount of the top earth fell in, and through this he could plainly see two sentinels apparently looking at him. One said to the other, " I have been hearing a strange noise in the ground there !" After listening a short time, the other replied that it was " nothing but rats." The working party had not been seen. After consultation, this opening was carefully filled with dirt and shored up. The work was then recommenced, and after digging about fifteen feet further the objective point under the shed was successfully reached.

This tunnel required about thirty days of patient, tedious and dangerous labor. It was eight feet below the street, between sixty and seventy feet in length, and barely large enough for a full-grown person to crawl through, by pulling and pushing himself along with his hands and feet. Among the officers entitled to merit in the execution of this work, Col. T. E. Rose, of Pennsylvania, deserves particular mention.

When all was complete, the company was organized into two parties ; the first under the charge of Major McDonald, of Ohio, and the second was placed under my direction. The parties having provided themselves with citizens' clothing, which had at different times been sent to the prison by friends in the North, and having filled their pockets with bread and dried meat from their boxes, commenced to escape about seven P. M., on the 9th of February, 1864; Major McDonald's party leaving first. In order to distract the attention of the guard, a dancing party with music was extemporized in the same room. As each one had to pass out in the immediate presence of these Confederate soldiers, when he stepped into the street from the outside of the line, and as the guard were under orders to fire upon a prisoner escaping, without even calling upon him to halt, the first men who descended to the tunnel wore that quiet gloom so often seen in the army before going into battle. It was a living drama ; dancing in one part of the room, dark shadows disappearing through the chimney in another part, and the same shadows re-appearing upon the opposite walk, and the sentinel at his post, with a voice that rang out upon the evening air, announcing : " Eight o'clock, Post No. One," and " All is well !" and at the same time a Yankee soldier was passing in his front, and a line of Yankee soldiers were crawling under his feet. The passage was so small that the process of departure was necessarily slow ; a few inches of progress only being made at each effort, and to facilitate locomotion outside garments were taken off and pushed forward.

By this time the proceedings had become known to the whole prison, and as the first men emerged upon the street, and quietly walked away, seen by hundreds of their fellows, who crowded the windows, a wild excitement and enthusiasm were created, and they rushed down to the chimney, clamoring for the privilege of going out. It was the intention of the parties, organized by those who constructed the tunnel, that no others should leave until the next night, as it might materially diminish their own chances of escape. But the thought of liberty and pure air, and the death damp of the dark loathsome prison would not allow them to listen to any denial. Major McDonald and myself then held a parley, and it was arranged that the rope upon which we descended into the basement, after the last of the two parties had passed out, should be pulled up for the space of one hour; then it should be free to all in prison.[*]

Having joined my fortunes with Col. T. S. West, of Wisconsin, we were among the last of the second party who crawled through. About nine o'clock in the evening we emerged from the tunnel, and cautiously crossing an open yard to an arched driveway, we stepped out upon the street and slowly walked away, apparently engaged in an earnest conversation. As soon as we were out of range of the sentinels' guns, we concluded it would be the safest course to turn and pass up through one of the main streets of Richmond, as they would not suspect that prisoners escaping would take that direction. My face being very pale, and my beard long, clinging to the arm of Colonel W., I assumed the part of a decrepit old

---

[*] NOTE.—One hundred and nine prisoners escaped through this tunnel that night, of whom fifty-seven reached our lines.

man, who seemed to be in exceeding ill health, and badly affected with a consumptive cough.

In this manner we passed beneath the glaring gas-lights, and through the crowded street, without creating a suspicion as to our real character. We met the police, squads of soldiers, and many others, who gave me a sympathizing look, and stepped aside on account of my apparent infirmities. Approaching the suburbs of the town, we retreated into a ravine, which enabled us to leave the city without passing out upon one of the streets. While in prison I copied McClellan's war map of Virginia, which aided us materially in this escape. Our objective points were to cross the Chickahominy above New Bridge, then cross the Yorkville Railroad, then strike and follow down the Miamisburg pike.

After resting and breathing pure air, the first time for more than four months, we resumed our journey, agreeing not to speak above a whisper, avoiding all houses and roads, and determining our course by the North Star. In crossing roads, we traveled backwards, that the footsteps might mislead our pursuers.

We soon came in sight of the main fortifications around Richmond, and instantly dropping upon the ground we lay for a long time, listening and watching for the presence of sentinels upon that part of the line. Being satisfied that there were none in our immediate front, in the most silent and cautious manner, we crossed over the fortification and pursued our way through a tangled forest. Coming to a piece of low ground, tired and exhausted, we lay down to rest. Our attention was soon attracted by the presence of a series of excavations; and on a close examination we found we were resting upon the battlefield of Fair Oaks, and among the trenches in which the Confederates had buried our dead; and, although it was the midnight hour, a strange feeling of safety stole over me, and I felt as if we were among our friends. It was the step and voice of the living that we dreaded.

At early dawn (Wednesday) we crossed a brook, and went upon a hillside of low, thick pines to conceal ourselves, and rest during the day. The Valley of the Chickahominy lay before us. While in this concealment, we saw a blood-hound scenting our steps down to the place where we jumped over the brook; it then went back and returned two or three times, but finally left without attempting to cross the little stream. Late in the evening, we went to the river and worked till after midnight to make or find a crossing. The water was deep and cold, and, failing to accomplish our purpose, we turned back to a haystack, and, covering ourselves with hay, rested until the first light of morning (Thursday).

Going back to the river, we followed down its course until we found a tree which had fallen nearly across the stream. Discovering a long pole, we found that it would just touch the opposite shore from the limbs of this tree. Hitching ourselves carefully along this pole, we reached the left bank of the Chickahominy River.

We now felt as if escape was possible; but, hearing

GENERAL HOBART'S NARRATIVE.

a noise like the approach of troops, for we were satisfied that the enemy's cavalry must be in full pursuit, we fled into a neighboring forest. As we approached the center of a thicket, my eye suddenly caught the glimpse of a man watching us from behind the root of a fallen tree. I concluded that we had fallen into an ambush; but our momentary apprehension was joyfully relieved by the discovery that this new-made acquaintance was Colonel W. B. McCreary, of Michigan, and with him Major Terrence Clark, of Illinois, who had gone through the tunnel with the first party that went out, and were now passing the day in this secluded place. The Colonel was one of my intimate friends, and when he recognized me he jumped to his feet and threw his arms around me in an ecstasy of delight.

By this time the whole population had been informed of the escape, and the country was alive with pursuers. We could distinctly hear the reveille of the rebel troops, and the hum of their camps. Thus reinforced, we agreed to travel in company. It was arranged that one of the four should precede, searching out the way in the darkness, and giving due notice of danger.

At dark we left our hiding place, and cautiously proceeded on our way. Late at night we crossed the railroad running from Richmond to White House, our second objective point. Here Colonel West saw a sentinel sitting close by the railroad, asleep, with his gun resting against his shoulder. Just before daybreak we went into a pine woods, after traveling a distance of more than twenty miles, and, weary and tired, we lay down to rest.

The morning (Friday) broke clear and beautiful, but with its bright light came the bugle notes of the enemy's cavalry, who were in the pines close by us. We instantly arose and fled away at the top of our speed, expecting every moment to hear the crack of the rifle, or the sharp command to halt. We struck a road and about faced to cross it, the only time that we looked back. We pursued our rapid step until we came to a dense chaparral, and into this we threaded our way until we reached an almost impenetrable jungle. Crawling into the center, we threw ourselves upon the ground completely exhausted. A bird flew into the branches above us as we lay upon our backs, and the words burst from my lips: " Dear little bird! Oh, that I had your wings!"

As soon as friendly darkness again returned, we moved forward, weary, hungry, and footsore, still governed in our course by the North Star. During all this toilsome way, but few words passed between us, and these generally in low whispers. So untiring was the search, and so thoroughly alarmed and watchful were the population, that we felt that our safety depended upon a bare chance. Again making our way from wood to wood, and avoiding farm houses as best we might, till the light of another morning (Saturday), we retired to cover in the shade of a thick forest.

Saturday night the journey was resumed as usual. It was my turn to act the part of picket and pilot.

While rapidly leading the way through a forest of low pines, I suddenly found myself in the presence of a cavalry reserve. The men were warming themselves by a blazing fire, and their horses were tied to trees around them. I was surprised and alarmed; but recovering my self-possession, I remained motionless, and soon perceived that my presence was unobserved. Carefully putting one foot behind the other I retreated out of sight, and rapidly returned to my party. Knowing that there were videttes sitting somewhere at the front in the dark, we concluded to go back about two miles to a plantation, and call at one of the outermost negro houses for information. We returned, and I volunteered to make the call while the others remained concealed at a distance.

I approached the door and rapped, and a woman's voice from within asked, " who was there?" I replied, that " I was a traveler and had lost my way, and wished to obtain some information about the road." She directed me to go to another house, but I declined to do so, and after some further conversation the door was opened, and I was surprised to find a large, good-looking negro standing by her side, who had been listening to the interview. He invited me to come in, and as soon as the door was closed, he said: " I know who you are; you're one of dem 'scaped officers from Richmond." Looking him full in the face, I placed my hand firmly upon his shoulder, and said: " I am, and I know you are my friend." His eyes sparkled as he repeated: " Yes, sir; yes, sir; but you musn't stay here; a reg'ment of cavalry is right thar'," pointing to a place near by, "and they pass this road all times of the night." The woman gave me a piece of corn-bread and a cup of milk, and the man accompanying me, I left the house, and soon finding my companions, our guide took us to a secluded spot in a canebrake, and there explained the situation of the picket in front.   It was posted on a narrow neck of land between two impassable swamps, and over this neck ran the main road to Williamsburg.   The negro proved to be a sharp, shrewd fellow, and we engaged him to pilot us round this picket.   After impressing us in his strongest language with the danger both to him and to us of making the least noise, he conducted us through a long canebrake path, then through several fields, then directly over the road, crossing between the cavalry reserve and their videttes, who were sitting upon their horses but a few rods in front, and then took us around to the pike about a mile beyond this last post of the rebels.   After obtaining important information from him concerning the way to the front, and giving him a substantial reward, we cordially took his hand in parting.   If good deeds are recorded in Heaven, this slave appeared in the record that night.

The line of the pike was then rapidly followed as far as Diascum river, which was reached just at light Sunday morning.   To cross this river without assistance from some quarter was found impossible.   We tried to wade through it, but failed in this attempt. We were seen by some of the neighboring population, which largely increased our danger and trepidation;

for we had been informed by our guide that the enemy's scouts came to this point every morning. After awhile we succeeded in reaching an island in the river, but could get no farther, finding deep water beyond. We endeavored to construct a raft but failed. The water being extremely cold, and we being very wet and weary, we did not dare attempt to swim the stream ; and expecting every moment to see the enemy's cavalry, our hearts sank within us. At this juncture a rebel soldier was seen coming up the river in a row-boat with a gun. Requesting my companions to lie down in the grass, I concealed myself in the bushes close to the water to get a good view of the man. Finding his countenance to indicate youth and benevolence, I accosted him as he approached.

"Good morning ; I have been waiting for you; they told me up at those houses that I could get across the stream, but I find the bridge is gone, and I am very wet and cold; if you will take me over, I will pay you for your trouble."

The boat was turned into the shore, and as I stepped into it I knew that boat was mine. Keeping my eye upon his gun, I said to him, "there are three more of us," and they immediately stepped into the boat. "Where do you all come from?" said the boatman, seeming to hesitate and consider. We represented ourselves as farmers from different localities on the Chickahominy. "The officers don't like to have me carry men over this river," he said, evidently suspecting who we were. I replied, "that is right; you should not carry soldiers or suspected characters."

Then placing my eyes upon him, I said, " pass your boat over !" it sped to the other shore. We gave him one or two greenbacks, and he rapidly returned. We knew we were discovered, and that the enemy's cavalry would very soon be in hot pursuit, therefore we determined, after consultation, to go into the first hiding place, and as near as possible to the river. The wisdom of this course was soon demonstrated. The cavalry crossed the stream, dashed by us, and thoroughly searched the country to the front, not dreaming but we had gone forward. We did not leave our seclusion until about midnight, and then felt our way with extreme care. The proximity to Williamsburg was evident from the destruction every where apparent in our path. There were no buildings, no inhabitants, and no sound save our own weary footsteps; desolation reigned supreme. Stacks of chimneys stood along our way like sentinels over the dead land.

For five days and six nights, hunted and almost exhausted, with the stars for our guide, we had picked our way through surrounding perils toward the camp-fires of our friends. We knew we were near the outposts of the Union troops, and began to feel as if our trials were nearly over. But we were now in danger of being shot as rebels by scouting parties of our own army. To avoid the appearance of being spies, we took the open road, alternately traveling and concealing ourselves, that we might reconnoiter the way. About two o'clock in the morning, coming near the shade of a dark forest that overhung the road, we were startled, and brought to a stand, by the sharp and sudden command, "Halt!" Looking in the direction whence it proceeded, we discovered the dark forms of a dozen cavalrymen drawn up in line across the road. A voice came out of the darkness, asking, "who are you?" We replied, "we are four travelers!" The same voice said, "if you are travelers, come up here!" Moving forward the cavalry surrounded us, and carefully looking at their coats, I concluded they were gray, and was nerving myself for a recapture. It was a supreme moment to the soul. One of my companions asked, "are you Union soldiers?" In broad Pennsylvania language the answer came, "well we are!" In a moment their uniforms changed to glorious blue, and taking of our hats we gave one long exultant shout. It was like passing from death unto life. Our hearts filled with gratitude to Him whose sheltering arm had protected us in all that dangerous way. Turning toward Richmond, I prayed in my heart that I might have strength to return to my command.

I was afterwards in Sherman's advance to Atlanta; the March to the Sea and through the Carolinas; entered Richmond with the Western army; and had the supreme satisfaction of marching my brigade by Libby Prison.

INDEX.

(399)

34